A Miscellany for
BIBLIOPHILES

A Miscellany for
BIBLIOPHILES

Edited by

H. George Fletcher

Foreword by William Targ

GRASTORF & LANG.

New York

Contents

[*v*]

Foreword

William Targ

IT IS A SENTIMENT UNIVERSALLY UNDERSTOOD that book-collectors would rather gossip about their possessions than almost anything else. "Your typical book-collector," said Carlos Baker, "has at least this in common with the old soldier and the young philanderer: nothing pleases him quite so much as the chance to talk about his conquests."

Bookmen talk (or gossip) a great deal; but then, isn't their preoccupation generally with words, in one form or another? I have been guilty, countless times, of biblio-garrulity, of reminiscing endlessly, wistfully, of "the big ones that got away"; or boastfully, of the little ones that turned out to be big, thanks to my vision and acute perception. Perhaps we talk too much ...

Of late I find myself thinking of the books I foolishly parted with: sold, traded off—the books I no longer own. Collecting should mean *keeping*. After parting with a treasure, we find that remorse usually sets in—and depression too. We talk about these experiences, and even write essays about them. Sometimes the subject is a melancholy one.

I once owned a first edition of Moxon's *Mechanick Exercises* (the Hoe copy in two volumes, mint) and also a first edition of Geofroy Tory's *Champfleury,* in its original binding. I was persuaded to part with both these jewels (yes, for a profit), and they now reside in Texas; of course you may surmise *where* in Texas. I should not have sold those books; I was not in need of money, missing no meals. But I remembered that some cliché-ridden millionaire once said something about the salutary effects of making a profit. My point, dear reader, is this: making a profit on a truly rare book (when you are not a dealer) is not always a wise decision. It so happens that money is not quite so rare as a rare book.

By the same token, neglecting to buy a great rarity because of the cost usually brings tears of regret. I am not referring to expensive Caxtons or First Folios. Confidentially, I have often gone into debt in order to acquire a desirable book. The debt *per se* rarely bothered me. Eventually bills do get paid; guilt and unease vanish. The book remains and brings joy and comfort.

As you can see, one can start talking about books at the drop of a 42-line Gutenberg leaf; most of our breed are unstoppable talkers. Eventually, each collector gets equal time. But the point is—there's no talk like book talk.

Pursuing and finding a rare book—that is a great sport. One bibliomaniac called it the greatest sport—after women. Perhaps. A. Edward Newton wrote passionately about his acquisitions and attendant experiences in his pioneering work, *The Amenities of Book-Collecting,* which he published in 1918. That book fired the imagination and appetite of many thousands of collectors, young and old. It is a perfect example of a good Book about Books. As is the present volume.

Here, in our present book, a group of highly cultivated collectors—professionals and educated amateurs—are talking about books: collecting, inscribed and association copies, printing, designing, binding, papermaking, and other related matters of interest to bookmen. I am happy to have been invited to this gathering because, among several reasons, there is the fact that some of the contributors are fellow members of "my Club," the Grolier, where rare and beautiful books are revered, housed, and well displayed; where scholars and collectors and printers gather in bookish fellowship.

You will find here much of value and interest and entertainment, with some fresh insights all along the line. Among the offerings is a warm and affectionate portrait of an authentic New York antiquarian bookseller, Dave Mendoza. He was one of the last of the Mohicans, an honest secondhand dealer with good will toward all book lovers.

There is a fine essay here on crime/detective fiction, by Otto Penzler, and the essay will add zest to anyone's life if he is involved in collecting the so-called Police Novel. Crime fiction offers all sorts of byways for specialists, as Mr. Penzler points out. But puzzlingly, it is not as popular a category as, say, science fiction or the modern first. There are hills and valleys of activity in most fields, however, and collecting fashions change. For example, there are several virtually unreadable novelists in our midst today who are ardently collected. Books of modest reader interest — cult attraction — become eagerly sought, especially when inscribed by their authors. Often, books of little literary interest fetch enormous premiums for byzantine reasons including the fact that successful movies were made from them, or simply because the books were inscribed by their authors, celebrities of a sort.

Returning to crime fiction: there are a few areas worth considering by the specialist. For example, first books only, by distinguished crime fiction writers. Or, periodical appearance (pre-book publication) of authors such as Poe. And then, for the ultimate dreamer, there are the first editions of Poe's tales in book form — probably an exercise in futility. Finding a copy of the first edition of *The Prose Romances of Edgar A. Poe* (Philadelphia, 1843), in its original wrappers, is about as likely as being struck by a comet at high noon . . . in Times Square

(Baudelaire's French translation might not be too hard to find, though).

Next to talking about books comes the pleasure of reading them, especially books about books. This is an extra category I would recommend to collectors. Regardless of your other interests, no one should be without a hundred or more miscellaneous books *about* books: biographies of great collectors and booksellers, printers, papermakers, typefounders, publishers, etc. Bibliographies are essential tools, as are catalogues. Actually, good rare book catalogues are often the best possible bedtime reading, and one always learns something from them. But getting back to books about books: I would be hard put to prepare a list of the hundred best — there are so many excellent works in this field. And I am not referring only to the so-called how-to books.

Some of the bibliolatrous brethren may protest at the absence of price-talk in the following pages. What, no prices! No, alas. But I will not quarrel about this; for I know full well that many collectors and dealers consider price-talk unfit for parlor conversation. Does one discuss the price of one's new suit, or a new watch, or rug? Many dealers feel that lists of book prices are immoral, that price guides should not be published. They are obscene, vulgar, misleading. One buys a book out of love, asks the price, and places the money inconspicuously on the mantelpiece . . . and changes the subject. Thus speaketh many a bookseller. Not I.

As a long-time book editor, I have been privileged to be involved in the publication of a number of books about books. Among my favorite assignments was the biography of A. S. W. Rosenbach by Edwin Wolf 2nd and John F. Fleming. That book, a landmark work, would be like a bouillabaisse without salt or seasoning were the cost and sale prices not included in many of the transactions described therein. Cost *vs* selling price: there's always a bit of drama there. The sex appeal, if you will. The last bookish work I was involved in as editor — before departing from the commercial publishing arena, in the winter of my discontent,

1978—was Hans P. Kraus's splendid autobiography, *A Rare Book Saga*. Rich in personal and professional anecdote and bookish lore, it would have been far too bland for most palates if prices had been excluded from the work. Of course, I have been burned in effigy (together with Van Allen Bradley) for my participation as editor in the publication of the three editions of *The Book Collector's Handbook of Values*. Now, that book would be totally without point if it lacked prices. I know that most booksellers have a copy of the book at their elbows, for ready and constant reference. But usually, in speaking of it, one would think they (the anti-price faction) were referring to a salacious or evil book. No matter.

I'll conclude with a moral: Don't sell your rare books. The fleeting pleasure of realizing a good profit vanishes; but it is not easy to erase the exquisite sense of possession, the recollection of the physical book in one's hand or visually enjoyed on the shelf.

To the newcomer or laggard: it is never too late to start forming a collection; even if you have only six books in your house, consider the excitement of adding a seventh to your shelf—just as you would add another flower to your window box. Consider the oceanic challenges and opportunities before you, once you've decided to invest some of your energy and imagination in this exhilarating pursuit. What will that next book be?

ACKNOWLEDGMENTS

THE PUBLISHERS would like to thank the following institutions and individuals for their assistance in gathering illustrations: The Grolier Club, Dr. Theodore Grieder of New York University, The New-York Historical Society, the Princeton University Library, Dr. Lola L. Szladits of The New York Public Library, and Janey Tannenbaum of the Gotham Book Mart.

Photo Credits: Henry W. and Albert A. Berg Collection, The New York Public Library, Astor, Lenox and Tilden Foundations, pp. 50, 196, 198, 207; Matthew J. Bruccoli, pp. 52, 60; ©Sotheby Parke-Bernet, Agent: Editorial Photocolor Archives, pp. 56, 64; Rare Book Division, The New York Public Library, Astor, Lenox and Tilden Foundations, p. 215; Library of Congress, p. 299.

Editor's Preface

OF RECENT YEARS we have seen not a few new books about books come off the presses. The theme of many of them has been a deliberate concentration upon the pragmatic—in particular, the monetary—side of bibliophilia. Believing this emphasis misguided (prices, for example, are especially susceptible of obsolescence, and single-minded speculators are rarely affable), the publishers determined to swim against that current in this, their inaugural work.

This collection is thus deliberately fashioned into the sort of volume which one would have expected to find a generation or more ago. There is, to be sure, the occasional if rare discussion of prices and what return one might expect eventually to see on one's investment; however, the general tone is a literary one. In other words: if you are looking for a hard-headed, objective manual on book-collecting, look elsewhere. The publishers sought to assemble a new, representative gathering of interesting

studies on a perennially enjoyable theme; they brought us together within these amenable confines, and asked me to see to
the editing. All of us are reasonably satisfied with the results,
and we trust that you will favor us with your patronage, and
thus signal your agreement with our sentiments. One particularly
striking feature of this *Miscellany* is the very rich quantity of
illustrations. Let me mention briefly the other kinds of riches to
be found between these covers.

Robert Taylor begins our gathering with a discussion of the
two poles of bibliophilia—the dealer and the collector. In the
genteel, polished manner which we have learned to expect from
him, Mr. Taylor offers us some of the wisdom gained from his
more than half-century addiction to this pleasant ailment.

Robert Nikirk takes up the matter of the previous owners of
rare books, and how their sometimes cryptic signs of ownership
may be identified. Some of the more obvious signs of the trans-
mission of particular copies are then discussed by Salvatore Iacone
in his essay on the significance of copies presented by some
important modern English-language authors.

Leonard Schlosser, out of his singular knowledge of the history
of paper and printing processes, contributes a work of seminal
importance on what he views as a watershed confluence of
technical developments at the beginning of the nineteenth
century. Dyke Benjamin then follows with a work on that Victorian
giant, John Ruskin. Around Ruskin, Mr. Benjamin develops a
study which may serve to show how the results of one collector's
hobby can become a scholarly resource for our generation and
the future.

Jamie Shalleck has assembled within surprisingly brief compass
a most useful guide to dating fine bindings made during the
last half-millennium. Between her verbal descriptions and the
many illustrations showing bindings in comparative groupings,
she has given us a helpful and compendious tool for research.
Philip Sperling offers us a lovingly crafted study of the long-time
object of his book-collecting, William Pickering, who kept taste
alive in bookmaking in the early Victorian age. Barbara Kline

presents us with a look into the relationships between certain publishers and their authors who were knowledgeable about book design and who had a strong say in the production of their own books.

Otto Penzler treats an area which was not even thought worthy of a collector's attention half a century ago, but which has been booming since the '30s: detective fiction. Roger Mohovich discourses concisely on almost the first two centuries of American newspapers, an important topic about which the average book-collector is sadly uninformed. My slight memoir of an old friend and guide is, I fear, sadly inadequate to its task, but I am at least glad of the chance to say thanks especially in type on paper. All of us are grateful to William Targ for his kind comments in the Foreword. Many of us owe our love for the world of books to his splendid collections of essays on a favorite theme, and we return to them regularly to recharge our batteries. It is fitting that his anthologies have themselves become rare and sought-for among collectors.

But I have already kept you too long from our authors, and I wish you joy in making their acquaintance.

H. G. F.

New York City

ROBERT H. TAYLOR *has been a collector of English (and, to a lesser degree, of American) literature for over fifty years. He is a past president of The Grolier Club, of The Bibliographical Society of America, and of The Keats–Shelley Association of America.*

Of Dealers
and Collectors

Robert H. Taylor

THE DEALER is the heart of book collecting. This is as it should be, for most antiquarian booksellers began young and kept at it despite the vicissitudes and misfortunes incident to the trade. And whatever affinities attached them to the business in the first place become reinforced by increasing knowledge and experience.

This being so, you might think they would have common and identifying characteristics; but no, there do not seem to be any—none, at least, that I have been able to discover. Like the rest of humanity, dealers are of all kinds, and this makes explorations of their shops—and personalities—more interesting.

I know of no greater pleasure for a young collector than carefully ransacking the shelves in a bookshop new to him. I say "young" because the middle-aged and elderly tend to be set in their ways, and the charm of novelty is no longer so strong as it used to be. They went through that stage years ago; they remember their first visit to that very shop, when they wished the proprietor would go about his business instead of asking what they were interested in. They could not afford his prices, they knew; but they did want to see the kind of thing that was on the shelves, even if they were engaged only in a bit of comparative shopping. But they could not very well say so. And then, perhaps once in a great while, they found a modest item they really wanted and could pay for. What an encouragement that was to come back! And that next time they were probably not so shy of conversation with the dealer. That is how it started, they recall; and they do not realize, now when they drop in for an occasional chat, that the bookseller would probably rather have the ardent young neophyte examining his stock than listen to talk of the golden years and the fearful state of the present market. After all, the dealer knows that he needs to renew his customers as well as his supply of books.

This renewal is not always easy. If dealers come in all sorts of temperamental personality, what is one to say about the bewildering variety of collectors? I remember one who believed that every dealer was a crook; he made nearly all of his purchases at auctions, where he bid for himself. He did have to buy the occasional item he wanted from one dealer or another, but he was not pleased about it. As one who regards auctions as necessary evils, I feel he had hold of the wrong end of the stick; but he was passionately devoted to his collection, and as happy as though he had been rational. Happier, maybe.

Contrast his behavior with that of two good friends of mine. They were also long-time friends of each other, and had for years collected in the same field without clashing. One of them, hearing that I was about to leave for England, sought me out to impart some wise advice. It was by no means my first trip, as he was aware, and I still have no idea why he suddenly became so serious, almost paternal. There were two things he wanted to tell me. "Of course," he said, "I don't have to urge you to go

[2]

to X's. They have the books, after all. But I do want to warn you of one thing: don't let anyone in England know that you ever heard of Y.'' Slightly mystified, I thanked him; and within two days I encountered the second friend, who greeted me breezily. ''I hear you're off to England,'' he said. ''Well, I don't have to tell you about that booby-trap of X's; but there is a bookseller who has a great flair for books; he and his wife stay with us when they're in this country, and I wish you'd look him up—and that's Y.'' The curious symmetry of these two admonitions has always struck me as astonishing. It helped to explain why the two collectors had not clashed, certainly; but to me it proved what I had always believed: you should hunt for the dealer who can do the most for you and whom you find most congenial. I never had much luck with either X or Y.

You will have to share your dealer's time with his other customers, but, if he sees that you are in earnest, he will make time for you. Try not to create difficulties for him. I remember another two friends (I hope the reader does not find these anonymities perplexing) whom I met in a bookshop in the late 'thirties. We had none of us progressed very far in the mysteries of our particular Eleusis. I was still concentrating on Trollope, while, of the other two, one was collecting Restoration drama and the second, a foreigner, was becoming acquainted with America by assembling Merle Johnson's *High Spots*. The bookseller was happy with three steady (if cautious) customers, and no conflict of interests.

It was too good to last. A copy of Ford's *The Broken Heart* was in a forthcoming auction, and this caused trouble. I had one or two of his plays, and wanted this item; the Restoration collector was moving backward in time and, though he had nothing of Ford, regarded that as a strong reason for acquiring *The Broken Heart*; and the Merle Johnson collector had discovered The Grolier Club list of *One Hundred Books Famous in English Literature*—in which the play is included. And then we, who had been gentle and compliant before, suddenly became stubborn and aggressive. Nobody would withdraw from the competition. In vain the dealer tried to reason with us, separately and together. In vain he promised sumptuous treasures in the future to any two of us who would yield on this one point. None of us three would budge. *The Broken Heart* took on an importance quite unjustified by its literary significance.

I do not know what the others did, but I finally gave my bid to another dealer. In the event, none of us succeeded: we were all outbid. This was probably the happiest solution; at any rate, we kept our slightly shaken friendship, and each of us managed to get along without the book. Some twenty years passed and took their toll; both my friends died, and so did the bookseller. And then I was offered that very copy of *The Broken Heart*—that same apple of discord of so many years before. Well, I am glad to have it now. But if my friends were still alive, how would I feel? Not altogether comfortable with it, I expect.

Then there was the occasion, a very long time ago, when I entered a London bookshop in August. Apparently I did not know that that was the worst time in all the year to find a bookseller. Naturally, he was not in—he would be back in September, as I was informed by the young attendant, who seemed in sole charge. Since I was there, I began looking around, but the books in that first room were mostly window dressing: the eighth edition of *Tristram Shandy* in full red morocco, and so on. And the attendant became over-helpful, calling my attention to a series of books I had no interest in. Evidently I discouraged him a bit emphatically—I have always wanted to do my own looking— for he abruptly began describing a Caxton the firm had recently sold to a titled client for £20,000 or thereabouts—anyhow, a staggering sum in those days.

I did not really care for what seemed to me his boasting, and in an effort to stem this tide I observed coldly that my own copy of the *Canterbury Tales* was imperfect: it lacked everything but one leaf. One should never try to be funny outside one's own

[4]

country, of course: that wretched youth misunderstood me. In a voice that now verged on the obsequious, he inquired, "What leaf is it that is missing, sir? Perhaps sometime we might be able to supply it."

There was no help for it; I had to climb down, I had to explain my pathetic little joke. It was not agreeable, it was even humiliating, for I do not think he understood the explanation. I did not return there for a long time, though, you will observe, it was not the fault of the dealer but my own *amour propre* that kept me away.

Then there was the time in more recent years when I went to a shop I had never visited before. It had dealt largely with scientific books—a large and important area, but not my field. It had begun to add literature to its stock, so I dropped in—just to see. I found myself alone in the shop, and began looking at the contents of the shelves. Presently a man emerged from an inner office and appeared startled at finding an intruder. I asked if I might continue browsing and he assented, staring at me rather suspiciously. Finally he said quite sharply, "Might I ask your name, sir?" And, when I said, "Taylor," he asked, "Not *the* Mr. Taylor?" Well, how does one reply to downright idiocy? I mumbled that that was the name, and he went on: "I don't believe we have anything that would interest you .... Oh, there is perhaps one. Did you ever see Browning's *Paracelsus* in wrappers?" No, I had not, nor had I ever heard of it. He disappeared for a moment and returned with a small volume bound in red levant. It was *Paracelsus*, however, and when the binder decked it out in fancy dress he had bound with it two pieces of dark-brown paper. These were evidently supposed to be the "wrappers."

"You don't think," I said, "that these two leaves are simply the paper soaked off the original boards?"

"Why," he replied swiftly, "do you know, that never occurred to me."

[5]

But his voice did not carry conviction, and I extricated myself from this unsatisfactory situation as soon as I civilly could.

One final anecdote, reflecting more on me than on the firm. I had wandered into the Conduit St. shop of Elkin Mathews (at last a real name!) and bought there a Trollope novel. This must have been about 1930; for I paid cash for it, not knowing then that a book could be obtained except for ready money. About a month after I returned home, a bill for it arrived. Well, I thought, their accountant will find their error sooner or later, and tossed the bill aside. But another one came several months later, and I was a bit perturbed. A general disinclination to correspondence kept me from explaining the situation, and besides, what could I say? Why had I not answered the first communication? I certainly had not kept a receipt—had they even given me one? I thought not. And when a third statement arrived I thought the best plan would be to stay out of England altogether. At all events, the firm gave up the effort to extract a second payment from me.

Percy Muir, to whom I told this story years later, scoffed at it, saying it could not possibly have happened. No one, he said, ever paid cash at Elkin Mathews; none of the staff would have known what to do with the money. (I thought they seemed to know very well what to do with it, but let that pass.) And, he continued, as for sending out a series of bills—! No, no, I must have dreamed the whole of it. Nobody is more familiar than he with the glittering eccentricities which marked that firm's brief transit in and out of brilliant success; but I know what I remember.

All these reminiscences which have floated to the surface of my memory have been merely of slight *contretemps*. This is understandable: no *contretemps*, no story. What I want to make clear is that they are the exceptional occurrence, and that really nothing more untoward has happened in my more than half a century of collecting. The satisfactory episodes, the times of good talk, of happy acquisitions, are most of them dull in the recounting. Shall we try one?

[6]

I was arguing once with a bookseller about some detail of the Robert Hoe bookplate. This was a mistake; the bookseller will almost invariably know more than you in such matters. Sure enough, he said, "You're wrong—here, I'll show you," and picked up a book from a table behind him. Of course he was right and I told him so; and having looked at it—Webster's *The White Devil*, 1612—I added, "I'll take this." To my surprise, his face fell; he had intended to offer it to someone else. But since he had not already done so, he let me have it. I now remember that this tale has appeared in print before, but without the questions I now append: if I had not engaged in that foolish argument, would I have this very scarce book? And what moral is to be drawn from the answer?

Another: one day when I was in Scribner's rare book department, presided over by Dave Randall, the mail arrived, and included a package from Italy. Now Dave did not deal in Italian, or indeed Continental, books, and my curiosity was aroused. "What in the world is that?" I asked, always curious about things that were none of my business. "I haven't the faintest idea," he said; "Let's see." He opened it, and found a note from the elderly Olivia Rossetti asking if he could sell the enclosed items for her. They consisted of a manuscript poem by Swinburne, written to her when she was a baby, and a series of letters from Walt Whitman to her father, William Michael Rossetti, about the first English edition of *Leaves of Grass*. A nice little clutch.

I knew that Dave had several customers who would buy anything of Whitman; but I coveted those letters—they were (and are) extremely interesting. I said, "Dave, I'm going to get you out of a terrible difficulty. I'll take these off your hands and then you won't have to decide which of your Whitman enthusiasts you'll offer them to first." He thought for a moment—apparently the problem was hard one—and then said, "All right. But don't tell anybody for a while." Well, I suppose the moral of that is: be at the right place at the right time.

I have so far not mentioned auctions, save to call them necessary evils. They can be exciting occasions, of course, when something spectacular is up for sale. Moreover, they are the darlings of executors who have valuable books to dispose of. In such a case they are suspicious of any offer made for the collection—how are they to know that it is not too small? But a public sale! No one can criticize them for relying on that, no matter what the outcome, which may be affected even by the weather. A blizzard on the day of the sale may reduce the total sum realized well below expectation; while if the sale-room is crowded with the curious, auction fever may overtake them and, though they may not have intended to bid, they may find themselves running up the prices and even surprising themselves by buying a few items. (This does not happen in London, where virtually all bids are made by dealers and no effort is made to encourage buyers from outside the book-trade.)

All collectors are faced with auction-buying at some time or other, and indeed a few appear never to tire of it. There is the excitement at receiving a prize, the disappointed astonishment that others are willing to out-bid them by such large sums, and so on. For most of us, however, these affairs soon become routine; and we soon realize that the dealer more than earns his commission with his expertise and his attendance at dull sales where he will try to buy only two or three books.

I speak advisedly of his expertise. Unless you are very knowledgeable indeed, he will be better able to judge a book's value than you are. It is his responsibility, if you have given him a bid, to know whether or not that particular book should have a half-title, to tell you what he thinks it will fetch, or rather, perhaps, tell you how high he thinks your bid should go. Sometimes he will have to tell you that some book is out of your financial range, and that it is better for you to concentrate on less expensive but still desirable items. Once in a while he will tell you that he has a bid from an old customer and cannot act for you: he might even ask you not to bid on it, but this would be very seldom indeed.

[8]

There are those, also, who give bids to several dealers. The late A. Edward Newton was one of these, and here is his rationale on the subject:

> My own plan, after years of experience, is to give my bids to the particular bookseller most likely to buy, for stock or for a client, the item that I especially covet. For example, if an item like *Robinson Crusoe* is coming up, to free myself from Dr. Rosenbach's competition I will give my bid to him with the highest limit I am willing to pay. He in turn will have to outbid Lathrop and Walter Hill and Gabriel Wells. If, on the other hand, I want a *Songs of Childhood* ... or *A Shropshire Lad* ... I would give my bid to James F. Drake and take my chance with Rosy. If then, having secured the good will of the trade, some little odds and ends come up of no special importance, I do not hesitate to bid myself. But an important item I would never attempt to buy myself, and I have seen thousands of dollars spent uselessly by persons giving commissions to the wrong agent.

Yet I recall the late Carroll Wilson telling me that his copy of the 1620 Marlowe's *Faustus* was the favorite among his books; and when I asked him why, he said that it was because he had successfully bid for it himself—at the Newton sale, incidentally. But I have never understood why he took particular relish in the mode of acquisition; to me this would mean nothing. Most of the early purchases I made when bidding for myself (because I had to be careful with small sums and the dealer's commission seemed to be something that could be saved) were mistakes.

In any case, I would rather look through a bookseller's stock than go to an auction. It is more leisurely, there is time to reflect, time to explore, there is no one competing with you, and one is free to accept or reject the prices without their being raised against you. And there is, very likely, good conversation. (After all, at a book sale, the auctioneer does practically all the talking.)

Mention of prices—always a vexing subject—brings up the fact that during this period of inflation and increasing scarcity of rare books it is difficult to judge what is a reasonable price and what is not. This holds true for both parties, especially if they have long memories. The dealer has a hard time bringing himself to pay so much for stock, and the customer is outraged to find that something he rejected as too expensive ten years ago may now be five times as much. The old rule still holds, however: do not haggle. The dealer has priced his books because he hopes to sell them at that figure, and his hopes are based on experience. If you cannot afford them, do not buy them. It does not cost anything to look at them, however; and perhaps prolonged contemplation may cause you to understand why he has to ask this figure. He will explain, if you ask. But do not try to beat him down. You are not, presumably, in the Near East, and do not need to follow its customs. No one who has read it has ever forgotten the forceful simile in John Selden's *Table Talk,* when, after urging the payment of the stated amount for a book in earnest of favors to come, the author adds, "So 'tis in giving a bawd her price."

For the most part, what the customer pays for is not merely the books, but learning about them, discovering new fields, making friends from among other collectors, librarians, and scholars. What more can you ask for? All this can come out of bookshops; at least, it has for me, and there is abundant testimony that it has happened that way for others.

It is sometimes said nowadays that there are fewer bookshops than there used to be. Certainly, all the senior collectors can recall many shops that are no more. It is frequently a one-man business, and dies with the founder. But others start up, and the outlook for the immediate future seems reasonably cheerful.

Though, as I say, there are those who disagree. Lord Clark, opening the London Antiquarian Book Fair of 1978, ended his talk with

    ... the book collector has more freedom of action than other collectors, and a chance discovery in a bookshop may open up a

[10]

new line. Alas, old bookshops are disappearing. There was a time when they could be found in every country town. Now I am told that collectors buy from specialized catalogues posted from accommodation addresses in the country. I have never bought a book in that way, and, since the practice arose, I have ceased to be a book collector; just as well, as my shelves are full. There must be others who feel as I do. Rummaging in an antiquarian bookshop was one of the pleasures of life, and like so many other pleasures, it is now almost unattainable.

It should be borne in mind that this speech was delivered to an audience which included some seventy-five dealers who each had a stall filled with samples of his wares, and a great many other dealers who had come to seek what they might devour. No, I think Lord Clark was rather gloomier than necessary. Moreover, I must admit that I had never heard of the "specialized catalogues" which he spoke of, and am constrained to add that I myself continue to receive the customary variety in the mail. But the passage that really betrays him is the sentence which declares it a good thing that he has abandoned collecting, because his shelves are full. What true collector ever stopped for that reason?

Still, Lord Clark remembers the past, when, it is true, dealers' catalogues contained richer ore than is now generally the case. They also appeared more often. But rising costs of printing have curtailed their frequency, and a diminution of the number of rare books has made it more difficult to hoard the supply necessary for a catalogue. Then, too, catalogues represent a great deal of hard work; and in view of an increased demand, a dealer will ask himself whether his books will not sell as readily without this additional trouble and expense. This is a pity, for they made excellent reading, and some of them are so informative that they are still on reference shelves.

Moreover, in earlier days there did not seem to be the same urgency about ordering from them. No, perhaps I am wrong here; one must not let memory render the past too iridescent. Now that I think of it, I recall receiving a catalogue from the firm of Lathrop Harper one morning about twenty years ago. In it was listed a scarce poem by John Gay, and I reached for the telephone and ordered it. Also, I said I would be in the following day to pick it up. On my arrival, I proffered my check to Douglas Parsonage, together with some withering comments on the price they had seen fit to attach to the volume. "Yes, well," said Doug, as soon as he found an opening, "we've had nine orders for it since you telephoned yesterday. So, if you don't really want it ..." I hate interruptions like that; they destroy all rational argument—and I still had in reserve several trenchant remarks I was never able to use.

Even earlier, in the 'forties, a Maggs catalogue listed a copy of George Herbert's *The Temple* for, I think, £150. This elicited some seventeen cables and many other orders from the United States, all of them unsuccessful. John Carter had wandered into Maggs's the day the catalogues were sent out, and walked away with Herbert in his pocket. No, I suppose it was always true that prompt action is advisable in the case of a book you really want.

However, I shall always feel that the most rewarding way of acquiring a book is to buy it from a dealer's stock. He may have set it aside for you, or you may surprise both yourself and him by finding something out of your usual line and deciding that it ought to be in your collection. You can examine its condition at length, and hear whatever he can tell you about it, and learn its provenance, and—but this list is endless, as all bookmen know. You are not rushed into a decision; indeed, if there is any doubt in your mind, he will give you plenty of time to think about it. The whole episode will be one more link in that lengthy chain of discussion, bibliography, gossip, friendliness, and acquisition with which collectors delight to fetter themselves.

Among my books is a copy of Trollope's *The Warden* which formerly belonged to Carroll Wilson. Now, Carroll was a reticent New Englander; but on the front endpaper he wrote a brief note to the effect that the purchase of this volume marked his entry

into serious collecting; that he had given it to himself as a birthday present in 1925 "and thereby opened the door to the most
pleasant hours of my life." I wish I knew what dealer sold it to him.

ROBERT NIKIRK, *Librarian of The Grolier Club, has been involved with the antiquarian book world nearly continuously since the age of eighteen. He says that he was bitten by the book bug on first reading the works of A. Edward Newton and John Carter's* ABC for Book Collectors *in the excellent public library of his native Corning, New York. While in college he worked for a displaced German* Antiquar *and in 1965 joined a New York bookseller specializing in scholarly art books. In 1967 he went to the book department at Parke-Bernet Galleries as a cataloguer where he worked until joining The Grolier Club in 1970.*

Looking into
Provenance

Robert Nikirk

PROVENANCE is a word used frequently in the collecting
world, sometimes seemingly to annoy those outside it. To
begin at once by borrowing from John Carter's still irreplaceable
ABC for Book Collectors, provenance is "the pedigree of a
book's previous ownership." After rarity and fine condition, it
is the quality most prized by collectors. But it must be stressed
that a *distinguished* pedigree is the only sort that counts. It is
pointless to record in catalogues or boast about a string of previous
owners who are today unknown as collectors or historical figures
of note. The purpose of this essay is to outline how a present
owner of a significant book may, by using the evidence available,
obtain information about his predecessor owners. Specifically,
it will introduce to the reader antiquarian booksellers' catalogues,

All of the books illustrated in Mr. Nikirk's article are from the library of The
Grolier Club.

[15]

auction catalogues and records, and private library catalogues.

Book collectors greatly enjoy discussion of provenance. What is an outsider to think, overhearing at some bookish gathering, "And do you know, it is the La Vallière–Wodhull–Hoe–Bishop–Wilmerding copy?" and the breathless rejoinder from his friend, "No, you don't say?" Arcane to the uninitiated, perhaps, but such talk is meat and drink to the collector. For a classic, detailed examination of the subject, read Seymour DeRicci's *English Collectors of Books and Manuscripts (1530–1930) and Their Marks of Ownership* (Cambridge, 1930).

All evidence of provenance, admonish Carter and DeRicci, is to be cherished and never destroyed or tampered with. But what *is* the evidence? Possibilities are numerous, from the obvious to the obscure. On bindings, armorial bearings stamped in gold can hardly be missed, nor can stamped names, initials, or sensible mottoes such as that of Jean Grolier (1479–1565), perhaps the most famous of all bibliophiles: PORTIO MEA DOMINE SIT IN TERRA VIVENTIUM ("May my inheritance, O Lord, be in the land of the living"). Occasionally, a binding style or decoration traditionally identified with a particular collector provides a ready link in the chain of provenance. The book bindings made for great collectors of the past are well recorded in monographs and articles, and would certainly be easily identified after only minimal research. From access to a good reference library, identifications can be made for books with distinctive coats of arms or mottoes stamped on their covers. English armorial bearings can usually be identified with reasonable ease because the issuance of coats of arms in Britain has been strictly regulated, like coinage, since the Middle Ages. English heraldic literature is very extensive, and much information has been extracted and published for the sole purpose of researching the provenance of books, in cluding Cyril Davenport's *English Heraldic Bookstamps* (1909). For France, armorial data are well recorded up to the time of the French Revolution in such reference works as Oliver, Hermal, and Roton's *Manuel de l'amateur de reliures amoriées françaises*

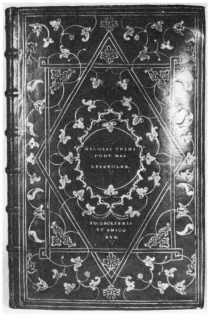

The upper cover of a binding for Jean Grolier showing the famous ownership inscription, "Jean Grolier's and his friends'."

The lower cover of a binding for Jean Grolier showing his motto.

An armorial binding of the English collector Michael Wodhull (1740–1816).

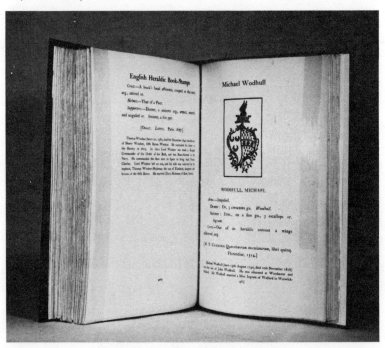

Cyril Davenport's reference book on English Heraldic Book-Stamps *(1909), showing the arms of Michael Wodhull.*

(Paris, 1924). Considerable reference literature also exists for the coats of arms of Germany and the Low Countries. But for elsewhere in Europe, the available heraldic literature is sparse and difficult to use. The subject is much complicated with respect to Italy, for example, because she can claim, in addition to the royal,

The most important reference work on French armorial bindings.

princely, and noble coats of arms granted by the temporal powers, the ecclesiastical bearings which the Vatican for centuries has issued to prelates and lay papal nobility.

* * *

The fact that a particular volume has stamped on its covers the arms of an historical figure does not necessarily mean that

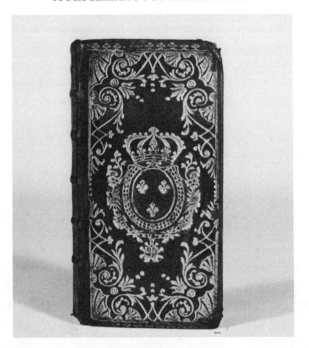

A French court calendar for the year 1779, stamped with the arms of King Louis XVI, possibly for presentation to a member of the royal household. Royal bindings on this type of book are common, and rarely if ever are valid evidence of provenance.

the book ever belonged to or was in the library of such a person. This is especially true of books bearing the arms of French and English monarchs, of popes, and of certain other individuals such as Napoleon. For example, a copy of an *Almanach Royal* bearing the arms of Louis XV is almost certainly *not* the king's own copy but one of the many copies given by him as gifts each year. Persons desiring to present a copy of any book to their sovereign would normally, as a matter of course, have the monarch's coat of arms stamped on the binding. But whether the book was ever given, or if given received, or if received kept, is entirely another matter and not determinable from the stamping

[20]

on the binding. The same caveat must also be given for books bearing papal arms or the crests of other famous "public" persons.

Moving from the binding to the interior of a book in the search for evidence of provenance, one may find one or more book-plates displaying arms or a name or both; a name or a motto written on a fly-leaf or on the title page; perhaps a shelf mark or auction lot number; or a clipping from an old catalogue. Shelf marks are usually large and awkward inscriptions of letters and numbers that are designed to pinpoint the exact location of the book on a particular shelf in a particular bookcase. A great many volumes that were once in the library of Benjamin Franklin and Horace Walpole have been discovered solely by virtue of their shelf marks. For the handwritten shelf marks of these men are, to the trained eye, as distinctive and as easily recognizable as their signatures. The shelf marks of other collectors may be distinctive by reason of the particular system of library arrangement which they reflect. Sir Robert Cotton (1571–1631), the great collector of manuscripts, arranged all his volumes in fourteen bookcases and above them, for identification, placed busts of the twelve Roman emperors and Cleopatra and Faustina (wife of the Emperor Antoninus). Thus the shelf mark of the famous Lindisfarne Gospels is Nero, D.IV. As this method was not unique to Cotton, not every book bearing a shelf mark incorporating the name of a Caesar can be said to have come from his library, but it certainly is evidence to be considered.

The evidentiary value of the signature of a former owner is self-evident and requires little or no special knowledge to recognize and appreciate. Some education is required, however, in order to spot a book once owned by Thomas Jefferson, for he did not use a bookplate. Rather, he preferred to incorporate his initials into the corresponding lettered signature of a volume. In other words, before the signature lettered "I" in a book, Jefferson would write a tiny "T." Even less obvious are mottoes or epigrams which some famous collectors inscribed in their books, often in lieu of all other marks or indications of ownership. A familiarity

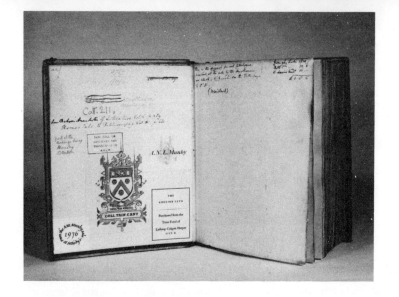

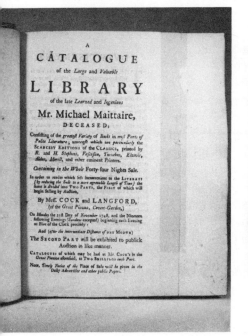

A plethora of evidence of provenance, including ownership inscriptions, purchase data, shelf marks, and bookplates in a rare complete copy of the auction catalogue of Michael Maittaire (London, 1748–1749). This was the auctioneer's own interleaved working copy in which he inscribed the names of buyers and prices realized.

with a few of the more famous of these mottoes might conceivably lead to the making of a significant discovery. For example, a book belonging to Ben Jonson would have "Tanquam explorator" written on its title page.

Bookplates may seem to be crystal-clear evidence of previous ownership, but unfortunately this is not always true. It is all too possible that a bookplate was added later to a book to lend it allure and value. Mr. Wilmarth Lewis, writing in *Collector's Progress* (New York, 1951), and *One Man's Education* (New York, 1967), recounts plenty of stories along these lines in reconstructing the library of Horace Walpole. An old bookseller of my acquaintance has told me that during his apprentice days before the First World War, his principal kept near him a large pile of fresh bookplates from the estate of a prominent and deceased collector. These were added at will to a marginally valuable book which might not otherwise have sold quickly.

The fact that a distinguished provenance can drastically increase the value of an otherwise ordinary volume has been well known to unscrupulous individuals for many years. Charles Dexter Allen relates in his *American Book Plates* (1895) that a counterfeit of George Washington's armorial bookplate was first discovered at an auction in 1867 in Washington, D.C. This particular fake is readily detected if one is alert and knows what to look for. There were also, however, plenty of restrikes made from the original copper plate, and these can be distinguished from original impressions only by differences in printing and paper. The collector who has done his research is also aware that it was Washington's habit to write his name in the upper right-hand corner of the title page in each of his books, in addition to affixing his bookplate. So any volume with bookplate but without signature should be carefully examined.

It must always be kept in mind that a genuine bookplate, unlike a genuine signature, may be added to a volume long after the death of its owner. In fact, on occasion this has been done openly and legitimately. For example, a few years ago a portion

[23]

tanquā Explorator

DICTA POETARVM
QVÆ APVD
IO. STOBÆVM
EXSTANT

EMENDATA ET LATINO CARMINE
reddita ab HVGONE GROTIO.

*Accefferunt Plutarchi & Bafilii Magni de ufu
Græcorum Poetarum libelli.*

PARISIIS,
Apud NICOLAVM BVON, in via Iacobæa, fub fignis
S. Claudij, & Hominis Siluestris.

M. DC. XXIII.   *Su Ben: Jonson*

CVM PRIVILEGIO REGIS.

*A book from Ben Jonson's library showing his typical ownership
inscriptions: his motto and signature.*

of the library of E. M. Forster was acquired and sold by an English bookseller by means of a special catalogue which, as will be discussed later, has become a valuable addition to the literature of provenance. E. M. Forster sometimes used a small printed label to denote his ownership of a book. And as the sale catalogue of books from his library clearly stated, "A number of E. M. Forster's books already contained this label when we received the residue of his library; shortly afterwards, a box of labels was discovered by Dr Munby in Mr Forster's rooms in King's College, and these were affixed to the remaining volumes. The labels left over have been destroyed." The insertion of these labels by the bookseller was designed to provide a sort of certificate of provenance, as many of the volumes would otherwise have had no mark of ownership in them. But one can't help but wonder if perhaps a couple of the books listed in the catalogue and now bearing the requisite label had merely been borrowed by Forster and were unreturned at the time of his death, or had accidently been left in his room by a visiting friend.

The vast majority of affixed bookplates are indeed valid indications of prior ownership but, in the absence of any other evidence of provenance, catalogues should say "With the bookplate of Count X" rather than "From the library of Count X, with his bookplate." But perhaps the former ownership of Count X can be documented beyond question, and it is the purpose of this essay to introduce to the collector the sources wherein such proof may be found.

Let us now begin to consider the three types of documentary corroboration for provenance mentioned at the outset—bookseller's catalogues, auction catalogues and records, and private library catalogues.

Lacking clear-cut evidence, our establishing that a certain book was sold by a certain bookseller is a very chancy game. Moreover, long runs of booksellers' catalogues are the rarest and least accessible of the documentary sources discussed here. Always of a strictly ephemeral nature until the twentieth century,

[25]

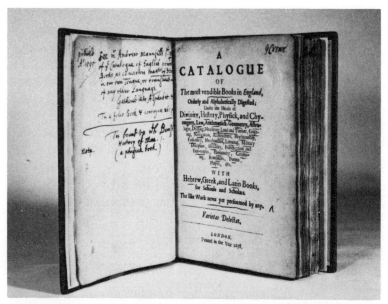

The title page of A Catalogue of The most vendible Books in England *(London, 1658), an important early bookseller's catalogue.*

few important caches survive even from the past one hundred and fifty years. Although the earliest surviving catalogue or list of books for sale dates from the fifteenth century, only a single copy of which is known to exist, booksellers' catalogues began to appear in quantity in the seventeenth century, reaching a high tide by the early nineteenth century and continuing at flood tide today. Unlike almost all of their ancestors, the catalogues issued by twentieth-century booksellers are not infrequently real contributions to bibliography and can be of great intrinsic interest by virtue of their typography and illustrations. Long runs of the modern major booksellers' catalogues thus tend to be preserved by collectors and librarians. One substantial archive of catalogues from all periods is in the library of The Grolier Club.

Since booksellers' catalogues reflect the collecting tastes and

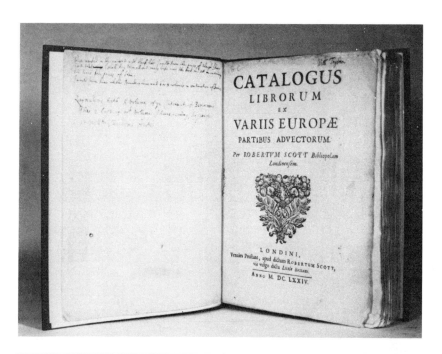

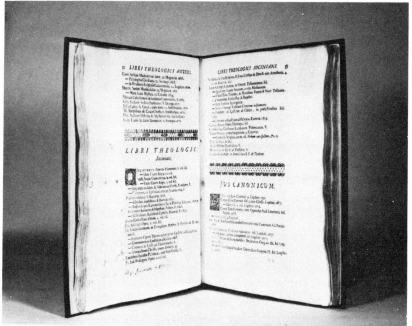

A catalogue issued in 1674 by the London bookseller Robert Scott, once owned by Sir William Twysden and later by Sir Thomas Phillipps. The writing on the front free endpaper consists of a query from Twysden to Scott, beneath which Scott has written his answer.

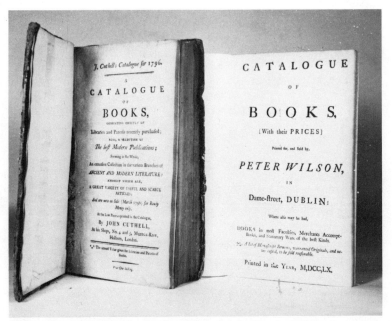

Two typical eighteenth-century booksellers' catalogues.

standards of their time, until comparatively recently catalogues listed only author, title, place of printing, date, and size. For up until at least the early nineteenth century, few collectors bought books from the viewpoint of provenance. The eighteenth-century collector's ideal was to acquire the most correct edition of, say, a classical author, while looking for a handsome edition into the bargain. James Logan of Philadelphia is a shining example of this kind of fastidious book buyer, as amply demonstrated by Edwin Wolf II's reconstruction of the Loganian Library (*The Library of James Logan of Philadelphia* [Philadelphia, 1974]). In the palmy days of collecting in Regency England, certain scholarly booksellers such as Payne & Foss and Thorpe began to catalogue with an eye on provenance. It took seventy-five years for this approach to come to America, eventually flowering in the catalogues of the George D. Smith and Dr. Rosenbach eras.

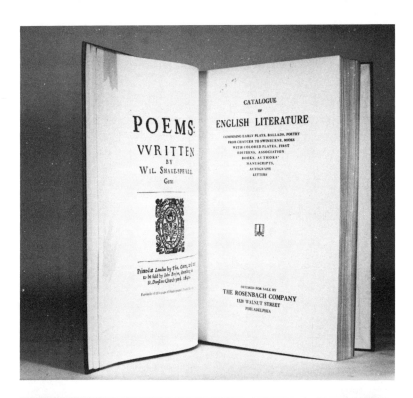

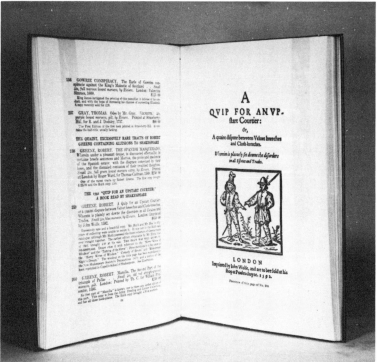

A catalogue issued by The Rosenbach Company, the most eminent American bookselling firm in the first half of the twentieth century.

But what use can be made of booksellers' catalogues in the search for provenance? Sometimes a notation of purchase from a bygone bookseller will be written near the front of a book:

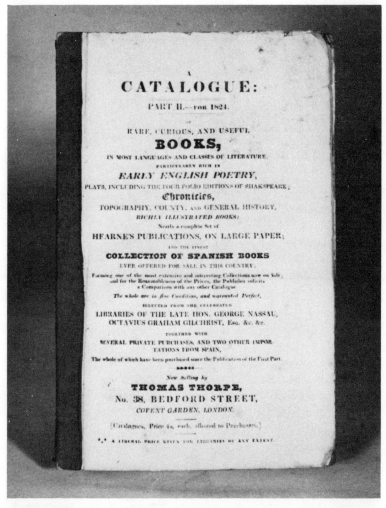

A catalogue issued in 1824 by Thomas Thorpe, one of the best-known booksellers of nineteenth-century London.

"Bought of Thorpe, July 1830," for example. Finding the very book listed in a Thorpe catalogue, if you can locate the catalogue, is a long shot but does forge another documentary link. Also, a clipping from a catalogue may be present, but if not annotated with a bookseller's name it will be of little help unless a trained eye can identify a characteristic typography. Occasionally, the bookseller's own code for cost and price is present (often in the form of a string of letters spelling no known word), and certain of these codes are so distinctive and well known to the trade as to be the only clue needed to identify the original bookseller.

A bookseller's catalogue composed entirely of the contents of one person's library is of fairly infrequent occurrence, as through the centuries a tying-up of capital required to acquire entire libraries of persons of note has not been characteristic of the antiquarian book trade. And yet it is precisely this kind of catalogue that often proves invaluable in the search for or confirmation of provenance. The catalogue of books from E. M. Forster's library mentioned earlier is one recent example of this sort, and the catalogue of the library of Charles Dickens issued by Sotheran's shortly after his death in June 1870 is another. As restrikes of Dickens' bookplate from the original plate are not uncommon (one was issued with certain modern editions of Dickens' works published by the Piccadilly Fountain Press in London), it is extremely useful, when one is offered a volume supposed to come from Dickens' library, to be able to check the Sotheran's catalogue to ascertain whether the volume is listed there and if so, whether according to the catalogue it should contain an inscription or other independent evidence of provenance. Except for those rarely issued catalogues that consist of books from one collector's library, finding documentation for a book's previous ownership through the use of booksellers' catalogues can be frustrating and complicated.

On the other hand, the history of book auctions as revealed in sale catalogues is virtually the history of book collecting. Certainly far more significant libraries have ended up on the auction block

CATALOGUS
Variorum & Insignium
LIBRORUM
Inftructiffimæ Bibliothecæ
Clariffimi Doctiffimiq; Viri
LAZARI SEAMAN, S.T.D.

Quorum Auctio habebitur *LONDINI*
in ædibus Defuncti in Area & Viculo
Warwicenfi, *Octobris* ultimo.

Cura *GULIELMI COOPER* Bibliopolæ.

LONDINI,
Apud {Ed Brewster & Guil. Cooper} ad Infigne {Gruis in Cæmiterio *Paulino*, Pelicani in Vico vulgariter dicto *Little-Britain*. 1676.}

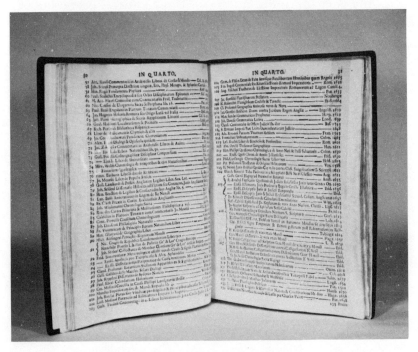

The first English book auction catalogue (October 31, 1676).

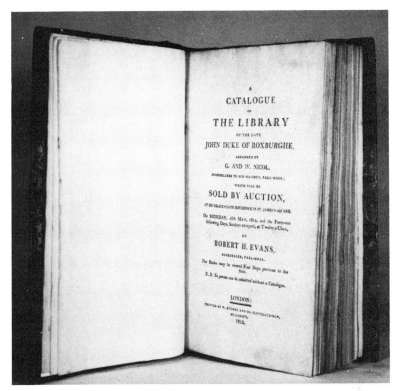

*The catalogue of the epoch-making auction of the library of the
Duke of Roxburghe (London, 1812).*

than have been bought by individual dealers or acquired by
institutions. The library of John Evelyn, dispersed in the London
sales of 1977–78, is just a recent instance of the public dispersal
of books of superb pedigree. In fact, so scarce are books of interesting provenance in today's market that many of the Evelyn
books appeared in booksellers' catalogues only a few weeks after
their appearance in the auction room, at substantially increased
prices.

When a significant book has come from a significant sale, this
information tends to have been recorded in the book itself. Per-

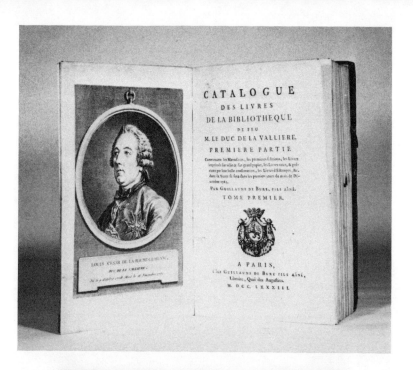

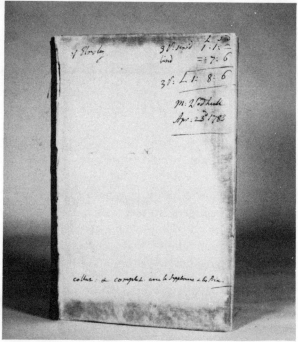

The title page and front free endpaper of Michael Wodhull's copy of the sale catalogue of the Duc de La Vallière's library (Paris, 1783). In addition to inscribing his name, Wodhull noted the price paid for the catalogue and the cost of having it bound.

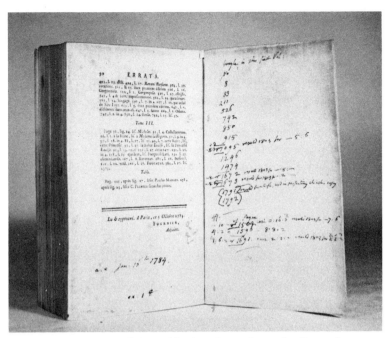

Wodhull's holograph list of his purchases from the first volume of the La Vallière sale.

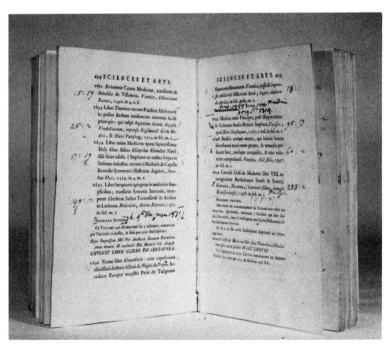

Two pages from the La Vallière sale catalogue showing Wodhull's annotations.

haps it has something to do with recording for posterity the satisfaction of having won out over competition. To the contrary, most run-of-the-mill books sold at auction, especially in London, are "bought for stock" by booksellers, and their source at auction will usually not be known to the ultimate purchaser.

The holograph noting of the source of a newly acquired book by collectors became common in the eighteenth century, and progressed to the insertion of clippings from catalogues in the late nineteenth (often leaving acid stain marks where laid in).

If he knows the name of a former owner of the book to be investigated, the collector might best begin by consulting the various "named sale" indexes to find out whether that person's library was ever sold at auction. Such indexes now exist for named sales in England up to 1900 in *List of Catalogues of English Book Sales, 1676–1900* (London: British Museum, 1915), revised by Munby and Coral to 1800 as *British Book Sale Catalogues 1676–1800* (London: Mansell, 1977); for the United States up to 1934 in George L. McKay's *American Book Auction Catalogues 1713–1934: A Union List* (New York, 1937); and in manuscript form for France up to 1969 (currently on deposit at The Grolier Club). For the period prior to 1900 in France, the first place to turn to establish if a known collector's books were sold at auction is the indispensable *Répertoire des catalogues des ventes 1600–1900* by Frits Lugt. Other countries await such named-sale indexing, the inquiring researcher being at sea in all of Continental Europe except for France. And as can be seen, all of the latter part of the twentieth century awaits diligent indexers.

By consulting these indexes, it is relatively simple to see whether or not a sale catalogue for the library of the person in question exists and where a copy may be found, because the indexes for England, France, and the United States already mentioned list representative major libraries or reference collections that contain a copy of each named-sale catalogue. Brief, polite inquiries will generally elicit an answer, perhaps accompanied by a photocopy of the catalogue page listing the lot in question. Be

[36]

aware, however, that until well into the twentieth century, auction catalogues gave little more information than did booksellers'—in fact, rather less. Until the pressure of scarcity occurred in post-war times, not even a Gutenberg Bible up for sale in the old London auction houses would move the cataloguers to paroxysms of description. By contrast, on the other side of the Atlantic, the American auction houses of the late nineteenth century indulged in the most extreme puffery. If you are fortunate, the copy to be consulted will be "named and priced," that is, with marginal notations of the purchasers' names and the prices paid. This information is essential in the search for provenance, as with it you confirm not only when and where your copy was sold

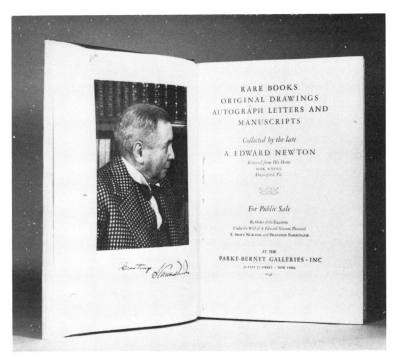

One volume of the auction catalogue (New York, 1941) of the collection of A. Edward Newton.

[37]

but to whom it was sold, thus adding yet another name to the list of previous owners.

Often the quest for provenance in old auction catalogues will abruptly end with a named and priced entry listing a bookseller as purchaser. As is nearly always the case, a book bought by a bookseller will be put into the trade and the trail lost. It is usually futile to seek assistance from the named bookseller (assuming that the firm happens to survive, of course), because most book-sellers are quite properly unwilling to release the names of their customers. The American auction houses, when they do answer an inquiry, generally will release only the name of a bookseller–buyer, because he is considered to be a "public" person.

Another source of auction-related evidence, applicable only to books sold in the twentieth century, are the printed auction records. These generally accurate and reliable volumes record the book auction year alphabetically by author, and list a short title, perhaps an outstanding feature of the book (in a special binding, for instance, or containing a presentation inscription), the price fetched, and usually, except for American sales, the name on record of the purchaser. This last, however, may be a *nom de vente*, a fictitious name given to the clerk in order to conceal the name of the real buyer. This practice is more prevalent in Paris than in the London, New York, or German auction houses.

For sales in England and America, two annual compilations record auction information. The older of the two is American, the *American Book Prices Current*, which commenced publication in 1895. It currently records all printed books sold at auction that fetched twenty dollars and up (with the judicious inclusion of less expensive volumes), and also similar information for broadsides, maps, charts, autographs and manuscripts. Its English equivalent, *Book Auction Records*, or BAR, founded in 1902, does list the names of purchasers because the lists of prices realized published after each auction by the English houses include them. Of greatest value to the researcher into provenance

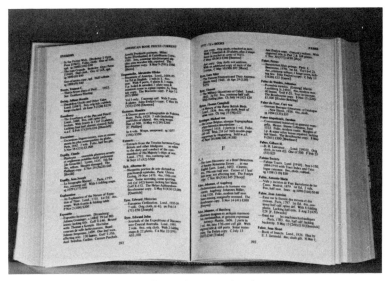

The format of American Book Prices Current.

is the index at the front of each volume of ABPC and BAR listing all the named sales reported in that volume, thereby providing a less compact and more awkward but nevertheless useful modern addition to the named-sale indexes discussed earlier. These auction records are vital tools which are used daily by everyone in the antiquarian book trade, and are often available in the reference sections of ordinary public libraries.

Less commonly found in American reference libraries are the printed auction records for France and Germany. In France, Delteil published an *Annuaire des ventes de livres* between 1918 and 1931. It was succeeded in 1941 by the *Annuaire des ventes*. The German printed auction records, the *Jahrbuch der Auktionspreise*, began in 1906 and continue today. In addition to the annual volumes, a five-year summary volume is, except for the French, issued by all the auction record publishers.

In summary: the printed auction records may, through their listing of all named sales (and sometimes the names of buyers)

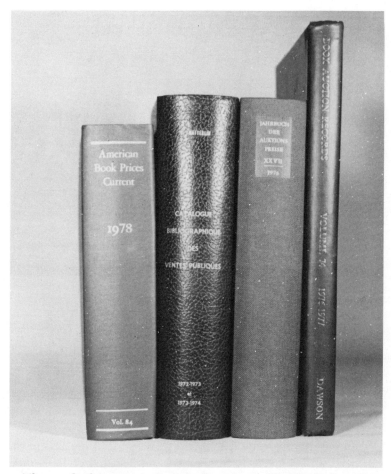

*The standard American, French, German, and English reference
works on book auction prices.*

provide a clue to the provenance of the book being researched.
The most important auction evidence in the search for provenance,
however, remains the original sale catalogue itself.

Finally, standing far apart from the catalogues issued by
booksellers and auction houses in both purpose and appearance

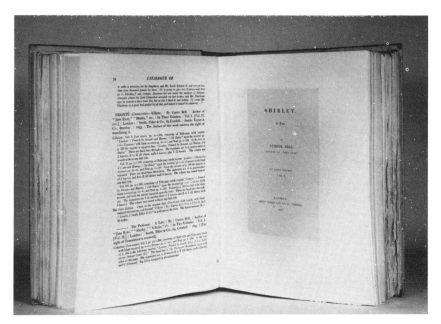

Volume I of Thomas J. Wise's 11-volume Ashley Library catalogue (1922–1936).

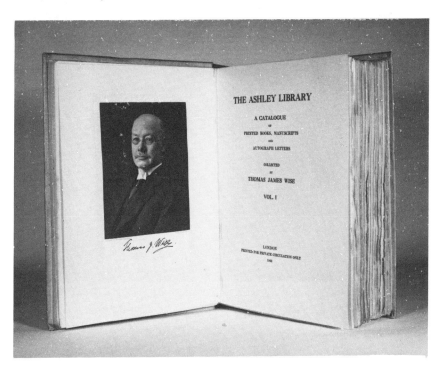

The format of the Ashley Library catalogue.

are the printed private library catalogues commissioned and often written by the proud owners of libraries, or on occasion by the institution that inherited them. Of course, in the search for provenance, private library catalogues are only useful if the catalogue records books which have been dispersed by sale and not donated to an institution, except where the institution has subsequently disposed of them. Thus, the otherwise very important catalogue of the Ashley Library formed by Thomas J. Wise (published in eleven volumes, London, 1922–36) is of little value to the collector researching provenance, as Wise's collection was acquired *en bloc* by the British Museum (now called the British Library) shortly after his death in 1937.

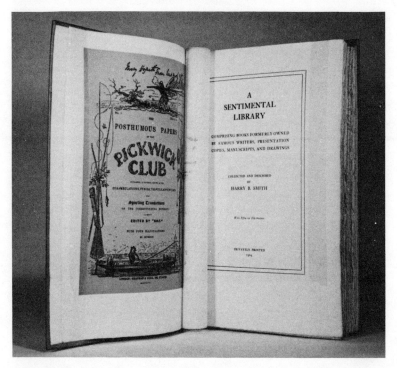

Harry B. Smith's privately printed catalogue of his famous Sentimental Library.

The whole subject of private library catalogues deserves special attention and is interesting from many viewpoints. These catalogues constitute a record of private enterprise in book collecting, and some have become standard bibliographical reference works while others are splendid examples of fine printing (e.g., those of J. Pierpont Morgan, William Andrews Clark, and Harry B. Smith); still others may provide an insight into collecting motives, goals, and purposes. The field of private library catalogues is one with which many experienced collectors, dealers, and librarians are not very familiar.

It should be noted that the habit of producing private library catalogues seems to be more prevalent among the English than other nationalities, with Americans second, having taken their usual cue from their English cousins. Some important catalogues have been produced by Americans, however. There is, for example, the catalogue of the collection of Robert Hoe, Jr., who formed the greatest private library ever gathered in the United States, and which was dispersed at auction in 1911–12. Hoe's splendid catalogue in sixteen volumes was produced between 1903 and 1909, and was completed just before his death in 1910. So massive was the Hoe library that books from his collection are still common in the trade (with his leather book label having done its acidic mischief on the title page and beyond).

The collection of English private library catalogues in The Grolier Club library occupies thirty shelves (including related materials by and about individual collectors), and American catalogues fill twenty-two shelves, with all other countries trailing way behind. As The Grolier Club is nearly one hundred years old and has always actively collected this sort of material, the Club's collection is doubtless a representative one. Unfortunately, there exists no complete or even partial index covering private library catalogues, and it will therefore take some inquiries to institutions known to possess such catalogues to establish if a particular individual ever issued a catalogue of his collection.

The search for provenance can be difficult and frustrating,

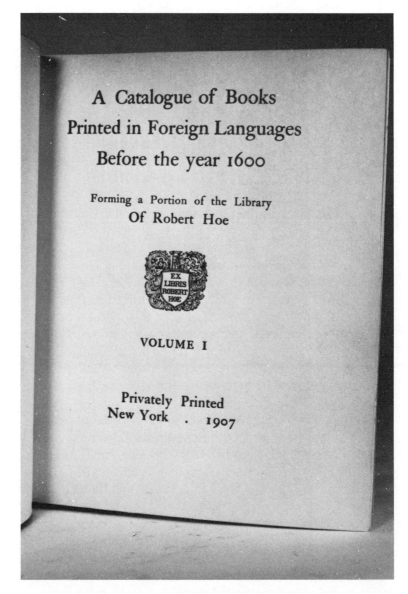

A volume of Robert Hoe's private library catalogue (1903–1909).

and often requires great patience and skill to evaluate the evidence properly and to use the documentary sources discussed in this essay. One outstanding example of painstaking research to establish provenance is found in Gabriel Austin's book, *The Library of Jean Grolier* (1971). In it, the 561 volumes known today to have been owned by Grolier are each followed by as complete a pedigree as it is possible to construct. In the family tree of each book, booksellers who once sold a Grolier volume are recorded in italic, interspersed with other past owners down to the present. Consider the work required to establish this provenance for Austin 3 (*Acta . . . Constantiensis Concilii* [Milan, 1511]): Baluze–Sunderland–*Ellis*–L. Techener–*Morgand*–Maglione–Hoe–Ives–Wallace–Wilmerding–*Rau*–Langlois.

Despite the many problems often encountered, discovering the provenance of a particular volume can be one of the most engaging pastimes associated with book collecting. A significant book will surely grow in interest and value for the collector if something of its past history can be documented.

SALVATORE J. IACONE *is a professor of English whose personal interest in book collecting focuses upon American and English literature, with special emphasis given to the first editions of Henry James, Ernest Hemingway, F. Scott Fitzgerald, and Gertrude Stein. He frequently lectures on the many delights of book collecting at various schools and libraries, and has also made guest appearances on radio and television. He is the author of* The Pleasures of Book Collecting *and he has contributed to* Harper's *and* Esquire *magazines.*

Inscribed Books
and
Literary Scholarship

Salvatore J. Iacone

INSCRIBED, presentation, and association copies of first editions have long fascinated collectors. Yet aside from the personal joy and satisfaction that many collectors experience in adding to their libraries, great or small, copies of first or later editions in which the author has set his or her pen, inscribed copies have another, and quite valuable appeal to scholars in terms of the biographical and bibliographical information they often provide.

To be sure, the purpose of this essay is not to suggest that all inscribed copies of first or later editions provide otherwise unobtainable information. Rather, this essay is intended to highlight the various ways in which inscribed books in general have served to provide scholars with information essential either to the specific theme of their research, or toward further insight and understanding of an author and his or her work. Due to the wide range of authors and topics that book collecting encompasses,

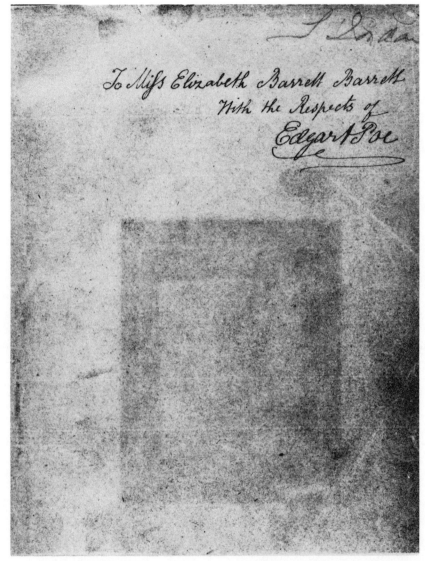

An inscription in a copy of The Raven and Other Poems *(1845) which, although brief, provides a tangible link between two great poets of the nineteenth century.*

[48]

the scope of this discussion is of necessity limited in nature, since emphasis will be solely on works of literature and representative authors, among them F. Scott Fitzgerald, Ernest Hemingway, T.S. Eliot, Sherwood Anderson, and James Joyce.

To begin, just what kinds of information do inscribed copies reveal? To be sure, they often provide accurate knowledge of an author's life, their relationship to other writers of their time, the circumstances surrounding or influencing the actual composition of a specific work, whether or not variant issues or states of a first edition were printed, and glimpses into the publication history of a work that was not otherwise known or available. To be sure, the nature of the information will often depend upon whether or not the author wrote revealing inscriptions. As Matthew J. Bruccoli states, with respect to F. Scott Fitzgerald:

> Fitzgerald was a serious inscriber. He rarely wrote best-wishes type inscriptions. He tried to be funny or say something about the book. For example, he was worried that *Tender Is the Night* would be judged by people who had read only the serial version— so in several inscriptions he urges the recipient to read the novel because it is better than the magazine version.

For example, in a copy inscribed to Dorothy Parker, famed wit of the Algonquin Hotel "Round Table" coterie of writers, Fitzgerald wrote:

> Dear Dotty
>
> This is better than the magazine.
>
> Love Always
>
> SCOTT
>
> Dorothy Parker
> c/o The New Yorker

Fitzgerald's equal concern with the formal critical reaction to this novel is apparent in a copy of the first edition inscribed to

An inscription from Fitzgerald to Dorothy Parker in a copy of
The Great Gatsby *(1925).*

Malcolm Cowley, then a book reviewer for *The New Republic*. The inscription reads:

> Dear Malcolm:
>
> Please don't review this—I know
> how you'd do it. Put a young man
> on it—oh hell—use your judgment,
> as you will anyhow.
>
> > Ever yours,
> > SCOTT

In one section of Dr. Bruccoli's bibliography of Fitzgerald's works, there are listed various examples of inscribed copies in which rather illuminating information, concerning either the particular work or the author himself, appears. For instance, in a first edition copy of *The Great Gatsby* (1925), inscribed to Charles T. Scott, Fitzgerald revealed a great deal about his conception of Gatsby's character:

> Gatsby was never quite real to me. His original served for a good enough exterior until about the middle of the book he grew thin and I began to fill him with my own emotional life. So he's synthetic — and that's one of the flaws in this book.
>
> > F. SCOTT FITZGERALD, Ellerslie,
> > Edgemoor, Delaware, 1927.

In another instance recorded in Dr. Bruccoli's bibliography, Fitzgerald disclosed how he felt about his first novel, *This Side of Paradise* (1920):

> For _____ This immature
> product of which, did I not feel an
> unnatural affection for it, I would
> be somewhat ashamed.
>
> > F. SCOTT FITZGERALD, April
> > 22nd, 1922, St. Paul, Minn.

[51]

Since many of Fitzgerald's novels and short stories treat the theme of the romance of money and the lives of the very wealthy, it is not surprising to find noted in an inscribed copy of *The Beautiful and the Damned* (1922) the following sentiments:

> To Mary Craven, who doesn't think
> it's fun to be rich—from one who's
> one idea is GOLD, from a sincere
> admirer of Mary & Frank Craven (&
> what's more—an imitator of the latter)
> Nov. 17th 1922

And in another copy of *This Side of Paradise,* we learn that Fitzgerald was a gracious encourager of aspiring writers:

> For Aiken Reichner Hoping you'll find
> your literary stride within the next year—
> and with a great deal of confidence that you
> will—F. SCOTT FITZGERALD March 28, 1920
> Princeton, N.J.

At times, inscribed copies of first editions will reveal how one author feels toward another, such as in the copy of *The Great Gatsby* inscribed to T.S. Eliot, in which Fitzgerald expressed his deepest admiration:

> For T. S. Eliot
>
> > Greatest of Living Poets
> > from his enthusiastic worshipper
> >
> > F. SCOTT FITZGERALD
>
> Paris,
> Oct,
> 1925

Sherwood Anderson's feelings are also apparent in a first edition of *Winesburg, Ohio* (1919) inscribed to Van Wyck Brooks:

> To Van Wyck Brooks, with love and
> admiration.
>
> SHERWOOD ANDERSON

or to Gertrude Stein, whom he first met in Paris in 1921 through
Sylvia Beach, and for whom he noted in her copy of *The Triumph
and the Egg* (1921):

> To My Friend Gertrude Stein,
>
> SHERWOOD ANDERSON

At other times, authors reveal something about their own
lives, such as the copy of Joseph Conrad's *The Shadow Line*
(1919), inscribed to his son Borys, expressing affection to the
wounded young man:

> To my dearest Boy to replace his own 1st. edition copy lost in
> March 1918 on the Somme front not withstanding his efforts
> to save it from the fire. J. C.

Sometimes an author is both affectionate and candid in his
inscriptions, as was Eugene O'Neill when he inscribed a first
edition of *The Great God Brown, The Fountain, The Moon of
the Caribees and Other Plays* (1926) to his longtime friend
Harold de Polo:

> To Harold de Polo—my friend from
> "those days" and these—
> The Donkeyman—"I done my share o'drinkin in my time.
> (Regretfully) Them was good times, those days. Can't hold up
> under drink no more. Doctor told me I'd got to stop or die.
> (He spits contentedly) so I stops!"
>> The Moon of the Caribbees.
>
> GENE—
> EUGENE O'NEILL.

Thus it is that the lines reveal a great deal about O'Neill's life

[53]

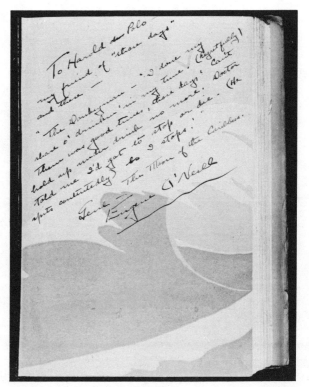

An inscription by Eugene O'Neill in a copy of The Great God Brown, The Fountain, The Moon of the Caribees and Other Plays *(1926).*

and his feelings toward his younger days, as well as his then deteriorating physical condition.

It sometimes occurs that there are gaps in the knowledge that has been gathered over the years about an author or his works. The pieces do not quite fit. Something is missing, and on occasion that "something" is discovered in an inscribed copy of an author's work. For instance, in concurring with this essay's premise that inscribed books often provide scholars with invaluable information, Dr. Donald Gallup, curator of the Collection of

[54]

American Literature in the Beinecke Rare Book and Manuscript Library at Yale University, noted a copy of the rare first edition of *Fanshawe,* published anonymously in Boston in 1828, bearing a laid-in inscribed endpaper on which, not the author, but someone close to him, the publisher James T. Fields, revealed the identity of the author, as well as his attitude toward the book:

> This story was written by Hawthorne. His wish that it should never be reproduced in print (expressed to me in a letter) should be respected.
>
> May. 1864   J. T. F.

Another book, also at Yale, which reveals the identity of the author is a first edition of *Hike and the Aeroplane* (1912), inscribed to the then fourteen-year-old Stephen Benét:

> To Stephen Benét,
>
> with the love of his friend
> Sinclair Lewis..
> who is also the author,
> 'Tom Graham'.

And in his definitive bibliography of the writings of T. S. Eliot, Dr. Gallup notes a rare pamphlet, *NOCTES BINANIANAE: Certain Voluntary and Satyrical Verses and Compliments as Were Lately Exchang'd Between Some of the Choicest Wits of the Age* (1939), in which the identity of the various "Wits" as well as the circumstances surrounding the book's publication are revealed by an inscription in one of the copies of John Hayward, one of the anonymous authors. The inscription reads:

> The following poetical effusions were composed for the most part in the summer & autumn of the year 1937. The pieces in French, Latin & German belong to the latter part of the following year. The authors were Mr. Geoffrey Faber, Chairman of the Publishing house of Faber & Faber Ltd, Mr. T. S. Eliot & Mr.

V. F. Morley, partners in the same, & Mr. John Hayward, their friend. The pieces, now printed, circulated among the authors in MS. for many months, until, through the kind offices of Mr. McKnight Kauffer, the artist, Mr. Eric Gregory, a genial & generous printer, undertook to see them through the Press at his own charge. The edition of 25 copies was distributed as follows:

Copies 1–6.	John Hayward, who prepared the copy for the printer.
7.	E. McKnight Kauffer.
8.	Anne Ridler, who typed the fair copy.
9–12.	T. S. Eliot.
13–16.	Geoffrey Faber.
17–20.	V. F. Morley.
21–22.	Eric Gregory.
23–25.	Reserved for the files of the Printers, Lund Humphries Ltd.

In terms of issue and state of a first edition, authors frequently can disclose a great deal of information, as did H. L. Mencken, who in a copy of the first edition of *The Artist, a Drama Without Words* (1912), wrote:

> This is the real first edition.
> There was but one printing of it.
> I know of no edition without
> "a Drama without words" on the
> title page.

Similarly, Paul Leicester Ford announced in a copy of the first edition of *The Honorable Peter Stirling* (1894) that it was the

> First edition with misspelling of
> name on binding.

The name "Stirling" was spelled "Sterling." Thus we have an example of an author describing priority of issue.

There have also been occasions where presentation copies have provided sufficient circumstantial evidence to lead to a logical assumption regarding a bibliographical matter. An interesting example of deduction using the evidence of presentation copies is found in the old controversy over whether the earliest copies of the first issue of Dickens' *A Christmas Carol* should have yellow or green endpapers. For almost a century after the publication of the *Carol* in December, 1843, conflicting statements regarding the priority of green over yellow or vice versa were made, but with little evidence to support either position. Then two men, Philo Calhoun and Howell J. Heaney, decided to conduct a careful investigation of all the hard evidence surrounding the publication of this little book, to see, among other things, whether the chromatic priority of the endpapers could be definitively established. In an article in *The Papers of the Bibliographical Society of America* (Volume 39, No. 4; 1945), they presented their discovery that all of the earliest dated presentation copies of the *Carol* had yellow endpapers. Each of these presentation inscriptions from Dickens to various people bore a date from December 17 to 21, 1843. On the other hand, the earliest presentation copy (or dated copy of any kind) with green endpapers was dated December 21, 1843. Thus it was in large part through the evidence of presentation copies that Messrs. Calhoun and Heaney were able to reach their conclusion that the earliest copies issued of *A Christmas Carol* had yellow endpapers.

Perhaps one of the most notable instances in which an author specifically disclosed the circumstances surrounding either the actual writing or printing history of a book concerns three books by Ernest Hemingway, inscribed to Dr. Don Carlos Guffey, the man who delivered two of the author's children. In a copy of Hemingway's second book, *in our time* (1924), he notes that:

> This book was printed and published by Bill Bird who had bought an old hand press and set it up on the Isle Saint Louis in Paris. It came out about a year after it should because I introduced Bill to Ezra Pound and Ezra suggested a series of books—"There'll

be me and old Ford and Bill Williams and Eliot and Lewis (Wyndham) etc.'' and Ezra said ''and we'll call it an inquest into the state of English prose.'' Eliot didn't include—nor did Lewis and finally Ezra had five titles—Bill said, ''What about Hem?''

''Hem's will come sixth,'' Ezra said. So when they were all printed and this one finally gotten out it was later than the Three Stories and 10 Poems although Bill had the manuscript long before Macalmon had the other set up.

An inscription from Hemingway to Fitzgerald in a copy of For Whom the Bell Tolls *(1940).*

When *The Torrents of Spring* was published in 1926, quite a number of Hemingway's friends and admirers (including Gertrude Stein) expressed shock at his somewhat cruel satire of Sherwood Anderson's writing. In an inscribed copy to Dr. Guffey, Hemingway disclosed not only the publication background of the book but his own feelings about it as well:

This book I wrote after the Sun also—starting it on a Friday and finishing it the following Thursday, which was Thanksgiving— Boni and Liveright turned down the Mss and Scribners accepted it—Liveright did not want to publish it fearing it would offend

Sherwood Anderson.... I like it as well as anything I ever wrote and so do Pound, Joyce, Wyndham Lewis, Allen Tate, Even Shipman and some others altho plenty of citizens consider it worthless.

And in a first edition of *The Sun Also Rises* (1926), Hemingway wrote:

> Since you are a collector, marks, mis-spelled words and other evidences of seniority in a volume are probably more important than how it was written but if it is of any interest to you the first draft of this book was commenced on my birthday, July 21, in Madrid and it was finished September 6 of the same year—in Paris— It was written at Madrid, Valencia, Madrid, San Sebastian, Hendaye and Paris—after it was finished I wrote The Torrents of Spring in the week preceding Thanksgiving of that year.—In November we went to Schruns in the Voralberg in Austria and there I re-wrote the 1st part of this book—went to N.Y. and came back and re-wrote the rest—the portrait on the jacket was by a twirp who said he was making drawings for Vanity Fair and then sold this, which he got me to sign, to Scribners.

Similarly, in two of his books, Sherwood Anderson noted the personal circumstances concerning their composition. In *Mid-American Chants* (1918), Anderson inscribed:

> Having failed as a manufacturer, I had gone to Chicago where I made my living as an advertising writer. These, chants, were, I daresay, inspired by my own life, by the great industrial city around me and by my own grasping for an adequate form of expression.

and in a copy of his classic American novel, *Winesburg, Ohio* (1919),

> ... I wrote this book at 735 Cass Street Chicago while making my living by writing advertisements. It was written during one winter but was not published until at least two years later. Most

of it was written at night, sitting by an open window in my overcoat.

Additionally, in a copy of the first English edition of W. Somerset Maugham's classic *Of Human Bondage* (1915), the author saw fit to note both the writing and publishing background and the source for the title as well:

> This book was begun in 1912 & finished in 1914. The proofs were corrected in Flanders during the first months of the war. The title of course is that of one of the books in Spinoza's Ethics.

In a copy of Maugham's *Great Novelists and Their Novels* (1948), the author gives an indication of the difficulty encountered in writing this work, since the inscription reads in part:

> the result of a terrible lot of work.

And what could be a more pleasant inscription, in which the author expresses excitement and contentment with his or her own particular work, as did Gertrude Stein in a copy of the first edition of her monumental *The Making of Americans*, first published in 1925 in Paris under the auspices of Robert McAlmon's famed expatriate Contact Publishing Company. In a presentation copy for an acquaintance of Alice B. Toklas', Stein wrote:

> I am pleased that you have this book. It pleases me as a book and as bookmaking.

Since this title is an important one in the Stein canon, and since she encountered a great deal of difficulty in finding a publisher (the book was written nearly twenty years earlier), and because she was very anxious about the actual published quality of the book, this inscription is revealing in that it discloses at first hand the author's true feelings about the final form of her creative efforts.

In a copy of *Picasso* (Paris, 1938), Gertrude Stein paid homage to Maurice Darantière, famous for being the printer of Joyce's *Ulysses*, and Stein's own *The Making of Americans*, among others. Particularly interesting in this inscription is Stein's sense of humor:

> À Maurice Darantière
> who did such books for me
> who did so much for me
> who did so much for
> everybody including
> of course himself the
> most important
> GERTRUDE STEIN

Equally revealing are inscriptions in which an author discloses displeasure or embarrassment with a particular work, or admits of an error, as did George Bernard Shaw in two instances. In a copy of the first edition of his first play, *Widowers' Houses* (1893), Shaw some years later admitted his somewhat negative attitude toward his earlier work:

> To Beatrice Stella Cornwallis West from G. Bernard Shaw, this guilty relic of my past (I mean relic of my guilty past), the first disgraceful form of my first play, with old fashioned asides & soliloquies all complete. Collectors will give diamonds and rubies for this copy. Observe the preface—even at this early age— and the THREE appendices!!!
> 22nd May, 1914.

And in a copy of *In Good King Charles's Golden Days* (1939) presented by Shaw to H. G. Wells, the inscription reads:

> Dear H. G. The figures on page 24 are wrong: I added the leap years instead of deducting them. Jeans did the logarhythms for me, Eddington gasped at the perihelion of Mercury; but as it was a sure stage laugh (like Weston super Mare) I could not sacrifice it. G. B. S. 7th Dec. 1939

Shaw here also admits the poetic importance of the stage laugh

[61]

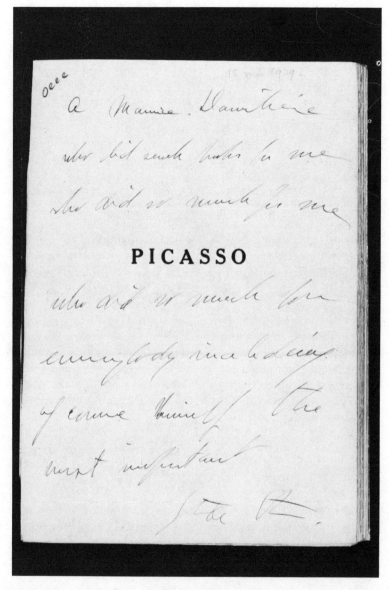

An inscription by Gertrude Stein in a copy of Picasso *(1938).*

over mathematical accuracy, divulging his sense of priority with respect to stagecraft.

Therefore, it is not difficult to understand how much information can be conveyed through inscriptions, whether of a biographical or bibliographical nature. And yet, perhaps something else should be borne in mind when noting these various examples of how inscribed books provide information, and that is that not every author either remembers or records such events always with accuracy. An example of this is pointed out in Donald Gallup's Eliot bibliography, with respect to one of Eliot's finest works, *Prufrock and Other Observations* (1917). In a note, Dr. Gallup states:

> A copy in my possession carries the following autograph inscription on the half-title: ''... One of twenty five numbered copies of which this is No. 3. Justification du tirage T S E'' Concerning this copy Mr Eliot wrote me on 8 September 1938: ''I had completely forgotten that any numbered signed copies of *Prufrock and Other Observations* had been issued.... I am sorry that my memory is so defective that I cannot tell you whether there were really 24 other numbered copies, or whether that was just my fancy, but if, as you say, the copy in your possession differs slightly from the ordinary edition, I can only suppose there was such a set, though what became of the other copies I have not the remotest notion.'' Although the dimensions of this copy are slightly greater than the average, other copies do exist uninscribed. The fact that no other numbered copies have been located would indicate that the inscription was not intended to be taken literally.

On occasion, inscribed copies of first editions serve more to provide the scholar with clues rather than actual information. For instance, when Leon Edel was in the process of writing his monumental biography of Henry James, he found inscribed copies to be of such use. In a letter he has stated:

> I attach enormous importance to presentation copies and in-

scribed volumes. Just how useful I found them can be seen in the chapters in *The Middle Years* and *The Treacherous Years* in which inscribed copies gave me clues to places, dates, meetings of Miss Woolson and Henry James. Also, dedications can be very significant.

In his work on F. Scott Fitzgerald, Matthew J. Bruccoli notes:

> I have pursued scores of leads from Fitzgerald inscriptions or notes. Most paid off. I have always felt that inscriptions should be regarded as letters and have been baffled to find that editors of authors' letters omit inscriptions.

Additionally, even though personal letters and interviews more fully served Carlos Baker's purpose when he was writing his wonderful biography *Ernest Hemingway: A Life Story*, he does admit that information can be deduced from an inscribed volume, as is the case with his own copy of Dickens' *Christmas Stories for Children,* presented to the little child Ernest by his Uncle Leicester at Christmas, 1904.

> A number of things can be deduced from this volume:
> (1) that books such as this were given to the Hemingway children by their uncle who wanted to help them along with their reading.
> (2) that Ernest was early introduced to this children's classic.
> (3) that EH saved this and other childhood books throughout his life, being a sort of packrat who did not throw much of anything away.

And certain inscribed copies have an appeal beyond their actual inscriptions, such as the copy of James Joyce's *Chamber Music* (1907) that Herbert Cahoon and John Slocum came across while compiling their standard bibliography of Joyce's writings, which was inscribed to Arthur Symons on May 4, 1907. As Mr. Cahoon states:

[64]

In his biography of Joyce Richard Ellman tells the story of Yeats's introduction of Joyce to Symons and of the considerable trouble Symons took to see that the little book was finally published, after at least two abortive attempts. In spite of his close association with *Chamber Music*, Symons saw fit to review it favorably and to promote it whenever possible.

Such is the influence of power, and of inscribed volumes oftentimes on the kinds of knowledge that scholars may seek about an author and his work, and of which the end result can only be a clearer understanding of the truth.

Leonard B. Schlosser *is president of the Lindenmeyr Paper Corporation, and he has written and lectured extensively on the subject of papermaking and graphic-arts history. His collection of books and documents related to the history of paper and writing materials is widely known through several exhibitions, catalogues of which have been published. His memberships in academic and professional organizations include positions on the councils of the American Antiquarian Society, the International Society of Paper Historians, and The Grolier Club.*

The Graphic Confluence of 1800

Leonard B. Schlosser

T HE HISTORY OF PRINTING is more than technological
evolution alone, for printed words and images record the
very fabric of history itself. The Renaissance invention of printing
has been called comparable only to the ancient invention of
writing and the modern one of the computer for its effect in
enlarging the application of intellectual effort to human problems. Like other technology, that of the reproductive arts has
evolved at an accelerating pace since its mid-fifteenth-century
origins, and has passed through periods when congruent demand,
precedent, and inventive genius made sudden, rapid change
inevitable. Such a period occurred at the beginning of the
nineteenth century, when the transition from handiwork to the
machine age was made possible by a series of developments
around the printing process, which was not itself to undergo

radical change for almost another hundred years. These seemingly peripheral events were to provide the foundation for the later evolution of printing.

Of the five graphic developments that are the subject of this essay, three deal with paper, one with printing equipment, and one with the invention of a new printing process. It is hardly surprising that the first three are interrelated, but the other two, each of separate importance, are related not only to each other but to the first three. Above all, the occurrence of all five within a short time span was the result of the needs of the day, individual inventiveness, and antecedents which themselves are common to several of the events of the Confluence.

* * *

PAPER had long preceded printing as a carrier of ideas. From the time of its earliest manufacture in Europe in the late thirteenth century, its raw materials had remained more or less the same, and the papermaking process had changed only through the application of water or wind power to the preparation of pulp. Rags—hempen, linen, or cotton—were in 1800 still the only source of fiber for paper, while techniques for the conversion of scraps of woven cloth to usable material for papermaking had become mechanized to meet increasing demand. The stamping mill, a European development of the thirteenth century, had been largely superseded by the Hollander beater, invented in the late seventeenth century, but the process of forming the sheet on a hand mould had undergone no fundamental change since its earliest Western origins. Rags were in continuing short supply, and their lack had stimulated researches into the use of alternative materials, but no commercially satisfactory substitute fiber had been found. The demand for white paper was being met in part by the increasingly widespread use of bleaching techniques, and the commercial availability of chlorine and related oxidizing agents was a recent development[1] which was to have its own profound consequences, almost unrecognized at the time, upon paper quality.

[68]

The first volume of Schäffer's great six-volume set of experiments in making paper out of a wide variety of plant fibers. The work of the German preacher–naturalist is the seminal research for modern paper-making materials.

Writing paper had begun to be differentiated from printing paper as early as the sixteenth century, mainly with respect to sizing and surface. Typographic printing required dampening paper for good ink receptivity, and the hard surface suitable for writing was less desirable for good printing. The intaglio processes, engraving, etching, and the later modifications, mezzotint and aquatint, required still more refined and receptive surfaces, and specific kinds of paper were by 1800 available for such use. The characteristically rough surface suitable for writing and desirable for drawing presented extra problems to the printer.

The most important precursory development to those which took place in 1800 was the invention of "wove" paper. From its earliest European origins, paper had been formed on a mould on which wires had been laid over supporting ribs of wood and sewn to the ribs with finer wire. The spaces between the wires permitted water to drain away, leaving the mat of fiber behind to be "couched" off on to a felt as a sheet of paper. The wires, probably originally of iron but by 1800 long since of brass, left their own characteristic marks[2] on the sheet, and, especially in early paper, imparted a rough surface to the finished product. Our conscious antiquarian interests prompt us to think of such surfaces as beautiful or interesting, but, like deckle edges, they were an imperfection to the printer striving for adequate reproduction of type, woodblocks, and engravings. John Baskerville (1706–1775) was such a perfectionist printer, and demanded more than could be gained from any available laid paper in the way of printing surface. He used paper of a new variety, made on a mould covered with woven wire cloth or screening, in order to gain smoothness of surface, devoid of laid or chain marks, for the fine-serifed types of his first book, the *Virgil* of 1757. Baskerville's use of wove paper, despite its seeming advantages for his purposes, was limited to only three books of his total production of fifty-six,[3] but there appears to be little doubt that he was responsible for the origin of a change in papermaking which was to have considerable effect upon later developments.

It is conjectural as to why wove paper appeared as it did in the second half of the eighteenth century, but it is likely that advances in wire drawing and metallurgy, combined with the invention of an improved loom by John Kay about 1733 and the power loom about 1750, made the weaving of wire cloth possible. The earliest papermaking moulds in Europe were covered with laid wires made from plates that had been cut into thin strips and the strips then hammered round. Wire drawing by means of the draw plate, using the additional power needed to draw brass, a metal of relatively low ductility, began in the fourteenth century. The verse accompanying the woodcut of the wire drawer (*Drahtzier*) in the Jost Amman book of trades (1568) speaks of brass wire, but the drawing of brass wire fine enough to weave into screening may well have had to await the development of hard steel or gem dies in the later eighteenth century. However and whenever wire cloth came into being, it was available in 1754 or 1755 when the paper for Baskerville's *Virgil* must have been made to permit the book's publication in 1757. It is likely, according to modern research, that Baskerville did not make the paper in his own establishment, but that it was made for him by James Whatman.[4]

Wove paper was highly-enough regarded for its refined surface by the most critical printers of Europe to have been fought over for priority in France, where it was first made by Johannot of Annonay at the insistence of François-Ambroise Didot in 1780,[5] and was named *papier vélin* for its beautiful look-through and its vellum-like appearance. Both the Didot family and wove paper itself were to play an important role in one of the turn-of-the-century events, the invention of the papermaking machine.

The nephew of François-Ambroise Didot, Pierre-Francois Didot-Saint-Leger (who later shortened his name to Leger Didot), was in charge of the family paper mill at Essonnes. There was employed in 1794, as head of the accounting department, a 33-year-old former artilleryman named Nicolas-Louis Robert (1761–1828), who had first been employed after his military discharge as a proofreader in the printing house of Leger Didot's father. Robert's duties were more than those of a book-keeper, and included the function of "clerk-inspector" of the 300 workmen employed in the mill. Paper for *assignats*, the paper currency of the Revolution and the First Republic, was produced in the Essones mill, and because of inflation and the rapidly escalating need of the printing presses (among them the Didots') for more currency paper, the output of the mill's vats was under considerable pressure.[6] Robert, whose responsibilities with regard to the workmen were made difficult by what his biographer[7] calls "the ideas and events of the time," conceived the project of a machine for making paper as a way to reduce the work force. His own mechanical abilities and his persistence, along with the encouragement of Leger Didot, resulted in the building of several preliminary models and, finally, in Robert's application for a

[71]

Nicolas Louis Robert's own ink and watercolor drawing of a longitudinal section of the first paper machine, one of six prepared for submission for the British patent. Five are still extant, and all bear the names of John Gamble, Robert's brother-in-law, and Bloxham and Fourdrinier, the firm which financed the machine and gave it its name.

patent in September 1798. The application was for a patent to be issued gratuitously, for Robert was unable to pay the tax called for. The first response of the Minister of the Interior was to deny the issuance of a patent free of tax, but within three months Robert had received, based on the submission of his drawings, a national award, and in a month more received the patent[8] he had requested.

Both Robert's drawings for the French patent and those for the English one[9] show a machine approximately seven feet in length, consisting of a wooden vat to contain the pulp and water suspension, from which a paddle wheel throws the papermaking mixture onto an endless belt of wire cloth. Both the paddle wheel and the endless belt are turned by a system of gears motivated by a hand crank, and other gears turn the pair of press rolls which squeeze water from the wet web after much of the water has drained through the wire. The pressed, but still damp, web is wound upon another felt-covered roller, which, after some buildup of paper upon it, is removed and a new roller put in its place to continue taking up paper without stopping the machine. An early account in English by John Gamble,[10] Leger Didot's brother-in-law, speaks of the practical difficulties of pressing and drying the paper which limited its length to twelve yards, but, theoretically at least, the length which could be produced on Robert's machine was unlimited. The first machine of working size was of about 24 inches in width, and the paper it produced was sold in long sheets to the paper-stainers of Paris for making into wall hangings.

It was Gamble who, during a cessation in hostilities between Britain and France, went to England to take out a British patent on the paper machine, his compensation to come out of any profits that might result from the sale of the machine in England. He was introduced to the Fourdrinier brothers, Henry and Sealy, and when they saw the rolls of paper which had been produced on Robert's machine and which Gamble had brought with him, they offered to purchase a share in the patent. The British patent of 1801 was issued in Gamble's name, and the Fourdriniers bought a one-third interest by agreement with Gamble. Thereby began the developments that took place under their direction and their financing, which were to culminate in the Fourdrinier names' being permanently identified with the machine, but, unfortunately, also in their ultimate bankruptcy. Bryan Donkin, the engineer who was the real developer of the paper machine, was engaged by the Fourdriniers, and his efforts resulted in the first full-scale model (about 48 inches wide) being put into operation at Frogmore Mill, in Hertfordshire, in 1804, to be followed by the first commercial machine, at Two Waters Mill, in 1805. The improvements engineered into this machine by Donkin form the real basis of the modern paper machine, and were

[73]

covered by a patent issued jointly to the Fourdriniers and Gamble in 1807.[11] The Fourdriniers ultimately had withdrawn £60,000 from their stationery business to finance these developments, and in 1810 were declared bankrupt. Bryan Donkin, on the other hand, continued to design and build paper machines until his retirement in 1846, and by 1832 had built more than 100 machines.[12]

Clapperton's exhaustive account[13] of the paper machine and its development does not dwell on Robert's model and its significance outside the paper industry, and there is one area affecting the machine's product that shows curious inconsistency between patent drawings, patent descriptions, and subsequent use. It does not appear logical to assume, as Clapperton does and as have the builders of working models after Robert's drawings, that the machine's endless wire cloth is of the laid variety. Clapperton's reference to the wire cloth of Robert's machine[14] as being made of laid wires like a modern laid dandy roll cover is without foundation in the French patent of 1799, where the continued reference to *toile métallique* fails to describe its nature. The drawings do show what appears to be a belt of wire cloth composed of laid wires held together at intervals by chain sewing, and subsequent model builders have interpreted it that way, but the difficulty of retaining the shape of such an endless belt under tension is obvious. Early commercial machine-made paper is all of the wove variety, and, since woven wire cloth was available and far more suited to the purpose, and, moreover, since wove paper had considerable acceptance by 1800, it would appear probable, lacking evidence to the contrary, that it was intended by Robert that the *toile métallique* be woven. Further, the relationship of the inventor to the Didots and the Essonnes mill make certain his thorough acquaintance with wove paper.

Be that as it may, the commercial development of the paper machine rested heavily upon woven wire cloth, and it was not until 1825 and the invention of the dandy roll that ''laid'' machine-made paper became available. The quotation marks are necessary, for unlike the hand-made product formed on the wires of a laid mould, Fourdrinier machine paper is wove paper watermarked by a dandy roll covered with wires in a laid pattern to create the appearance of the earlier type of paper.[15] The paper-makers' term "laid finish" is more properly descriptive.

The impact of the paper machine upon printing was enormous. First, it made available, even at a time when pulp sources remained limited to the traditional papermaking fibers obtainable from rags, large quantities of paper to feed the multiplying printing establishments fulfilling the demands of literate population growth. Second, while the economics of machine production were not of supervening importance in that age of abundant, low-paid labor, they were soon to become so, and the replacement of large numbers of highly skilled artisans with fewer workers

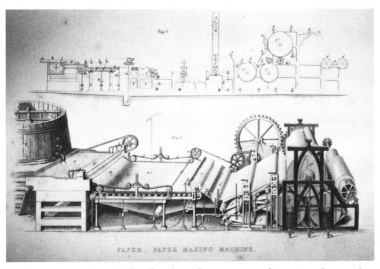

A more or less fully developed paper machine in the mid-nineteenth century, from Charles Tomlinson's Cyclopaedia of Useful Arts & Manufactures *(London, 1857). The headbox design is still primitive, but the general arrangement of wet end and dryer has completed its first period of development.*

not requiring long handcraft training resulted in geometrically increased production of units per worker. Sheets of large size were difficult to make by hand (Antiquarian, 53 × 31 inches, remains a supreme achievement), but even the earliest paper machines were easily able to produce paper to exceed these dimensions. Applications for such large sizes were limited, except for wallpaper use, but were soon to grow in importance. Finally, although the immediate significance of the paper machine to printing was not realized, the accelerated development of printing presses beginning with the iron hand press and culminating in a few years in the cylinder press and the application of power to printing machinery was again to increase demand for paper. These later needs were not only for larger sheets, but by 1837 required paper in continuous rolls for printing purposes. The paper machine, which had been invented to cope with the problems of undisciplined workers, and whose first product had been used for wall hangings, had found its ultimate justification. Other papermaking machines followed on its heels, but Robert's was the first, and, in its modernized versions, far and away the most successful and widely-used.

*   *   *

WHILE the principal thrust of the invention of the paper machine was in its own time economic, the invention of the iron printing press by Charles, Earl Stanhope[16] in 1800 presented both a labor-saving device and one which simultaneously improved the quality of the printed page. The printing press had been essentially unchanged for 350 years, and while the crude wooden screw press of the mid-fifteenth century had undergone evolutionary improvement, it was, before the Stanhope press, still built of wood, except for the screw which operated it and the platen which created the impression. More important, the limitations of pre-1800 printing-press construction required the type form to be printed in two pulls by the pressman, each covering half the form. The iron press enabled the full form to be printed with one impression of the platen, squeezing the paper against the type.

The origins of the printing press are uncertain, but when Johann Gutenberg perfected the type mould in about 1440 he was faced with the necessity of finding a way to transfer ink from type to paper. Paper before Gutenberg had been a writing material, made with a firm, hard surface to resist the scratching of the quill pen and the penetration of early writing inks. It was totally unlike its Oriental ancestor, which was soft and flexible to accommodate the needs of brush writing with moistened carbon black, or wood block printing performed by rubbing the paper against the image to transfer the water-base inks that had been applied to the xylographic surface. Transferring the ink made of oil and lampblack, which it was necessary for Gutenberg and his successors to use to prevent reticulation when ink was applied to type, required more pressure than could manually be applied to the hard-sized Western paper. The principle of the screw press, earlier used for oil, wine, and for water removal in papermaking, was applied to printing, for it provided the firm, sharp impression that was needed. Between 1450 and 1800 the impression screw and platen of the press evolved from wood to metal, and the method of hanging the platen free of the screw was improved to permit evenness of impression, but the wooden supporting members and their inherent elasticity prevented firm, unyielding contact over a large area from being developed. Further, the screw itself, even though it was required to travel only a short vertical distance when brought down by a pull of the pressman's bar, did not provide sufficient mechanical advantage to permit even the strongest pressman to close the press adequately on a large type form.

These limitations are not unrelated to paper dimensions and the desired page size of books. The typical folio sheet of about 19 × 25 inches yielded a finished page about 12½ × 19 when printed two pages on a side. The lack of impressional strength of the wooden press necessitated closing the press twice on each side of the sheet, once for each page.[17] The platen covered about one-half of the folio sheet, and the inked form was positioned for impression on half its area and then slid further under the platen to permit a second pull of the press on its other half. As Moran[18] points out, the earliest printing presses may well have had platens, type forms and paper all of approximately the same size, but when larger paper required the printing of more than one page on a sheet, the limitations of available power made necessary the printing of half a sheet at a time with two pulls of the bar.

The interval of 350 years since Gutenberg had seen the complexities of printing increase, especially with regard to the reproduction of illustrations. The woodcuts of the early books, however imperfectly printed because of the difficulties attached to press-work, were able to be locked up in the type form and printed at the same time. As the intaglio processes (engraving, etching, mezzotint) came into being and were used for illustration of books and other typographic materials, the complications of registration of a sheet printed by two totally different processes on different presses made the letterpress printer's job more difficult. Paper that had first been printed on a rolling press with intaglio illustrations and then had to be re-dampened for printing of type presented handling problems (equally true if the letterpress came first, a less usual procedure) which strongly influenced book design toward the use of large illustrations on separate sheets without type matter. The advent of wood engraving in the last two decades of the eighteenth century brought into being a relief illustration process that permitted, once again, blocks and type to be printed at the same time, but the fine lines of wood engraved blocks presented new requirements for impressional strength. The wood engravings of Thomas Bewick, for example, with the notable exception of his *Poems of Goldsmith and Parnell* (1795),[19] are almost always seen to better advantage in later printings from the original blocks.

Paper had, by 1800, improved to make printing easier. The

early hard-sized writing papers used by the first printers had by mid-sixteenth century given way for printing purposes to papers made for impression with oil-based printing ink, and the intaglio processes had in turn commanded modifications of their own. Within the limits of the hand papermaking process and its fiber sources a comparatively sophisticated assortment of products was available in 1800, ranging from writing paper through printing paper and on to paper especially made with a lesser degree of sizing for intaglio printing. The advent of wove paper had made that more refined surface useful for printing of fine lines and small type. Despite this improvement in one of the basic raw materials, however, the wooden press continued to place limits on printing in terms of both production and quality.

Stanhope's invention provided for the first time the solidity of an iron press coupled with a new system of compound levers for activating the screw, and the resulting power that made one-pull printing of a full form possible. The typical platen size of the wooden press[20] could be doubled, and in spite of the geometrically increased pressure necessary to close the larger bearing area, the pressman's work was made easier and the result considerably improved. No better description of the dramatic improvement thus gained could be given than that by Hansard[21] in 1825:

> The advantages of the iron presses in working are very considerable, both in saving labour and time. The first arises from the beautiful contrivance of the levers, the power of the press being almost incalculable at the moment of producing the impression.... In the Stanhope press, the whole surface is printed at once, with far less power upon the lever than the old press, when printing but half the surface. This arises not only from the levers, but from the iron framing of the press, which will not admit any yielding, as the wood always does, and indeed is intended to.... Indeed, it is so different from the other press, that when an experienced pressman first tries it, he cannot feel any of the reaction which he has been accustomed to, and will not believe, till he

sees the sheet, that he has produced any impression at all; ... and men who are accustomed to the iron presses only, would scarcely be able to go through the work of the old press.

There were difficulties encountered with the press of Stanhope's first design, for the power of the compound lever system often caused the straight "cheeks" (vertical sides) of the cast iron frame (staple) to break. From about 1806 onward the staple was strengthened, and the typical Stanhope press of the second design, of which more have survived, has characteristic round cheeks. For this reason and other technical ones, as well as the press's high price,[22] Hansard was critical of the Stanhope press of the "first construction" (although it is of this one that he shows an illustration[23]), while being full of praise for its ease of operation and fine printing ability.

Stanhope, described by biographers as a public-spirited man of noble motives, refused to patent his printing press himself, and while it was first manufactured by Robert Walker, an ironsmith, by arrangement with Stanhope (it was Walker's high price about which Hansard complained), there were later at least five other British makers. Stanhope's system of levers was used by other printing-press makers, notably by George Clymer in his Columbian press, and, as Moran points out, this method of providing impressional power was the link between the screw of the old press and the toggle joint of the later nineteenth-century presses, like the Albion and Washington. Stanhope's work in stereotyping and in attempting to develop an inking system are each spoken of at length in Hansard, but it is for his press, among all his printing and non-printing technological and scientific endeavors, that he is best remembered. The arrival on the scene in 1800 of a method for printing which not only eased the work of the pressman and improved the art, but made possible relief printing of fine-line illustrations, had implications that were to last beyond the fourteen years which lay ahead before the introduction of the cylinder press. The iron hand press continued to dominate all but newspaper and large-scale book printing well into the age of power.

* * *

Just prior to 1800 an entirely new method of multiplying images had been invented, and for almost the first time in the history of printing the originator was a known person, all of whose early work was documented by himself and by his contemporaries as well as by later historians. Alois Senefelder (1771–1834) is virtually undisputed as the inventor of lithography, although Twyman[24] and Weber[25] properly point out that the work of others, contemporary with or earlier than Senefelder's, should be credited in the beginning history of printing from stone. It is Senefelder's technical achievement in making lithography a chemical process, rather than the use of stone as a replacement for the printing plate, that sets him apart as its originator. His own manual, published finally in 1818,[26] describes in its first section the detailed history of his successes and failures, and later interest in the process has prompted the writing of lengthy discussions of its origins, so there is little point in reviewing that here. There are numerous points of contact between Senefelder's invention of "chemical printing" in 1799[27] and the other elements of the Confluence, and his work and its later influences may be seen differently in that context.

The word "lithography" was not in common use to describe the process, for even its inventor did not use the term until 1808,[28] and entitled his own manual of 1818 as dealing with *Steindruckerey*. The name "lithography" seems to have been coined in France,[29] and the early English name for the process was "polyautography," but it is in any case its *chemical* and *planographic*[30] nature which sets it apart from its predecessors and makes it the foundation of the most important reproductive method of the twentieth century. Planographic printing depends for its success upon the mutual repellence of grease and water, and the essence of Senefelder's discovery was that it made available for the first time a method which permitted the multiplication

[81]

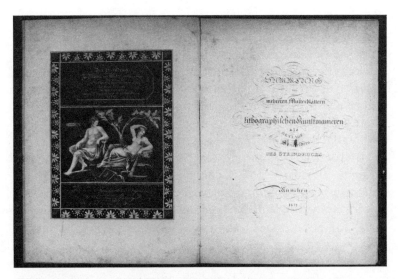

Senefelder's Musterblätter *(Munich, 1818): the plate volume, published separately in larger size, to accompany the German issue of his manual. Shown is the title page and a plate in the "Etruscan" style, dating the author's invention.*

of original material, drawn or printed, without the necessity for an intervening craft process that caused alteration, however slight, of the original. Lithography was the first truly autographic process, and remained essentially an artist's medium from the time of the first published artists' lithographs[31] until the intersection of photography with lithography in 1853[32] and the invention of the offset press about 1905. There were commercial applications of lithography from its earliest days, primarily in the printing of music (Senefelder's earliest business association was with the composer Franz Gleissner in a music publishing venture) and for the printing of maps[33] and official circulars,[34] but the main thrust of nineteenth-century use of the process was for illustration. Type, with a few notable early exceptions,[35] continued to be printed letterpress for a hundred years, and all the early lithographic manuals themselves, except for handwritten

[82]

ones (Houbloup, 1828, and Desportes, 1834), consist of typographic text matter and lithographed plates.

Senefelder's transfer method made possible the printing of type or other material printed or drawn on paper (it is by this means that *The Parthenon* was printed), and, although this portion of his invention was considered by him to be its most important aspect,[36] it has not been emphasized in the published histories. That is understandable, for Weber and Man[37] treat the history of lithography from the artistic point of view, although the Pennells'[38] earlier work, despite its factual defects, does underscore the importance of transfer. The use of transfer paper not only permitted the artist the freedom of working in a medium familiar to him without losing most of the advantages of lithography, but is the real basis for lithography's nineteenth-century commercial development. All of the editions of Senefelder's manuals contain examples of lithography transferred from paper, with the original image either drawn or printed from type, and the French edition[39] contains plates showing transfers of wood engraving, etching, and handwriting as well.[40] Artists' lithographs continued to be made either by direct drawing on the stone or by the transfer method, but the latter made easier not only the production of maps, music, and circulars, but the preparation of facsimiles of earlier works, so important in the development of German lithography[41] and a major application of the process until photomechanical methods came into use.

Choice of paper was vital to lithographic printing, and the subject is discussed in all of the technically oriented early manuals. Descriptions of the process before Senefelder's 1818 treatise are primarily from an artistic point of view and do not deal extensively with the process of reproduction itself, but rather with the preparation of the stone. Beginning with the inventor's own manual, however, stress is laid upon paper selection both for printing and for transfer use. Senefelder begins the section on paper in the German edition with the statement that "Nicht jeder Art von Papier ist für den Steindruck gleich vorzüglich...,"

[83]

and goes on to describe the desirable properties of paper for use in printing from the stone.[42] Paper such as is normally used for copperplate printing, preferably unsized or partially sized, is described as the best for the purpose, and although wove paper is not specified, it is made clear that a smooth surface, free of lumps or imperfections which would spoil the impression by holding the paper away from the stone, is necessary. Copperplate printing, especially in the years immediately preceding 1800, was often done on wove paper to avoid the interference of laid lines: so it is obvious, by implication at least, that the wove product was thought preferable for lithography. It is not surprising, therefore, that the majority of early lithographs, and the demonstrations of the process in Senefelder's manual, are on wove. Later manuals often specify wove paper as a necessity, and Raucourt (1819), Tudot (1833), Desportes (1834), Chevallier (1838), and Engelmann, in his exhaustive treatise (1835–40), all stress the point. Even lithography's earliest bibliographer, E. G. Peignot, stresses the quality of wove paper for illustration, although not applied specifically to the new process.[43] Considerable emphasis is laid on the nature of sizing materials, as well as on their quantity, and virtually every manual cautions against the use of paper that is excessively acid, for fear of counter-etching the stone and destroying the image. Warnings against paper that is acidic because of residual chlorine from bleaching the rags, from the presence of excess alum, either on the surface or used in sizing preparations, and against the use of colored papers[44] are common in descriptions of lithographic printing.

The best transfer paper is specified by Senefelder as being wove, and although different methods are given for its preparation, depending upon its use, it is clear that the absence of surface disturbance caused by the wires of the laid mould is an advantage in paper used either for transfer or for tracing.

Lithography, which from the first stimulated artistic endeavor in new directions, had several declines and resurgences in the nineteenth century, and, especially after its mid-century growth

[84]

as a reproductive process, had its detractors among critics of "pure" art (Ruskin's statement "Let no lithographic work come into the house if you can help it" is often cited[45]). It had critics among professional printers, too: not alone because it was disregarded as an adequate graphic process, but because it was not competitive economically with letterpress. Hansard writes disparagingly about lithography in the latter sense,[46] although he devotes considerable space to a complete description[47] and makes the point that it is in the preparation of autographic materials that the process excels. From the printer's point of view, lithography was not a competitor to relief printing, and even photography and the offset press failed to change that until the evolutionary advent of photocomposition a few years later. Senefelder's invention, however, provided new artistic freedom, made facsimile printing possible and simplified the printing of music and maps even in its earliest years, and, with the application of color to the process just before 1840, entered, full-scale, the world of commercial printing. Written histories of the subject do not deal at length with this aspect, and have devoted themselves primarily to lithography's origins and early development and its later growth as an artistic technique. The growth of chromolithography alone is responsible for much of the process' mid-century expansion, and while its application to books has been discussed,[48] its commercial use remains a fertile field for exploration. The lithographer, as the process grew, became the modernist among printers (although remaining differentiated, in their view, as a "Lithographer") and was involved with change both within the process itself and outside it. Photography, for example, was adapted for continuous-tone reproduction to the grained stone of lithography long before the halftone screen permitted its use in relief printing.

The study of early lithographic manuals provides source information about this graphic process in a way unlike that obtainable in any other area of reproduction, and Senefelder's own writing remains the only first-hand account of the invention of a major printing method. While the direct contemporary relationship of the invention of lithography to the other events of the Confluence is tenuous, it shares common antecedents with them and, like them, is the basis for later graphic expansion. Seen from a modern viewpoint, lithography, along with the paper machine, is one of the most important achievements of the Industrial Revolution.

* * *

WHILE Robert's invention of the paper machine had provided a mechanical means for increasing the production of paper, no way had been found by 1800 to alleviate the perennial shortage of raw materials for papermaking. The preceding two centuries are replete with laws governing the gathering of rags and restricting the exports and imports of raw materials (as well as the finished

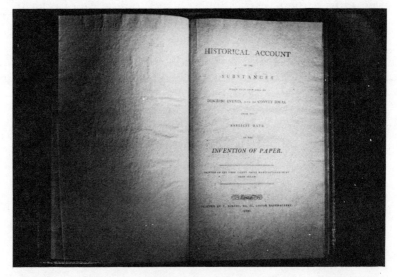

The first edition, in small folio, of Koops's Historical Account *(London, 1800). This copy is signed by Koops, with the address 18 Queen Street, Ranelagh. The straw paper is yellow (probably its original color), and is very strong and crisp.*

[86]

product), and, despite such regulations, the price and sheer availability of rags had continued to be a problem for paper-makers. The revelation that Oriental paper was made from woody plants had appeared in the West in the early eighteenth century,[49] and Réaumur had suggested that wasps had their own way of preparing paper-like fiber from wood,[50] but serious research into non-rag materials for papermaking had not been performed until Schaeffer's work in 1765.[51] Even Schaeffer's extensive labors and the more narrowly-focused, far more successful ones of Léorier de l'Isle,[52] who produced paper with no rags in the pulp mixture, did not result in commercial-scale applications of the use of plant fibers. It was not until 1800 that Matthias Koops operated a paper mill using straw as its basic fiber source and carried on experiments with waste paper and wood pulp that the door was opened—briefly, it turned out—for the making of paper from non-traditional materials.

Little is known about Koops or his background, and were it not for the manuscript documents and other unique ephemeral material in the Dard Hunter collection,[53] virtually nothing would be known about his enterprise, which survived only until 1803. Koops's published writings, fortunately, provide a brief description of his efforts as well as samples of his work, for the three volumes are printed on various papers of his making.[54] The first edition of his book appeared in September of 1800, after a patent[55] had been issued to Koops for a method of removing ink from "printed and written paper," making the old paper into pulp, and then making paper from it. Although old paper had earlier been pulped and re-used, primarily for board, Koops's work in de-inking was new, at least in England, and, what is more, was intended to provide fiber for printing and writing paper. In August of the same year, Koops received another patent,[56] this time for making paper from straw and other plant fibers, as well as "different kinds of wood and bark," and early in 1801 still another patent,[57] similar to the second of 1800, but extended to paper "fit for printing and other useful purposes." The reasons for Koops's researches and for the establishment of his mill are stated clearly by him in his 1800 publication,[58] and are largely economic. The consumption of rags for papermaking exceeded their availability in England despite Parliament's efforts to improve the situation (laws were in effect requiring the burial of the dead in wool so as to save linen, and no import duty was imposed on rags, old nets, rope, and waste paper). Koops had observed the manufacture of "several thousand reams of perfectly clean and white paper, since the 1st of May, made from old waste, written and printed paper,"[59] and proposed to make "the most perfect" paper from straw and other plant fibers. The 1800 edition was published as a first specimen of his straw paper, not yet perfected, but intended to demonstrate his progress to the king[60] and to the public at large.

Koops closes the 1800 edition of his book with an exposition of his thesis that his use of new materials will reduce the necessary importation of rags, increase the value of land, and reduce the price of paper. He goes on to say that if he is successful in making bank note paper, forgery may be prevented by keeping secret the mixture of vegetables used. Even more important for its future impact, there is an appendix added, printed on paper made entirely from wood, with no added rags, waste paper, straw, or bark, and this portion of Koops' book, even though brief and not descriptive of the process, is most portentous of the future. He suggests not only that printing and writing paper be made of wood—not successfully done on any scale for another fifty years— but that laminated paper, similarly made, be used for buildings and furniture.

Obviously the issuance of the three patents and the presentation of the book was helpful in getting the commercial enterprise started, for in 1801 a stock company was set up by Koops and 24 other investors, with a capital of over £70,000. A new building was erected, and 20 papermaking vats were installed, along with other equipment needed to operate so large an enterprise.[61] The production of straw and re-made paper was 700 reams (350,000 sheets) per week by the time of the publication of the 1801 edition of Koops's book,[62] and the author states[63] that before many weeks the output of the mill will be doubled. This quantity of paper, large for a hand papermaking operation at any time, was being produced at the Neckinger Mill in Bermondsey,[64] and not, as Koops says, in a new mill, built for the purpose (presumably the mill of the new stock company, which could hardly have been expected to have gotten into operation in the seven months since its incorporation). Whatever occurred after the new mill was built, it was disastrous, for by December 1802 the workers were laid off and the pulp was rotting in the vats. The mill may have operated again, but it was soon declared bankrupt, and was sold at auction in October 1804. It appears clear that the larger mill was built, and the invested capital finally approached £100,000, for the auction notice contains descriptions of the new buildings and mentions the amount invested.

The re-made paper would be difficult to identify, and one doubts that much of the experimental wood-pulp paper was made, but even the straw paper, clearly identifiable, now turns up only rarely. Aside from Koops's published works themselves, a few engravings—possibly demonstration trials—are known, but much of the mill's output must have been used for ephemera or has gone unnoticed.

Despite the tragic ending (and Koops's personal obscurity), the fact of his accomplishment remains on the record as one far ahead of its time. Even the production of paper from straw, a field in which experiments were later carried on with scientific thoroughness by the author and papermaker Louis Piette,[65] was only the initial beneficiary of Koops's work (and Piette acknowledges the debt). It was the demonstration, known to the graphic arts community at the time,[66] that usable paper could be made from other materials which helped to prepare the demand for and acceptance of the bleached straw paper and the wood pulp paper that came later. Hunter states it succinctly: ''In the search for new papermaking materials, Matthias Koops towers above all his predecessors, for Koops is responsible for the growth of the paper industry as it is today'';[67] if that is hyperbole, it contains a considerable germ of truth.

* * *

THE least-known event of the Confluence, but one which in its application was far-reaching and in its ultimate effect a sort of time bomb, was the invention of rosin and alum sizing of paper pulp. The originator of the process, Moritz Illig (1777–1845), was a papermaker of Erbach, near Mannheim, and began his experiments about 1800 in his father's mill, but did not publish the results until 1807.[68] His pamphlet, only 74 pages in length, was sold for 50 guilders, along with the right to use the process. It contains not only a complete description of the necessary materials and their use, but a theory of sizing which is supported by later, more scientific research.

Before 1800, Western paper had been sized in finished sheet form by drenching the sheets in small packets (''spurs'') in a tub of animal glue in warm water. The sizing process was necessary to permit the paper to be handled by giving it water-resistance, to prevent the penetration or spreading of writing ink, to make the surface firm, and to give the sheet stiffness and ''snap.'' Animal glue as a sizing material is thought to have originated in Italy in the fourteenth century, and improved on, and replaced, the earlier boiled starch used by European papermakers and their Arab predecessors.

The paper machine and the production of a continuous web of paper made sizing in pulp form (''engine-sizing,'' from the beater ''engine'' as opposed to the older ''tub-sizing'' of finished sheets) necessary, and although Illig's process was slow to take hold, it was in existence at the time of the earliest development of the paper machine, if not in wide use. The process involves the application of a rosin soap (rosin dissolved in a potash solution) to the pulp mixture and the precipitation of the rosin onto the fibers by means of the addition of alum to the mixture. The same process, in increasingly sophisticated form, has been in use for engine-sizing since about 1830, when its use spread rapidly throughout the paper industry, until the present time, and has only in the past few years been partially replaced, for general purpose use, by synthetic compounds. Rosin has many advantages as a sizing agent, but the excessive amounts of alum added to precipitate the size, especially before the chemical refinements of the early 1900s, left the paper highly acid in nature and subject to serious deterioration. Alum is not unique to rosin sizing for use in papermaking, and it was added to tub sizing materials to slow the spoiling of the glue; but its excessive use, combined with the speeded-up process of paper manufacture and the early, unsophisticated use of wood pulp, is in large part responsible for the ready deterioration of much nineteenth- and early twentieth-century paper. The destructive potential of excess alum was recognized early; John Murray speaks of its action in destroying pulp (by hydrolysis) in 1829, [69] although he attached more importance to the excessive use of bleaching and to the adulteration of paper with mineral fillers.

Illig's work was long unknown outside Germany, and the search for a successful method of sizing paper in pulp form continued unabated until Piette developed a practical approach virtually identical with Illig's method,[70] and credited Illig with the initiation of the idea. The development of rosin and alum sizing runs parallel with the development of the paper machine (Piette mentions that Illig was an early paper-machine experimenter in Germany), and its use, or the use of some form of engine-sizing (now termed stock sizing), was essential to the growth of the paper industry. The days of the excessive use of alum (or, for that matter, of any papermaking chemical) are for the most part over so far as printing and writing paper manufacture are concerned, for economic and environmental reasons if not for the development of permanence. Illig's contribution to papermaking remains a vital, if an unsung one.

* * *

HAPPY ENDINGS were not a part of the Confluence of 1800. Nicholas-Louis Robert died in poverty, and his machine is to this day called "Fourdrinier" after its bankrupt developers, rather

[91]

than after its inventor or its successful engineer. Lord Stanhope's invention, unpatented at his own desire, was imitated and then supplanted by better iron hand presses and, after only a few years, by the cylinder press. Koops's short-lived enterprise left only the inventor's own books and his theories amid the debris of bankruptcy. Senefelder's invention was at first disputed, until the publication of his own manual, and then criticized as unworthy in some quarters, if exciting in others. Illig's development was at first unknown, then enthusiastically used (and abused), and its inventor made the implied target of complaint about paper deterioration.

The nineteenth century witnessed the transition from hand operation to power, and, at its close, dissatisfaction with mechanization gave rise to the handcraft movement. Craftsmanship was restored to printing, but handcraft archaisms and renewed interest in type and design were directed at the final fifty years of letterpress as a broad-scale reproductive medium. The twentieth century brought underlying change to printing: change from reciprocating to rotary motion, from relief printing to planography, and from metal to film as an image source. If printing, in the second half of the twentieth century, is better able to perform its function of spreading knowledge, it is because of its roots in the developments of 1800, and those events, along with the invention of photography, have provided the framework for the movement of printing technology into the electronic age.

NOTES

[1] Chlorine, discovered by Scheele in 1774, was found to be a powerful bleaching agent by Berthollet in 1785 and applied to papermaking use about 1792.

[2] The wires closely spaced on the mould surface and running in the long dimension of the sheet are responsible for the *laid* mark, while the sewing wires holding them to the ribs create *chain* lines.

[3] Philip Gaskell, *John Baskerville, a Bibliography* (Cambridge: Cambridge University Press, 1959), indicates that wove paper appears only in the *Virgil* (no. 1), *Paradise Regain'd* of 1759 (no. 7), and *Select Fables*, 1761 (no. 14).

[4] Ibid., p. 22.

[5] The whole episode of the earliest use of wove paper in France is charmingly told in Pierre Didot's *Epître sur le progrès de l'imprimerie* (Paris: Didot l'Aîné, 1786), on pp. 123-29 of the notes to this long poem.

[6] The *assignats* were printed on wove paper with a light-and-shade watermark. For an interesting discussion, see the article by Henry Morris in *A Pair on Paper* (North Hills: Bird & Bull Press, 1976).

[7] J. Breville, in *Le Centenaire de la machine à papier continu* (Paris: Firmin Didot, n.d. [1900]).

[8] Brevet d'invention, 29 nivôse, an VII (January 18, 1799).

[9] Patent no. 2487, 1801.

[10] R. H. Clapperton, *The Paper-making Machine* (Oxford and New York: Pergamon Press, 1967), pp. 16–17.

[11] Patent no. 3068, August 14, 1807.

[12] including the first of the Fourdrinier type in America, in Saugerties, New York, in 1827. The first American paper machine—a cylinder machine—had preceded it by ten years in the Gilpin mill on the Brandywine.

[13] See note 10.

[14] Ibid., p. 18.

[15] The few modern cylinder machines making printing paper may be used to produce paper formed on laid wires covering a cylinder mould, and such paper is more truly deserving of the appellation "laid."

[16] Charles Stanhope, 3rd Earl Stanhope (1753–1816).

[17] In the case of a quarto book, page size about 6¼ × 8½, four pages on one side of a 19 × 25 sheet, each pull of the press would print two pages (half the form); in the case of an octavo, four pages; and so on downward through the smaller book sizes.

[18] James Moran, *Printing Presses* (London: Faber & Faber, 1973), offers a complete and thoughtful history of the development of the printing press.

[19] A lengthy preface to this book, printed by William Bulmer, makes a particular point of the care taken with "Printing, Typefounding, Engraving, and Paper-making," and the book is printed on James Whatman's wove paper. Bulmer was among the earliest users of the Stanhope press.

[20] Given by Moran as about 12 × 18 inches on average.

[21] Thomas C. Hansard, *Typographia* (London: Baldwin, Cradock & Joy, 1825), pp. 424-25.

[22] 90 guineas for Stanhope's early model versus £60 for good wooden presses.

[23] Opposite p. 637.

[24] Michael Twyman, *Lithography 1800 –1850* (London: Oxford University Press, 1970).

[25] Wilhelm Weber, *A History of Lithography* (London: Thames & Hudson, 1966).

[26] *Vollständiges Lehrbuch der Steindruckerey* (Munich: K. Thienemann, and Vienna: K. Gerold, 1818).

[27] Senefelder's own history in his manual gives 1799, although most other accounts, as well as the commemorative illustration in the "Etruscan" style in the plate volume of

Senefelder's book, say 1798. Weber's conclusion is that it was at the turn of the year 1798/9.

[28] In the title of his *Musterbuch über alle lithographischen Kunstmanieren* (Munich, 1808).

[29] Twyman, p. 4.

[30] Printing from a flat surface, as opposed to relief (letterpress, typographic) or intaglio processes.

[31] *Specimens of Polyautography* (London: P. Andre, 1803).

[32] Lemercier, Lerebours, Barreswil, and Davonne, *Lithographie, ou impressions obtenu sur pierre à l'aide de la photographie* (Paris, 1853).

[33] Cartography was an obvious early application, for both speed and accuracy, and early presses were established in England (at the Horse Guards) and in Bavaria for government and military use.

[34] The earliest continuing Paris press was established by Lasteyrie at the Ministry of Police in 1815.

[35] Among them, *The Parthenon*, a short-lived London publication, whose first issue of June 11, 1825, carries the note that it is the first publication printed by "typolithography" in England or, the publishers believe, anywhere.

[36] "This manner is peculiar to the chemical printing, and I am strongly inclined to believe, that it is the principal and most important part of my discovery." Alois Senefelder, *A Complete Course of Lithography* (London: R. Ackermann, 1819), p. 256. The facing page is a transfer lithograph drawn on paper by Samuel Prout.

[37] Felix H. Man, *Artists' Lithographs* (New York: G. P. Putnam, 1970).

[38] Joseph and Elizabeth Pennell, *Lithography & Lithographers* (London: T. F. Unwin, 1898), p. 260–63 and numerous other refs.

[39] Alois Senefelder, *L'Art de la lithographie* (Paris: Treuttel & Wurtz, 1819).

[40] Plates VI, X, XV.

[41] Among the most important early major pieces of German lithography is the set of facsimiles of Albrecht Dürer's marginal drawings for the prayer book of the Emperor Maximilian, drawn by Johann Strixner and printed under Senefelder's supervision, published in 1808 in Munich.

[42] Op. cit., pp. 217–19.

[43] G. P. P(eignot), *Essai historique sur la lithographie* (Paris: A. A. Renouard, 1819), pp. 46–47: "Si je me suis un peu étendu sur l'origine du papier vélin, c'est qu'il paroît le plus propre au tirage des gravures."

[44] Because of alum needed to set the dyestuffs.

[45] *Elements of Drawing* (1857).

[46] Op. cit., p. 910.

[47] Ibid., pp. 888–910.

[48] See Chap. 11 and numerous other refs. in Ruari McLean, *Victorian Book Design and Colour Printing* (Berkeley: University of California Press, 1972).

[49] Engelbert Kaempfer, *The History of Japan*, trans. J. G. Schenchzer (London: Printed for the Publisher, 1728), 2 vols. Appendix, pp. 21–28, pls. XL, XLI, XLII. J. B. du

Halde, *Description ... de la Chine* (Paris: P. G. le Mercier, 1735), 4 vols. Vol. II, pp. 239–45.

⁵⁰ René A. F. de Réaumur, *Mémoires pour servir à l'histoire des insectes* (Paris: Imprimerie Royale, 1734–42), 6 vols. Vol. VI, pp. 223–24 (originally published separately, 1719).

⁵¹ Jacob Christian Schaeffer, *Versuche und Muster, ohne alle Lumpen oder doch mit einem geringen Zusatze derselben, Papier zu machen* (Regensburg, 1765–71), 6 vols., containing 82 specimens of experimental paper.

⁵² P. A. Léorier de l'Isle first showed experimental non-rag specimens in Pelée de Varennes' *Les loisirs des bords du Loing* (Langlée près Montargis, 1784), and then published an edition of the *Oeuvres* of the Marquis de Villatte (London, 1786) entirely printed on non-rag paper and containing specimens of his experimental papers.

⁵³ Institute of Paper Chemistry, Appleton, Wisconsin.

⁵⁴ Matthias Koops, *Historical Account of the Substances Which Have Been Used to Describe Events and to Convey Ideas from the Earliest Date to the Invention of Paper* (London: T. Burton, 1800), first edition, "printed on the first useful paper manufactured soley [sic] from straw." Ibid. (London: Jaques & Co., 1801), second edition "printed on paper manufactured solely from straw." Ibid. (London: Jaques & Co., 1801), second edition, "printed on paper re-made from old printed and written paper."

⁵⁵ No. 2392, April 28, 1800.

⁵⁶ No. 2433, August 2, 1801.

⁵⁷ No. 2481, February 17, 1801.

⁵⁸ Op. cit., pp. 73–79.

⁵⁹ Ibid., p. 78.

⁶⁰ Both the 1800 and 1801 editions are dedicated to George III.

⁶¹ From Dard Hunter's account of the material contained in the original Koops documents. Dard Hunter, *Papermaking: The History and Technique of an Ancient Craft* (New York: Knopf, 1957), 2nd edition, pp. 333–40.

⁶² August 30, 1801.

⁶³ Op. cit., p. 251.

⁶⁴ The straw paper of the second edition of Koops's *Historical Account* is wove, watermarked "Neckinger Mill," and the mill is mentioned thus on p. 250. The address in the Hunter documents is given as Mill Bank, Westminster.

⁶⁵ Louis Piette, *Die Fabrikation des Papiers aus Stroh und vielen andern Substanzen* (Cologne: Dumont-Schauberg, 1838), contains 160 specimens.

⁶⁶ Hansard, p. 235.

⁶⁷ Op. cit., p. 333.

⁶⁸ Moritz F. Illig, *Anleitung; auf eine sichere, einfache, und wohlfeile Art, Papier in der Masse zu leimen* (n.p. [Erbach], 1807).

⁶⁹ John Murray, *Practical Remarks on Modern Paper* (Edinburgh: William Blackwood, and London: T. Cadell, 1829).

⁷⁰ Published first in his *Traité de la fabrication du papier* (1831) and again, with Illig's complete text, in his *Strohpapier* (op. cit.).

RICHARD DYKE BENJAMIN *is an officer of the financial firm Lazard Frères & Co. As Deputy Head of his organization's institutional portfolio management group, Mr. Benjamin spends a good portion of his professional life in economic, financial, and securities portfolio analysis. A graduate of Harvard College and The Harvard Graduate School of Business Administration, and a member of The Grolier Club, Mr. Benjamin's interest in political economy, literature, and collecting books and letters has spanned almost two decades. In recent years, he has attended Ruskin conferences at The University of Leicester, at The Johns Hopkins University, and at The Speed Art Museum, Louisville, Kentucky. At the Louisville conference and at The Grolier Club, he has delivered several papers on the subject of John Ruskin, Mr. Benjamin's primary collecting and academic interest.*

John Ruskin:
The Development of
a Private Collection

R. Dyke Benjamin

PUBLISHERS' NOTE: *Is it yet possible, in the last quarter of the twentieth century, for a relatively young collector with limited financial resources to build a significant collection of the works of a recognized writer? This essay demonstrates that it can still be done; that with intelligence, expertise, patience, and scholarship a dedicated private collector can overcome the obstacles of rising prices and increasing scarcity of important material, to develop a collection recognized not merely as an admirable accumulation of related books and manuscripts, but as a valuable primary research facility.*

* * *

IN ADDITION to making general observations about the building of private collections and their value as research facilities, I shall in this paper provide a case study of my specific experience as a collector of first editions, manuscripts, letters, and related materials by the nineteenth-century art critic, sociologist, and economist John Ruskin. By means of this case study, I shall develop a number of points which I hope will be of universal interest to private collectors.

While my collection of Ruskiniana has a definite importance, the size of my collection is smaller than the vast institutional libraries of Ruskin materials at Bembridge School on the Isle of Wight, The Pierpont Morgan Library in New York City, and the Beinecke Library at Yale University. But, since I am a relatively young collector, I should expect my library of Ruskin materials to increase in size and significance. Certainly, Dr. Mary Hyde's collection of Samuel Johnson, Boswell, and Thrale memorabilia, Joseph Verner Reed's collection of botanical books, and Professor Richard Macksey's vast library of English and Continental first editions are current examples of extensive and important private collections formed by long-standing collectors. I must hasten to add, however, that size is not a prerequisite for an important collection. The Chapel Hill, North Carolina, Ruskin scholar Dr. Harold Shapiro once remarked that each Ruskin letter is important. Allowing for degrees of importance among collected materials, one may yet appreciate that each unique piece of Ruskiniana is significant. Even in seemingly average letters, important nuances in an author's temperament and opinion may be discovered; each letter provides the biographically oriented literary critic with additional information about the chronology and development of the subject's thinking.

Once formed to a meaningful degree, private collections may be utilized as research facilities in two ways. First, many private collectors graciously allow scholars to visit their collections and to take appropriate notes. Second, private collectors themselves often have a dynamic intellectual relationship with their collected materials; as a result, scholarly interpretations of the materials may result, and the collectors' own creative powers may be heightened. Also, through continued careful handling of their materials, and by living among their rare books and old letters, the collectors' sense of texture and antiquity may be refined.

[98]

One major private collector of my acquaintance is host to scholars in his country home almost every weekend. Another provides room and board for serious scholars wishing to visit her collection over an extended period of time. To house his magnificent collection, a third has added one large wing to his lovely residence, and a second wing is being planned. One of this collector's greatest joys is sharing his library's treasures with students and friends; he holds some of his university seminars in his library so that he may illustrate his classes with selections from his library's rarities. How all of us would enjoy spending hours with this learned man in his beautiful library! On the other hand, not all private collectors are characterized by generosity: Ruskin's very important translation of Plato is said to be in the hands of a recalcitrant private collector.

Often, the important collections of altruistic individuals are willed to institutions. Publically minded collectors derive satisfaction from the knowledge that their mature, lifetime unification and interpretation of a great person's ideas will become available to future generations of scholars. For monetary reasons, other major private collections must be sold at auction. Since the winning bidders at these auctions are often representatives of institutions, the auction may also be a vehicle for making the lifetime work of a collector available to future scholarship.

* * *

WITH regard to the formation of a private collection, the following questions may be asked: How does a private collection commence? What obstacles must be overcome? How is the emerging private collection made available as a research facility? In answering these and other questions, I shall draw upon my own case history. Implicit in my discussion is the idea that vast amounts of money are not required to establish important collections.

Fifteen years ago, my latent bibliomania was awakened by my discovery of a copy of John Ruskin's *Sesame and Lillies*. Nestled among the bargain-table books in the basement of Harvard Square's Pangloss Bookstore, this attractive red-leather-bound volume spoke ''Of Kings' Treasuries,'' the treasures hidden in books. Attracted by Ruskin's beautiful style and by his interesting ideas, I returned to the Pangloss shop to purchase an American edition of the complete works of Ruskin. Also residing upon the bargain table, this edition was well within my graduate-student's budget.

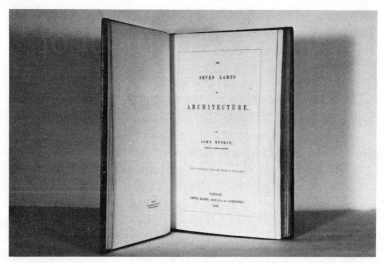

The Seven Lamps of Architecture *(London, 1849). The first edition, which contains 14 illustrations etched and signed in the plate by Ruskin.*

Mornings in Florence; The Stones of Venice; The Seven Lamps of Architecture; The Bible of Amiens: these and other Ruskin titles possessed me. I traveled to Florence to witness the sunlight falling upon a particular Giotto fresco as Ruskin had described it. With *The Stones of Venice* as my guide, I spent a week analyzing the Basilica of St Mark's. I visited Amiens to study the cathedral. "This apse of Amiens," stated Ruskin, "is not only the best, but the very *first* thing done *perfectly* in its manner, by Northern Christendom."

I shared Ruskin's enthusiasm for J. M. W. Turner's art. I understood Ruskin's respect for Tintoretto and his disdain for

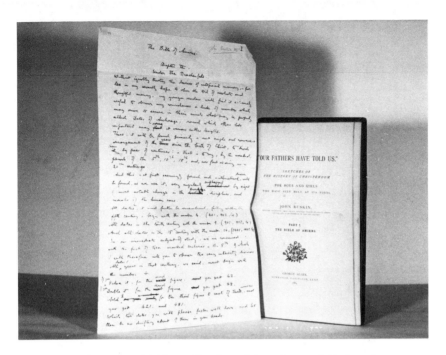

Our Fathers Have Told Us. Sketches of the History of Christendom for Boys and Girls Who have been held at its Fonts. *Part I.* The Bible of Amiens *(Orpington, 1884). First edition in book form. Also shown is a manuscript portion of Chapter II of Ruskin's* The Bible of Amiens *entitled "Under the Drachenfels."*

Founded by John Ruskin, the St. George's Museum in Sheffield contained specimens, copies, and casts selected by Ruskin to represent the highest forms of art. Shown are three early publications concerning the museum and its collections.

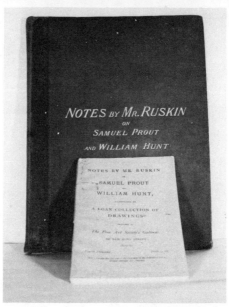

Notes by Mr. Ruskin on Samuel Prout and William Hunt *(London, 1880). The large paper edition is the fifth edition of these notes but the first edition to be illustrated. Also shown is a copy of the fourth edition in wrappers, from which the basic text of the illustrated edition was taken.*

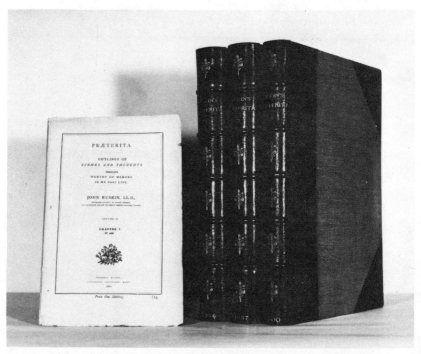

Praeterita. Outlines of Scenes and Thoughts Perhaps Worthy of Memory in My Past Life *(Orpington, 1886–1900). The first edition in book form, in three volumes. Also shown is the original part issue of Chapter I, Volume II.*

Claude Lorrain and Poussin. In the social and economic sectors, I sympathized with Ruskin's concerns about the needs of the working people. I agreed with Ruskin's wish to superimpose a human equation upon Adam Smith's laws of supply and demand. I recognized the importance of Ruskin's wish to maintain an incentive motive in England's economy while modifying the system. Finally, not only his theories and beautiful prose but also his friendships and his life experiences began to fascinate me.

Ruskin advised his followers to consider his theories from their own individual viewpoints. He scorned imitation. Following the Ruskinian spirit, my philosophy and taste began to form within the framework of Ruskinian theory. Many of my thoughts are in harmony with his; some of my ideas, in counterpoint.

The scope of Ruskin's theory, the beauty of his writing, and the romance of his life—all enhance the enjoyment of collecting his books, letters, manuscripts, and related materials. One of my first purchases was the first American edition (limited to 200 copies) of W. G. Collingwood's *The Life of John Ruskin*. My discovery of this two-volume work by Ruskin's friend and secretary was made in one of New York City's Fourth Avenue bookstores. Since the second edition of this excellent biography extends to Ruskin's final days, I was pleased to find a copy of that edition in a small bookshop located on the Upper East Side. In this competitive era, when a course in karate is useful during the rush of dealers at the opening of a church bookfair, it is a pleasure to discover books of gem quality in the quiet atmosphere of the worn-out Fourth Avenue and Upper East Side mines.

In Boston, there is an old bookstore whose floors are sagging under the weight of decades of book traffic. In this nursing home for books, I discovered a nice edition of Ruskin's *Queen of the Air*. Fortunately, my copy escaped the proprietor's malpractice of tearing out all marked flyleaves. Presentation copies, inscribed copies, or complete copies rarely emerge from this iconoclast's shop.

My greatest bookstore "find" was my discovery of the autograph edition of Ruskin's *The Stones of Venice*, limited to 1,500

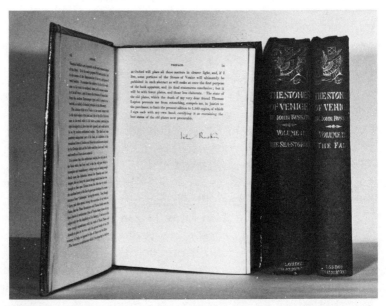

The Stones of Venice *(London, 1874). This three-volume set is generally known as the "Autograph Edition" since Ruskin signed the new preface in Volume I of each of the 1500 copies printed.*

copies, on the top shelf of a Charing Cross bookshop, in London. I located the three-volume set of this important edition in its pristine contemporary binding. Priced as a second-hand book, this rare edition became a foundation of my collection.

* * *

BESIDES discovering interesting bookstores in the New York, Boston–Cambridge, and London–Oxford areas, I have found a number of antiquarian bookshops in the State of Maine. Thirty-three were listed in the 1978/9 brochure of the Maine booksellers' association. While my own collecting interests are not likely to encourage me to travel to The Northwoods Funnies Book Shop in Dover–Foxcroft, my family would not be surprised if I rented our next vacation cottage near the Victorian House and The

Book Barn in Stockton Springs. Evidently, the combined inventory of these two Stockton Springs outlets exceeds 40,000 volumes.

In the summer of '78, our vacation home was situated near the village of Hallowell, which hosts more than twenty antique shops. While books are scattered among these stores, the major Hallowell antiquarian book outlet is Leon Tebbetts' Book Shop. Built up from a base of local library discards, many of Mr. Tebbetts' books are "Bumped but internally fine." Unlike one Maine book dealer whom I encountered, Mr. Tebbetts allows escorted children into his shop's numerous alcoves. As a result, my one-year-old son pulled down an old book which I subsequently purchased. An inscribed copy of Amos K. Fiske's *Midnight Talks at the Club* (New York, 1890), this volume has become a treasured possession.

Maine is well suited for collectors of English and Scottish literature. The stormy and craggy Maine milieu seems to attract books of Ruskin and Carlyle interest. The faith of many of the Down Easterners has brought English and Scottish hymnals, prayer books, and Protestant sermons into many of the bookstores. Two of Leon Tebbetts' offerings which I added to my collection were David G. Ritchie's 1889 edition of the *Early Letters of Jane Welsh Carlyle* and Edward Flügel's *Thomas Carlyle's Moral and Religious Development* (New York, 1891).

One of my friends takes annual book-purchasing trips to England, and he has three bookbinders working for him in London. A bachelor, this gentlemen has relocated his apartment to house his expanding collection. While these frequent London visits are enviable, New York, Boston, and possibly Stockton Springs in the Pine Tree State are all worthy of book collectors' interest.

* * *

THE HABITUÉ of the second-hand bookstore develops a sense of where treasures within the store may be found. While a typical eye-level shelf may contain such unwanted titles as Hendrick's *The Life and Letters of Walter H. Page*, Volume II, or Cozzens'

Morning, Noon and Night, relatively inaccessible high or low shelves sometimes house more desirable items.

Another good book-foraging area in many second-hand bookstores is the region near the proprietor's desk. Often, so carefully are books stored in the owner's corner that it almost seems as if he would rather not market books from that portion of the store. Even when a browser successfully invades the proprietor's sacred area, difficulties may arise. Well do I remember an experience early in my collecting career when I located the red-leatherette-bound individual volumes of Ruskin's *Mornings in Florence* in a well-guarded covey of a Cambridge, Massachusetts, bookstore; many of these small volumes were first editions. Thrilled that the low price of this set matched my budget, I handed my money to the proprietor and announced how pleased I was that these nice first editions were priced so reasonably. Thereupon, the cantankerous proprietor responded that he was now tripling his price. Stunned by this development, I left the store.

The book buyer's law of averages states that, for every "find" in a bookstore, the collector will pay too much for other volumes acquired. Thus, feelings of guilt are not required when a buyer happens to discover a volume priced under the market. Yet, despite my unfortunate experience in the Cambridge bookstore, I usually mention my discoveries to a bookstore's salesperson.

A hybrid form of second-hand bookshop is the rare-book department of a store which is primarily a purveyor of new books. Often the book prices in these departments are outrageous. Both books and prices are designed for the wealthy customer seeking a "fine binding" for a wedding or Christmas present. However, at inventory time or department relocation time, even these hybrid book outlets may become interesting. When Scribner's retrenched its rare-book department, C. E. Norton's translation of Dante's *La Vita Nuova* was drastically reduced in price; inscribed by Thomas Carlyle "T. Carlyle (from Charles Eliot Norton) 17 Sept. 1873" and carrying an Ashburton bookplate, this *Vita Nuova* now is one of my most valued association

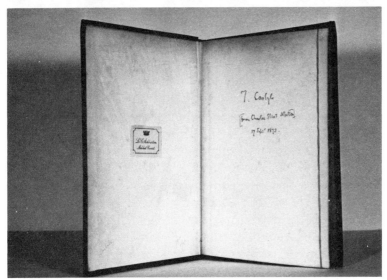

Thomas Carlyle's copy of The New Life of Dante Alighieri, *translated and with essays and notes by C. E. Norton. Presentation copy to Carlyle with a notation in his hand: "T. Carlyle [from Charles Eliot Norton] 17 Septr. 1873." Norton was one of Ruskin's closest friends; the poetry of Dante and the teachings of Carlyle were in the mainstream of Ruskin's intellectual development.*

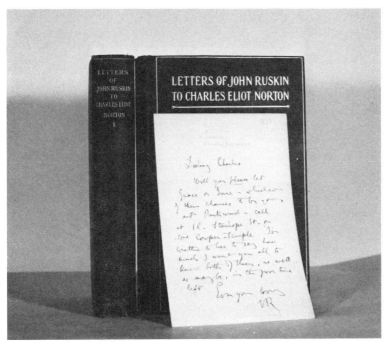

Letters of John Ruskin to Charles Eliot Norton *(Boston, 1904). First edition. Also shown is an affectionate letter written in 1873 from Ruskin to Norton.*

copies. Dante–Carlyle–Norton–Ruskin are all part of a vital intellectual link. Similarly, Brentano's underwent a shift in the location of its rare-book department. To clear shelf space, the Brentano's salespeople set up a "mostly $1.50–$5.00 odds and ends table." Through a careful analysis of these "odds and ends," I discovered a nice first-edition copy of J. A. Froude's three-volume edition of the *Letters and Memorials of Jane Welsh Carlyle* (1883), Robert Louis Stevenson's (alleged) copy of the first edition of Alexander Smith's *Dreamthorp, Essays Written in the Country* (London, 1865), and the first edition of John Greenleaf Whittier's *Hazel-Blossoms*, a memorial to Elizabeth Whittier published in Boston in 1875. The Brentano's discoveries

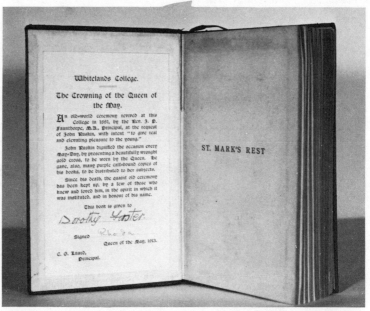

Whitelands College bookplate: "The Crowning of the Queen of the May." Signed "Rhoda," Queen of the May, 1913, this bookplate explains that Ruskin's quaint old May Day ceremony for the Whitelands College girls "has been kept up, by a few of those who knew and loved him...."

illustrate several additional points. Having discussed my Carlyle, Smith, and Whittier finds with the saleslady, and having explained how hard I had *looked* for them, she congratulated me and said I was a "good looker." I laughed and returned the compliment. By discussing well-bought books with salespeople, buyers may dispose of guilt feelings as they and their new-found treasures leave the store.

Another point illustrated by my Brentano's experience is that of collecting focus. While there were a number of interesting volumes on the Brentano's "odds and ends table," I limited my purchases, for the most part, to books relating to my major field of interest. Certainly, the Carlyle and Smith items were in the direct line of my collecting interest. Although the Whittier item was on the fringe of my collection, the book was irresistible. Perhaps twenty per cent of my library is in this "just plain irresistible" category. Unless one has abundant shelf space and resources, though, the eclectic collector may end in financial ruin. One of my friends must warehouse a significant portion of his collection. Since it costs him about $10 per volume to get access to his books, he often purchases duplicate copies, and his problem is compounded!

Another lesson to be derived from my explorations in Brentano's is that rare and scarce books are not always expensive. In addition to the aforementioned books, Brentano's inexpensively sold me an inscribed copy of Ruskin's 1865 lecture on *War* in its first edition limited to 100 copies. As early as 1905, Cook & Wedderburn stated that "This little book is one of the scarcest Ruskiniana." While *War* was an obvious find, other scarce Ruskin materials and association items might have escaped my notice if I had not made a continuing intensive study of my field over a period of many years. Although it should be self-evident that the more a collector understands his field, the more meaningful that collection is likely to become, I am surprised by the numbers of collectors who do not read their collected materials. Simple collection of a complete run of an author's first editions without reading these

[109]

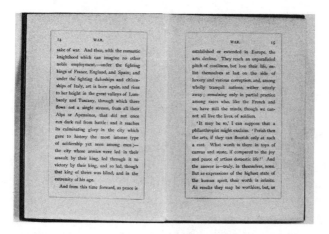

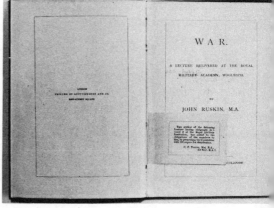

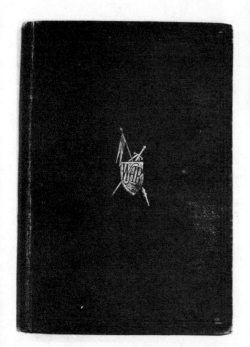

War *(London, 1865). This little volume, published for private circulation, is one of the scarcest items in the Ruskin canon.*

books and without an examination of relevant scholarship could result in a loss of depth and vitality for the collection and its assembler.

My final comment about the Brentano's "mostly $1.50–$5.00 table" is that, recently, one of the world's most distinguished collectors was seen rummaging through the table's books. While my witness commented that he was startled to see a man of this stature examining bargain-table books, he did say that he understood the ceaseless search by all serious book collectors for rarities, whether on bargain tables or in dealers' catalogues. Having heard this story, I wondered whether the great collector–scholar had focused one hundred per cent of his attention upon these particular bargain-table books. Perhaps a portion of his thought was directed to a bargain table "find" many years ago which started him upon his book-collecting adventure. While my question was entirely speculative and based upon my own discovery of Ruskin at the Pangloss Bookstore, it helps me to enjoy my image of this exceptional collector at the bargain table.

* * *

WHEN in a bookstore deciding whether or not to purchase a book within one's immediate field of interest, the individual generally has a fairly good idea of the value of most items. However, collectors vulnerable to impulse purchase require guidelines when deciding upon the acquisition of unrelated items. One such guideline is the price marked upon such omnipresent first editions as Hilton's *So Well Remembered*. Like *The Life and Letters of Walter H. Page*, the first edition of *So Well Remembered* seems regularly to appear in most second-hand bookstores. By cross-checking the prices of items within their immediate field with prices of "semi-precious" books which are available in a number of stores, collectors may orient themselves toward a particular store's pricing policies.

Another guide-post is the pricing of remainder books from such publishers' overstock stores as Marboro or Barnes & Noble. If the haunter of second-hand bookstores is also a regular browser at the remainder bookstores, this individual may readily check the extent to which the second-hand bookstore proprietor has marked-up the remainder books. If a book from a remainder store's "book for a buck" table suddenly dons a four- or five-dollar price tag for the privilege of entering a second-hand bookstore, the customer may become suspicious of that store's overall pricing policies.

The above guidelines presuppose that the collector does not arrive at a second-hand bookstore with a knapsack containing extensive records of book prices at auction and a copy of *American Book Prices Current*. Even if these resources were readily available, other guidelines, such as those which I have mentioned, are useful.

One of my favorite means of placing my collection into perspective—and acquiring reference materials relating to it—is visiting such large remainder bookstores as Marboro and Barnes & Noble. Like the maneuvering of a good conversationalist at an interesting cocktail party, the bibliophile may circulate among the "books for a buck" and the more sophisticated $1.98 crowd. Some of my associates in the book world are horrified by my frequenting of these vast literary emporia; they claim that book covers and pages—mere merchandise—are all that exist in these remainder-book department stores. Notwithstanding, at Barnes & Noble one day, I "talked to" (and purchased) Alan Menhennet's *Order and Freedom: German Literature and Society, 1720–1805*. How well this interesting book supplemented my efforts to trace the influence of Goethe's social environment and thought upon the social theory of Carlyle and Ruskin! Certainly, John Ruskin's Guild of St. George was concerned with the concepts of order and freedom. The same day, I purchased Sir John Hick's *The Crisis in Keynesian Economics* because another of my projects is to trace the development of twentieth-century economic thought from its nineteenth-century base. Did John Maynard Keynes incorporate many of John Ruskin's social concerns into his economic theories?

As a Ruskin collector, I am fortunate that overstocks of English publishers often find their way into Marboro and Barnes & Noble; not only covers and pages but also profound thought and beauty may be found in these stores. Silent conversations with a spectrum of scholars provide a useful way to locate a particular author's belief within the development of human thought.

It has been argued that public libraries provide a more coherent source of reference materials for collectors. Certainly, this is true in those cases where a library has collections which overlap the interest of a specific collector. Once one's collection is large enough, however, bookstores and dealer's catalogues as well as public and private libraries should be consulted by the private collector.

Second-hand and rare bookstores provide some individual collectors with a necessary respite from the stress of business and the oppression of tax payments. In these bibliophilic havens, sufficient treasure may be found to maintain the joy of the search. Even so, the major benefit of many bookstores is their restoration of a sense of peace to tense human beings. More important books and collectible materials are often found in dealers' catalogues. Well do I recall the moment when one of my early catalogue-inspired purchases, the thirty-nine-volume Library Edition of *The Works of John Ruskin*, arrived in my apartment! Limited to 2,062 copies, this Cook & Wedderburn edition is an Edwardian monument to scholarship. Emblazoned in gold upon each volume's red cover is Ruskin's motto, "Today." Adding further excitement to my set is the inscription upon each flyleaf, "H. H. Maharaja Janisaheb." In the hospital at the time of the arrival of this edition of Ruskin's *Works*, my wife almost suffered a relapse when she was told about the four shelves required for this giant dust-gatherer. On the other hand, she was responsible for the first Ruskin letter in my collection. In response to a catalogue notice, she visited a bookstore located in a New York City loft. How pleased I was to receive my birthday present, a Ruskin letter to Dr. F. J. Furnivall. Thrilled by this gift, I began my never-ending search for additional Ruskin letters. While I have occa-

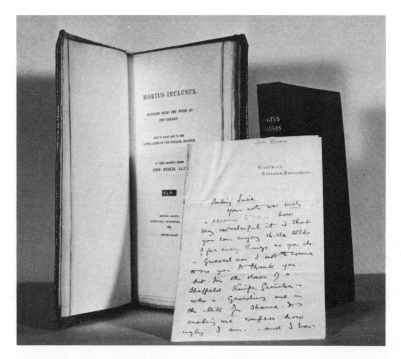

Hortus Inclusus. Messages from the Wood to the Garden, Sent in Happy Days to the Sister Ladies of the Thwaite *(Opington, 1887)*. *First editions. The larger volume is one of 250 copies printed on Whatman's handmade paper. The letter shown is from Ruskin to Susie Beever, one of the "sisters of the Thwaite," which refers to "a Sheffield Knife Grinder," Benjamin Creswick, who was visiting at Brantwood to sculpt a bust of Ruskin.*

sionally discovered Ruskin letters without the aid of catalogues, most of my collection has been built in response to catalogue offerings.

* * *

AS WELL AS bookstores and dealers' catalogues, professional bookfairs provide another means of collecting interesting materials. Although I prefer relatively quiet bookfairs such as those held in

[114]

London's Ivanhoe Hotel, even the fairs held at The Americana (now the Sheraton Centre) or The Plaza hotels in New York may serve a useful purpose. The bookfairs held at the large New York hotels may be compared with the auction market located on the floor of the New York Stock Exchange. Like stocks and bonds, books and letters are sold to the highest bidder. Each crowded dealer's booth is like a stock-exchange specialist's post. Over

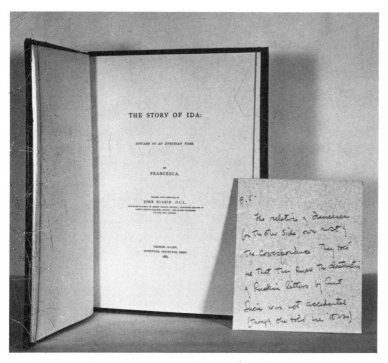

The Story of Ida: Epitaph on an Etrurian Tomb *by Francesca Alexander, edited with a preface by John Ruskin (London, 1883). First edition. Also shown is a letter from Constance Alexander, Francesca's cousin, to M. H. Spielmann, the Ruskin scholar. Dated October 13, 1928, this letter refers to Aunt Lucia's destruction of Ruskin's letters to Francesca "... because they were love letters and, so, should not be seen by anyone else."*

[115]

both dealer and specialist, an atmosphere of customer frenzy may prevail.

Although these bookfairs attract some serious collectors and scholars, unpleasant types of investors also appear. While the recognition of books' and letters' monetary values and appreciation potentials is necessary, the more appealing collectors de-emphasize the investment aspect of their collecting experience. At the bookfairs, however, one overhears such comments as, "Do you have any signed copies?" The baffled dealer is forced to respond, "Do you have a particular inscribed book in mind?" Another typical question is, "Do you have the most expensive of the Hemingway editions? I am willing to pay, since expensive items are supposed to appreciate the most rapidly." With no thought about the content or texture of great books, these investors cause discomfort to the bibliophile. Books contain the best thoughts of their authors. It is tragic to witness the auctioning and bartering of these records of great minds in the Plaza and the Americana markets.

Leaving the unpleasant features of the bookfair, I should point out that one occasionally finds in dealers' stalls good materials fairly priced. In addition, useful dealer contacts may be made. As the result of meeting a very nice dealer at one of the Plaza bazaars, I acquired an important series of letters from Ruskin to William Walker, the banker for Ruskin's Guild of St. George, which Ruskin believed to be the most significant project of his life. On a subsequent trip to London, I made an appointment with this dealer. After enjoying a cup of tea, I was shown the collection of thirty-five Ruskin letters. While his price was not inexpensive, the dealer's quotation was fair and transaction was completed. I am now editing this cache of St. George's Guild letters for a university press. Although Messrs. Cook & Wedderburn catalogued most of Ruskin's books and many of his letters, a number of the letters were not available at the time. Thus, my publication of the St. George's Guild letters, and related letters from my collection, is extremely important.

[116]

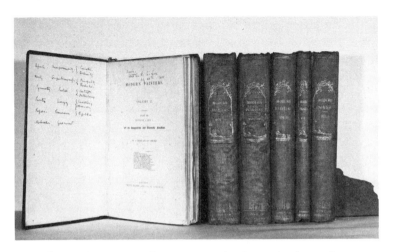

Modern Painters *(London, 1873). The first complete edition to include all five volumes (which were published separately between 1843 and 1860), this is generally known as the "Autograph Edition" since each new preface is signed by Ruskin. One thousand copies of this set were printed. Also shown is a copy of the first edition of Volume II (1846), annotated in Ruskin's hand and inscribed to Joan Severn, his adopted daughter.*

This is a good example of the formation of a building block for a private collection and its subsequent utilization as a research facility.

Just as bookfairs may lead the collector to interesting materials, so may one's fellow collectors guide one to important items. The rare-book librarian at Columbia University once told me that a dealer located in the Flatiron Building was planning to move to another state. Since he had seen some Ruskin items in the inventory, my Columbia friend suggested that I examine this individual's stock. My visit to the Flatiron Building resulted in my purchase of the four available volumes of Ruskin's own copy of *Modern Painters*. Ruskin had inscribed each copy to his cousin and adopted daughter, Joan Severn, and, during his latter years, he had annotated three of the volumes. Not only is it exciting to

[117]

handle the precise copies important to Ruskin, but it is important to recognize the research value of these corrected copies of his earlier works. I was pleased to report my purchase of *Modern Painters* to the Columbia rare-book librarian, who, incidentally, collects Burne-Jones materials. Edward Burne-Jones was one of Ruskin's best friends.

*　*　*

SINCE I am a New York City resident, and since this paper is in part a discussion of my own case history as a collector, I should like to discuss the New York "subculture" of book collectors. The vitality of this subculture encourages a dynamic relationship between collectors and scholars and collected materials.

Many of New York's book collectors, bibliophiles, and scholars circulate at functions held at The Grolier Club, The Century Association, The Pierpont Morgan Library, The Columbia University Library, The New York Public Library, The Typophiles, and The New-York Historical Society. Each locus of book-collecting activity and bibliophilic discussion is characterized by special features. Constructed of seventeenth-century paneling and Delft tiles, and bordered with clay churchwarden pipes, the Dutch room in The Grolier Club has provided a background for many fascinating discussions about book collecting. The beautifully arranged exhibitions of books and manuscripts at the marble-pillared Morgan Library have provided hours of pleasure for individual collectors and scholars. My memories of the Morgan Library opening featuring William Morris' collection of illuminated manuscripts and Kelmscott Press masterpieces continue to stimulate my imagination.

Unlike the meetings held in the book-lined Grolier Club and the massive Morgan Library, the Typophiles' discussions take place on the second floor of a restaurant located near Broadway and Forty-second Sreet. A special feature of the Christmas season's Typophiles meeting is the mystery bag of private-press books presented to each one who attends.

New York's bibliophilic subculture provides added stimulation for private collectors. To be able to come into contact with distinguished collectors and scholars on a continuing basis is tremendously important to private collectors. The occasion of the aforementioned Morgan Library William Morris exhibition was an individual collector's gift of Kelmscott Press items to the library. Enjoyment of the company of such a distinguished individual as this benefactor reminds private collectors not only of how significant private collections may ultimately become to scholarship, but of how agreeably one's collecting interest may blend into one's character. Critics of New York's bibliophilic subculture state that the same people tend to be present at all the functions at the different book-oriented institutions. Certainly, a reception prior to a Bancroft Awards dinner sponsored by the Columbia University Library looks similar to a Grolier Club reception. The obvious answer is that many *interesting* collectors and scholars attend comparable functions and that the scope of these individuals' ideas is such that they do not become tiresome. Also apparent is the point that friendships develop which make frequent reacquaintances a pleasure.

* * *

I HAVE described the importance of private collections as research facilities, some varied sources for books and manuscripts, and the significance of a vital bibliophilic subculture to the private collector. My final major point will be the difficulties associated with the formation and display of a private collection.

To establish a private collection, one must not only exercise self-discipline but also achieve a sense of balance. Ideally, part of the value of a collecting interest is increased mental stimulation and social contribution on the part of the collector. A monomaniacal collecting drive could become asocial and self-destructive.

One of my oldest friends is a professor who has declined the married state on the grounds that marriage would interfere with his collecting, research, and teaching. Similarly, one important collector of Ruskiniana was so enthusiastic about her author that she regularly wore a locket containing a clipping of Ruskin's hair. Confronted by her husband while she was working upon her collection, this lady was asked to chose between Ruskin or her spouse. Ruskin was selected! Since the academic output of both these celibate scholars is excellent, I respect them. The unmarried state, however, is no guarantee of successful collecting and research. One of my unmarried friends has accumulated a vast collection of books but has reduced himself almost to poverty. The resultant mental strain could impair his creative abilities.

This friend not only collects books through some of the means which I have suggested, but advertises his "wants" in bibliographic journals. Furthermore, he subscribes to auction catalogues, and, when he discovers desirable items to be sold at auction in New York or London, he asks selected dealers to bid for him. As a result, he is book rich and cash poor. I believe that marriage, love for one's family, and avid collecting interests are all possible if a sense of balance is maintained. Rather than drive a family into bankruptcy through over-collecting, the collector should take a discerning approach toward items offered for sale. Rather than incessantly speaking of a collection, the collector should quietly permit the collection to grow and to permeate thought and work.

Similarly, a business profession and book collecting are not necessarily mutually exclusive events. While my own profession, the management of investment securities portfolios, may seem to be distantly related to nineteenth-century English literature, art, and social criticism, strong links do exist: my profession requires a close scrutiny of the economy and the securities market outlook. In this context, my collection and study of Ruskin's books on the subject of political economy are most appropriate in terms of achieving additional academic discipline and background. Furthermore, as in the case of most professions, my business demands clarity of expression. Greater communication skills may be developed through continued exposure to the literary style and logic of many of the great nineteenth-century authors.

[120]

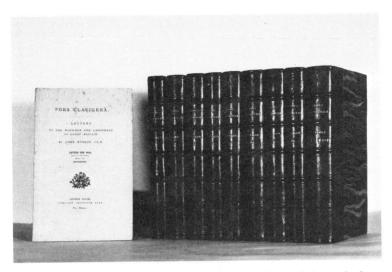

Fors Clavigera *(Orpington, 1871–1884). First edition of the bound parts, with illustrations by Kate Greenaway. Also shown as originally issued is letter 94 in this series of Ruskin's 96 letters addressed "to the workmen and labourers of Great Britain."*

During the early portion of my business school training, one of my classmates read Shakespeare rather than statistics. As a result, this poetically inclined individual did not graduate. Learning from this experience, the wise business person with book instincts is advised to submerge a desire for the book beautiful until after business hours. On the other hand, I know of an officer of a leading firm who instructs his associates to scout for volumes for his own library when these subordinates are on field trips. Since this officer is a controlling factor in his firm, he is able to unite book collecting and business successfully during office hours.

While a book collector should strive to achieve a balanced lifestyle, there are occasions when neurosis may prevail. One of my friends, a devoted collector of first-edition paperbacks, was recently on a cruise. Discovering a passenger keeping a bridge score on a title page torn from one of his cherished paperbacks, the irate collector threw the surprised bridge enthusiast overboard.

Preparing one's collection for public exhibition is one of the best methods of bringing one's collection forward as a research

[121]

facility. Whether such an exhibition of a private collection is held at a bibliophilic institution or a wine merchant's office (as was a recent important Ruskin exhibition), organization of one's collection for showing requires thoughtful application on the part of the collector. To get the most value out of private collections as exhibitions which lead to further research, the collector must temper by hard work the romantic atmosphere of bookstores and the lure of unopened dealers' catalogues. The private collector setting up an exhibition must be prepared for financial sacrifice, self-discipline, hard work, and some frustration. He must be satisfied about the security of the room, the extent of fire and theft insurance, and the safeguards against improper humidity and exposure to sunlight and tobacco smoke. To prepare a collection for presentation, the exhibitor not only must be pre-

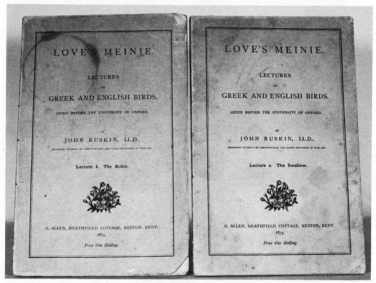

Love's Meinie *(Keston, 1873). Shown are Lecture I (The Robin) and Lecture II (The Swallow). First editions, limited to 1000 copies. Ruskin wrote, " 'Meinie' is the old English word for 'many'.... It passes gradually into 'menial', and unites the senses of multitude and servitude."*

[122]

pared to spend hours on travel and organization but also must be equipped to counteract a number of potential problems.

When the display is in progress, all the exhibitor's efforts may become worthwhile if only one visiting scholar remarks, ''You obviously understand your author from the inside out.'' If a catalogue is prepared in connection with the exhibition, and if this catalogue becomes a research source for future scholarship, a well-conceived show gains more permanent value. Finally, if a creative and relevant lecture—or series of lectures—is published, further enduring research qualities are added.

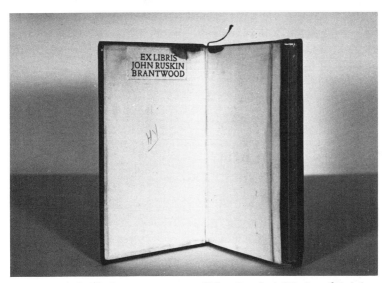

Ruskin's bookplate, in a copy of The Poetical Works of Leigh Hunt *(London, 1846). Printed on handmade paper in the Golden type designed by William Morris in 1889 and first used in 1891, this plate was printed some 16 months after Ruskin had ceased to take an interest in his own affairs. To document books which had once belonged to Ruskin, this and subsequent bookplates were inserted in Ruskin's volumes by Mrs. Severn, his adopted daughter. This book also bears Ruskin's signature on a page not shown here.*

[123]

As enjoyable as it is mentally to relocate into an earlier century through the collection and study of the writings of a great author such as John Ruskin, it is also important to interpret such writings and to carry them forward into the twentieth century. Critics have claimed that collectors live in yesterworlds and, at best, provide poor reflections of their authors' ideas. In fact, intelligent collectors, who strive to organize and to provide vitality to their collections, may make a significant contribution to the development of civilization. Through creative interpretation of their authors' philosophy and theory, they may add dimension to the collected legacy. By editing and publishing themes discovered in their collections, and by willing their entire collections to institutions, collectors may create centers of thought where future scholars may work toward an original development of ideas within their contemporary frameworks.

BIBLIOGRAPHY

J. L. Bradley (ed.), *The Letters of John Ruskin to Lord and Lady Mount-Temple* (Athens: Ohio State University Press, 1964).

V. A. Burd (ed.), *The Ruskin Family Letters* (Ithaca: Cornell University Press, 1973).

——, *The Winnington Letters* (Cambridge: Harvard University Press, 1969).

E. T. Cook, *Homes and Haunts of John Ruskin* (London: George Allen, 1912).

E. T. Cook and A. Wedderburn (eds.), *The Works of John Ruskin* (London: George Allen, 1903–12) 39 volumes.

W. G. Collingwood, *The Life of John Ruskin* (London: Methuen, 1900).

——, *Ruskin Relics* (London: Isbister, 1903).

J. S. Dearden, *Facets of Ruskin* (London: Charles Skilton, 1970).

J. S. Dearden (ed.), *The Professor: Arthur Severn's Memoir of John Ruskin* (London: George Allen & Unwin, 1967).

——, *Iteriad, or Three Weeks Among the Lakes, by John Ruskin* (Newcastle Upon Tyne: Frank Graham, 1969).

J. Evans and J. H. Whitehouse (eds.), *The Diaries of John Ruskin, 1835–1889* (Oxford: Clarendon Press, 1956–59).

D. Leon, *Ruskin, The Great Victorian* (London: Routledge & Kegan Paul, 1969).

M. Lutyens (ed.), *Young Mrs. Ruskin in Venice* (New York: Vanguard Press, n.d.).

C. E. Norton (ed.), *Letters of John Ruskin to Charles Eliot Norton* (Boston: Houghton, Mifflin, 1904).

H. I. Shapiro (ed.), *Ruskin in Italy* (Oxford: Clarendon Press, 1972).

M. Spence (ed.), *Dearest Mama Talbot* (London: George Allen & Unwin, 1966).

V. Surtees (ed.), *Sublime & Instructive* (London: Michael Joseph, 1972).

L. G. Swett, *John Ruskin's Letters to Francesca and Memoirs of the Alexanders* (Boston: Lothrop, Lee & Shepard, 1931).

R. Unwin (ed.), *The Gulf of Years* (London: George Allen & Unwin, 1953).

H. G. Viljoen (ed.), *The Brantwood Diary of John Ruskin* (New Haven: Yale University Press, 1971).

P. H. Walton, *The Drawings of John Ruskin* (Oxford: Clarendon Press, 1972).

T. J. Wise (ed.), *A Complete Bibliography of the Writings in Prose and Verse of John Ruskin, LL.D.* (London: Dawsons, 1974).

——, *Letters from John Ruskin to William Ward* (London: Privately printed, 1893).

Wyndham, G., *Letters to M. G. & H. G. by John Ruskin* (Privately printed, 1903).

JAMIE KLEINBERG SHALLECK *is a fine binder and book restorer, and the proprietress of The Stonehouse Bindery. Her conservation work at Princeton University Library, which included identifying and dating many of the fine bindings held there, formed the basis for her article.*

Identifying
and Classifying
Fine Bindings

Jamie Kleinberg Shalleck

A BOOKBINDER evaluates a fine binding by reversing it conceptually. First he considers the surface decoration. Is it aesthetically satisfying, and how was it accomplished? From the decorative ''finishing'' of the book, he turns to the details of the binding process itself. He examines corner mitering, inside hinges and joints, endband sewing, headcap shaping, and so forth, to measure the binder's skill. He looks for the meticulous attention to detail which distinguishes the master binder from the ordinary craftsman. Simultaneously, he will be gathering evidence of the structure of the binding. Was it sewn on tapes or cords? Is the spine ''flexible'' or ''hollow''? Are there hinges, and if so, how were they joined to the gatherings of the pages? Are the cords threaded into the boards, cut at the hinges, or spread out over the board surfaces? Finally, he handles the book, sensing how well it works. Does it open easily? Is it comfortable to hold? Is it conducive to reading, and does it protect the pages while they are in use?

An historian, by contrast, would concentrate almost exclusively on the decoration. He might consider the techniques of decoration, as distinguished from those required to build the book. But his interest is primarily to locate the binding historically: Who did it, when, where, and in relation to what broader artistic milieu? He might trace the provenance of a volume in order to answer these questions. He would probably analyze the heraldic device on an armorial binding to discover its owners. Finally, he might compare the design of a volume in question with others of the same suspected origins. One method for identifying a binding as the work of a particular craftsman consists of comparing the individual tools used in building up a design with those used by the alleged binder on his acknowledged body of work. The assumption here is that a binder's collection of tools is limited, and that he has favorites which he will use repeatedly in various combinations on different bindings over the years. But the drawbacks to this approach soon become apparent. If the binder did not design and make his own tools, several examples of the same tool may have been crafted simultaneously by a supplier and sold to a number of different binders. A fine binder's tools might be copied, either while he is still alive or years, even centuries, later. The tools may have passed from one generation of bookbinder to the next, or may have been used by several binders working at various times in one shop or for one entrepreneur or collector. (Such was probably the case in the Mearne bindery, founded by Samuel Mearne, who employed several binders, then went into partnership with his son Charles, who later took over the business, hiring, among others, Robert Steel.)

Tool identification is one small element in researching a fine bookbinding. Such limited evidence must be considered in the context of available biographical information, surviving business or bibliographical evidence, marks of provenance, and—certainly not least—the evolution of techniques.

Thorough knowledge of the history of bookbinding techniques can be as helpful in identifying a binding as that of the decorative motifs. A forger would have to have both skill and scholarship to duplicate the telltale structural details of a period binding, as well as imitating the appropriate decorative motifs. But rarely does it occur to the historian to learn how a binding is constructed; rarely does it occur to the binder to study the broad history of decorative arts. And without this combined approach, we will be a long time solving the mysteries of fine bookbinding.

For example, there is a handsome "medieval treasure binding" in the rare book collections at Princeton University: a German manuscript, *Expositio in evangelium Sancti Matthei* of Hrabanus Maurus, ca. 900, bound in stout wooden boards, possibly contemporary with the manuscript. The boards are covered in faded red velvet, which dates from the fifteenth century. The front cover is decorated with a painting on vellum under glass representing the Pascal Lamb and symbols of the Evangelists. This is

Hrabanus Maurus, Expositio in Evangelium S. Matthei *(MS, Germany, ca. 900)*.

surrounded by a twelfth-century Rhenish enameled border. The book has several times been displayed as a fifteenth-century rebinding incorporating the twelfth-century border. But consider the clear, smooth, machined glass covering the painting. It obviously dates from the nineteenth century. Was it added later to protect the fifteenth-century painting? How could the painting have survived in such perfect condition until this time? The nineteenth-century binder–collector Léon Gruel worked on and owned many of the fine medieval volumes now in various institutions and private collections Many of the practices which were praised by Gruel's contemporaries would now raise questions of ethics. In her volume *Bookbinders and Their Craft* (New York, 1903), S. T. Prideaux wrote of Gruel's shop:

> From its earliest days the business has always had the highest reputation, both for initiative in artistic matters, as well as for irreproachable execution in the detail of its many-sided achievements. It has indeed been the nursery of all the chief binders of the time, and no other house in any country has a roll-call of such distinguished names. Marius Michel père remained there twelve years.... Chambolle and Thouvenin were there also, as well as David, Thibaron, Motte, Joly, Loisetier and others.... Nor must we omit the names of Rossigneux, a designer of extraordinary genius, Liénard, the designer and carver in wood, the brothers Sollier, enamellers of exquisite taste, all of whom contributed to the revival of mediaeval bindings, of which M. Gruel discovered the traditions anew.... M. Gruel has employed all the decorative arts as adjuncts to the embellishments of the "livre de piété." Painted mosaics, enamels, wrought metal in clasps, corners and panels, sculptured wood and ivory, the monastic invention of "cuir ciselé," all these arts of many kinds and many ages have been applied in faultless workmanship to the Service Book of this century.... The possession of a very fine collection of ancient bindings has enabled M. Léon Gruel to become an authority on the history of binding....

The amalgams of reused materials and modern reproductions that such shops produced are misleading to say the least. Certainly

the anachronistic reappearance of old materials on newer bindings vastly complicates the question of authenticity.

In light of an awareness of such nineteenth-century practices,
a group of binders and curators re-examined the Princeton treasure
binding. Judging from the freshness of the trimming of the
inside margins of the binding, they concluded that the velvet
has been reapplied to the boards some time in the nineteenth
century, simultaneously with the enameled border, the painting
on vellum, and the protective glass. The painting itself was
probably executed in the nineteenth century. The border may
date back to the twelfth century, or might be the work of extremely skilled enamelers, such as the brothers Sollier. Because
the conference lacked an expert enameler or authority on medieval art, it could not resolve the questions raised about the
border or the painting.

Such bookbinding mysteries will persist because of the isolation
of the various approaches to the study of fine bindings. In addition
to the dichotomy between technical and historical experts, there
is a widespread prejudice in this country against Craftmanship
as distinguished from Artistry. In the United States in particular,
bookbinding has been considered less than fine art. Ironically,
now that crafts are becoming reputable, we are hampered by the
absence of experts. Here and abroad, experts are those who have
seen and studied a great number of bindings. These experts are
often old; their demise leaves astonishing gaps in the Authorities.
Their published treatises, too, are all too rare and largely un-
illustrated, simply because of cost. The body of identified bindings
in public collections in this country is relatively limited; and the
total body of fine bindings in America is largely uncatalogued.
No wonder it is difficult to compare a work in question with
several other examples of the work of a particular binder. One
does not know where to turn.

Consequently, attribution must be tentative—the exposure
of a binding to further comparison. Thus, one should not hope
to establish the infallible pedigree of a fine binding; rather, the
object should be to categorize it sufficiently to permit its entry,

over time, into a growing body of reference about fine bookbinding.

Most bindings cannot be ascribed to individuals. Many can be dated according to structural details, decorative technique, and style. For example, title labels were not used until the later seventeenth century; earlier, titles were tooled directly onto the leather of the spine. In the sixteenth century, they might appear as part of the cover decoration, or not at all. Before the sixteenth century, they were sometimes inked onto the edges of the pages. The earlier title lettering was large, brief, and uneven, as applied by means of individual handle tools; at the end of the seventeenth

Titling (left to right): 14th century — Magna Carta (MS, England, before 1311) — top-edge painted with arms of Edward I; 15th century — Johannes Nider, Praeceptorium *(Paris: Gering, 1478) — fore-edge titling; 16th century — Erasmus,* Colloquia *(Basel: Froben, 1537) — titling as part of the cover design for Jean Grolier; 17th century — Allestree,* Gentleman's Calling *(London: Paulet, 1676) — titled spine; 18th century — Heydon,* Harmony of the World *(London: Brome, 1662) — titled spine worked by Roger Payne.*

[132]

century, type pallets, in which loose type could be composed and fixed for stamping, came into use; titles became longer and more evenly tooled.

Title treatment is only one bit of technical evidence for dating a binding. In fact, every element of the binding has evolved over time, and a thorough knowledge of this evolution can provide convincing evidence for dating a binding. Together the peculiarities of all the elements of the binding may suggest, not only the origins of the binding, but also its use and ownership— in short, who fooled with the book, when, and why.

The spines of sixteenth- and early seventeenth-century books were barely rounded, if at all; the shoulders were small. During the eighteenth century, spines became semi-elliptical in shape, with heavy shoulders. Before the late eighteenth century, the leather was pasted directly down onto the spine; during the late eighteenth century a hollow tube of paper might be interposed between the spine and the covering leather. This allowed the books to open flat even when printed on stiff paper; but over the years, many such bindings have separated, the spine leather with the outer section of the hollow tube splitting away from the boards.

Earliest endbands were part of the sewing of the volume in figure 8's over double thongs. Separately sewn endbands formed around cord or thongs which were oversewn in natural linen next came into use. By the late sixteenth century, many endbands were sewn in colored silks. In the seventeenth century, double (2-tier) endbands appear; in the nineteenth century, flat endbands were formed over vellum strips.

The treatment of the excess leather turned in around the boards at the corners is also revealing. On medieval volumes the corners were sewn together. Tongue-cut corners were used into the sixteenth century. Until the mid-sixteenth century the excess leather might simply be cut off at a 45 ° angle. In the late sixteenth century, the excess leather might be overlapped from a trimmed-out hole just inside the corner of the board. During

[133]

Headcap and spine formations (left to right): 12th century — St. Augustine, Sermones X in Epistolam S. Johannis *(MS, France); 14th century — Magna Carta (MS, England, before 1311); 15th century — Johannes Nider,* Praeceptorium *(Paris: Gering, 1478); 16th century — Erasmus,* Colloquia *(Basel: Froben, 1537); 17th century — Richard Allestree,* Gentleman's Calling *(London: Robert Paulet, 1676); 18th century — John Heydon,* Harmony of the World *(London: Henry Brome, 1662); 19th century — Homer,* The Iliad, *translated by George Chapman (London: Nathaniell Butter, 1611).*

the sixteenth century, pared, folded corners appeared on the better class of bindings. During the eighteenth century, the excess leather was pared thin and beveled together, with the overlaps trimmed away. When covered with gold tooling these jointures were almost invisible.

Patterns of sewing the gatherings together have also varied over the centuries. Endpaper formation provides additional technical clues for dating a binding. And the materials themselves are revealing. Marbled papers, for example, came into general use in the second half of the seventeenth century; pink parchment was popular in the fourteenth century; morocco leather, little used before the sixteenth century. Even the quality of the paper and leather reveals whether it was manufactured traditionally or more recently by the "improved" methodologies that have caused both to carry the seeds of their destruction.

CORNERS

1. *Tongue-cut corner turn-ins (15th century)*

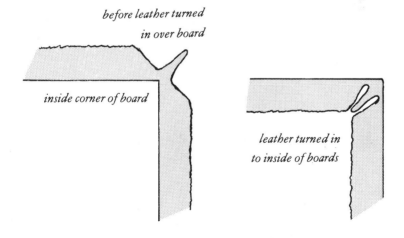

before leather turned
in over board

inside corner of board

leather turned in
to inside of boards

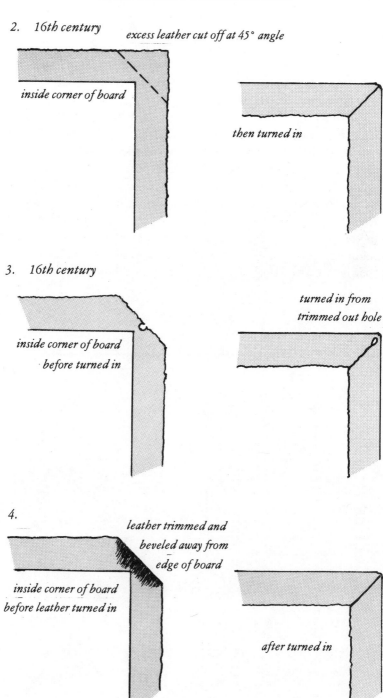

2.   16th century

excess leather cut off at 45° angle

inside corner of board

then turned in

3.   16th century

turned in from
trimmed out hole

inside corner of board
before turned in

4.

leather trimmed and
beveled away from
edge of board

inside corner of board
before leather turned in

after turned in

Decorative techniques can also help to date a binding. Gold-tooling was generally unknown in Europe before the fifteenth century. Panel stamps and decorative rolls came into use during the late fifteenth century. Gold blocking becomes common after the sixteenth century. The earliest decorative tools were intaglio-cut stamps; during the sixteenth century, the designs were raised on the tools so as to be depressed into the leather. The designs themselves were at first heavy and filled. Later they become lighter in feeling with open areas outlined.

Tooling (left to right): 15th century — French binding decorated with small intaglio animal stamps on Nider, Praeceptorium; *late 15th century — "Caxton's binder" used a combination of intaglio and direct-impression tools to decorate the* Testament de Amyra Sultan Nichemedy *(MS written for Edward, Prince of Wales, Bruges, ca. 1482); 16th century — gold-tooled and painted binding for Jean Grolier, on Erasmus,* Colloquia; *late 15th century — Parisian gold-blocked binding on a Book of Hours (Paris: Philippe Pigouchet, 1498).*

The recognized binding styles—e.g., Fanfare, Moorish, cottage-roof, dentelle—can be grouped more generally within the stylistic periods recognized in the art world: Gothic, Renaissance, Baroque, Rococo, Modern, and so on. Such groupings help to relate bookbinding design to the larger artistic movements. When one stops to consider that many fine bindings were executed for the same patrons who commissioned paintings, sculpture, and music, one need not wonder that bookbinding design should relate intimately to the overall history of art.

On occasion, despite all our attempts to consider the evidence of technique and style, a binding will still defy dating. The binding of the fourth-century Coptic manuscript in The William Scheide Library at Princeton is in such fine condition that, in spite of the fact that all elements seem to fit together technically, some doubts existed about its true age. The radiocarbon laboratory at The University of Pennsylvania was asked whether or not the archaeological tool of radiocarbon dating would be applicable. Unfortunately, at this time the process requires burning a considerable amount of the material to be dated, but the University is now developing a refined process which will require only the smallest fragment of the material in question. It was decided to wait.

Once the age and style of a binding have been determined, its authenticity must be considered. During the nineteenth century in particular, when book collecting was practiced on a truly grand scale and skillful binders were readily available, vast numbers of fine bindings were repaired more extensively than would be thought advisable today. Today's collector will try to preserve as much of the original in as untouched form as is compatible with the purpose of the collection. In the nineteenth century, collectors often rebound valuable old volumes to make them look beautiful, and to eliminate the imperfections which develop over time or are inherent in the various forms and styles of bindings. Repairs or restoration, when well done, should not detract from the authenticity of the binding. Ideally, the repairs are minimal, reversible, effected with the finest materials, and appropriate stylistically to the era from which the binding dates. They should not materially change the structure, style, or decoration of the bookbinding. Common repairs which must be considered when evaluating the authenticity of a binding include rebacking, joints mended with overpasted thin strips of leather, corner repairs, and replaced endpapers.

Rebacking requires removing the original spine leather and replacing it with new leather. Often the new spine was tooled more elaborately than the original. This is especially true of many sixteenth- and seventeenth-century books with rather plain spines, rebacked in the eighteenth and nineteenth centuries, when elaborately tooled spines were in vogue. In rebacking books, I have on occasion lifted the elaborately tooled, but anachronistic eighteenth-century spine leather to find the original plain seventeenth-century spine beneath. Today the meticulous restorer will try to save the original spine and paste it back down over the rebacking leather on the volume; otherwise, he will reproduce an appropriate style of decoration on the rebacked book.

Added tooling on a restored spine does not necessarily constitute a fake, but it is, perhaps unintentionally, a step in that direction. Any decorative additions to the original binding or elaborations upon earlier design elements must be suspect. Nevertheless, it has been fairly common practice to take, for example, a simple panel-tooled binding of the seventeenth century and add elaborate corner fleurons worked with nineteenth-century tools; or to add to a simple armorial binding, consisting of a center coat-of-arms, a panel border and corner fleurons. Such intermingling of earlier and later tooling is not easy to unravel. For example, one book in the Princeton rare book collections, Zarate's *Historia del descubrimiento y conquista de las provincias del Peru* (Seville, 1577), is pictured in a 1927 English dealer's catalogue as a Spanish sixteenth-century armorial binding bearing the arms of Don Francisco Perez Cabrera y Bobadilla, Marqués de Moya. It is a handsome reddish-brown

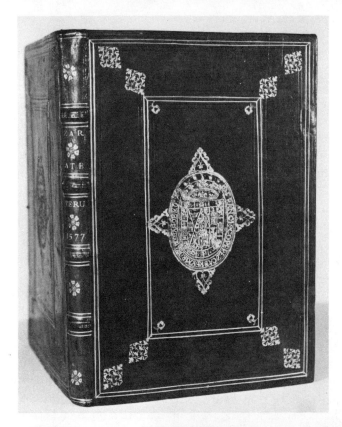

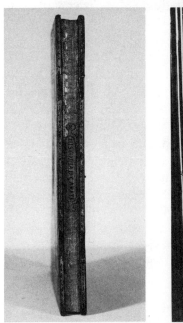

Zarate, Historia del descubrimiento y conquista de las provincias del Peru *(Seville, 1577).*

leather binding with panel borders, corner fleurons, and center coat-of-arms. The pages are sewn on four raised bands; the compartments of the spine are gold-tooled with large rosettes and titling. The headbands are red and blue silk. The edges of the boards are gold-tooled; the edges of the pages are gilt, gauffered, and handsomely titled. The tooling of the coat-of-arms on the front cover is "doubled," that is, the second impression of the tool through gold did not line up exactly with the first blind impression of the stamp.

The binding is undoubtedly very handsome, but it has the feel of a mid-seventeenth-century binding. The Marqués de Moya flourished in the late sixteenth century. It is an easy enough task for a binder to take the stamp of a man long dead and apply it to a bookbinding.

It is possible that the binding itself is sixteenth-century. The gilt, gauffered, and titled fore-edge seems authentic. Yet the titling on the spine suggests a late seventeenth-century date. The coat-of-arms may be sixteenth-century, but the fleurons that abut the edges of the armorial device were applied separately from the center ellipse of the coat-of-arms. This is obvious from the fact that they are clearly impressed, not "doubled." Furthermore, these fleurons overlap the blind panel borders. The color of the gold on the armorial device does not exactly match that of the panel borders or the decorative fleurons. And the gold-tooled panel borders overlap the blind, suggesting that they might have been applied later. Furthermore, the tools used around the coat-of-arms are azurée (impressed with an azured tool—i.e., one with close parallel lines running diagonally across its surface); the corner fleurons are not. The fleurons are deeply and unevenly tooled and the leather has been burned in places, both of which suggest a less-than-skillful hand. Finally, the plain endpapers are put down over reinforcing hinges of printed paper.

To decide the chronology of elements of this binding, one would have to research the coat-of-arms further, lift the end-

[141]

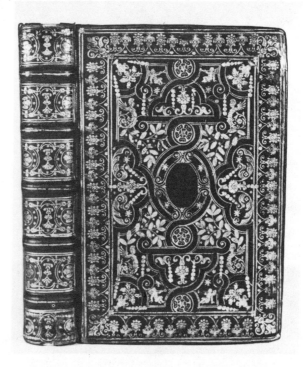

Euripides, Tragedies *(16th century).*

Pietro Barozzi, De modo bene moriendi *(Venice, 1531).*

papers and try to determine the date of the printed paper used for the hinges and compare this binding with other sixteenth-century Spanish armorial bindings.

There were binders and collectors, and there probably are today, who made a practice of adding decoration to earlier bindings. Sir Edward Sullivan (1852–1928) is known to have elaborated upon several earlier bindings. Curiously, several bindings in the Elmer Adler Collection at Princeton show signs of over-tooling. Adler seems to have known little about book-bindings. His own notes concerning the bindings of his books are usually wrong. It is, therefore, likely that he purchased the books as we see them today, failing to note the discrepancies that make them doubtful examples of fine bindings.

The most obvious example is the binding of a volume of Euripides' *Tragedies* now in The Graphic Arts Collection at Princeton. The book itself, in Greek, dates from the sixteenth century. The binding may be sixteenth-century—it is calfskin, sewn on double bands, with simple, linen headbands, rough turn-ins, plain endpapers, and titling on the edges of the pages. The gold-tooled decoration on the binding is later. The decorative motif resembles a fanfare design, but the tools from which it is composed are peculiarly rococo in feeling—vases of flowers, seated cupids blowing horns, winged mermen, and large leafy branches. A mask roll forms the border. I suspect that this pseudo-fanfare decoration was added to the original plain sixteenth-century binding in the late eighteenth or early nine-teenth century.

Another book which appears to be over-tooled is Pietro Barozzi's *De modo bene moriendi* (Venice, 1531), also in The Graphic Arts Collection. Adler dated the binding by identifying the armorial device of a sixteenth-century Venetian doge. But the elements of the binding belie any such early origins: marbled endpapers and double headbands put us into the late seventeenth century; the title label suggests an eighteenth-century date, as does the elaborate spine tooling. Even the coat-of-arms is questionable. It is not a single stamp as was customary; rather, it is made up from small curved tools, known as gouges. Any binder familiar with the arms of the sixteenth-century doge could have composed these insignia from tools he would have at hand.

Another problem involved in authenticating bindings is to distinguish what is and is not the work of the "known" fine binders. Is the binding really by Roger Payne, or is it simply a

Catholicon *(Mainz, 1460).*

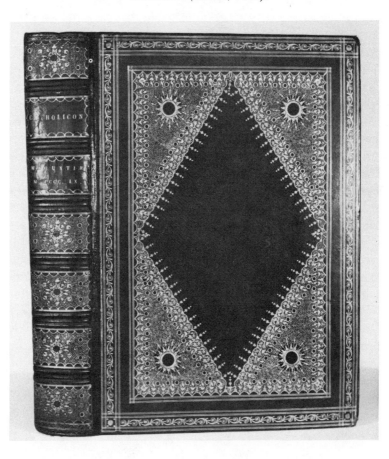

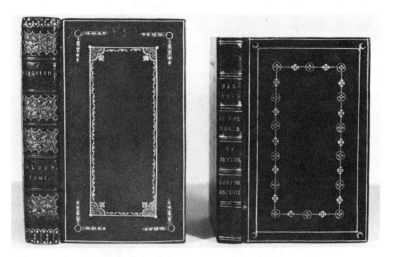

Roger Payne binding of Heydon's Harmony of the World, *and a similar binding, probably not the work of Payne, on* Virgil *(Venice: Aldus, 1501).*

beautiful eighteenth-century binding in a similar popular decorative style? The *Catholicon* in The Schiede Library provides a handsome example of an eighteenth-century gold-tooled binding in the style of Roger Payne, the impressions less precise than those of the known Payne bindings at Princeton. Moreover, the separated double spine binds are suspicious. And Payne usually avoided use of roulettes, stating in his bills that his designs were painstakingly compiled from small tools. With less convincing evidence, also questionable is a small red straight-grained morocco binding on an Aldine *Virgil* of 1501, Paynesque in design, but showing several doubtful discrepancies. It is not quite as finely worked as it might be. The use of blind tooling is unusual. The gold tea-chest paper endleaves are even more garish than the purple papers Payne affected. The raised bands are more pronounced and squared than those of the known Payne bindings. Again, I cannot say that Roger Payne could not have bound this volume, but I have no final evidence that he did.

[145]

Hanhagot Mikol Hashanah, Compilation of Jewish Customs
(MS, N. Italy, ca. 1475); lower (sic) cover.

There is one certain forgery at Princeton, significant enough
in its own right to be included in any exhibition of fine bookbinding. The small eighteenth-century wooden binding, inlaid
with mother-of-pearl and ivory, on a fifteenth-century northern
Italian manuscript, Hanhagot Mikol Hashanah's *Compilation of
Jewish Customs,* was manufactured to appear to be a fourteenth-
century binding bearing the arms and initials of Cardinal Gotio
Battaglia on the front cover, and the Malatesta arms and initials
on the back cover. The manuscript, too, bears marks of tam-
pering—e.g., the addition of a preface suggesting it was written
by Moses and illustrated by Giotto. Erwin Panofsky, who reported
his examination of both manuscript and binding in his article
"Giotto and Maimonides in Avignon" (*The Journal of the*

[146]

Walters Art Gallery, 4 [1941] 27–44), commented that the falsification is "like Falstaff's lies, 'gross like a mountain, open, palpable.' It has a likeably naïve, imaginative, and definitely non-professional touch...." He suggested that the binding and preface, etc., were probably manufactured for an eighteenth-century descendant of the Battaglia family, Marc Battaglini, Bishop of Cesena. Panofsky kindly speculated that the forger may not have had ignoble motives.

> The forger may have acted with perfect *bona fides* and sincere enthusiasm. The provenance of the ancient-looking book would automatically bring to mind the most famous member of the Battaglia family, that is to say the Cardinal Gotio—so great a figure in Avignon—yet so loyal to his native Rimini—, the favorite of Pope Benedict XII, and, presumably, a friend of Galeotto de' Malatesti who had been the "Permanent Vicar of the Most Holy Church of Cesena," the see of Bishop Marco Battaglini. If the volume had been in the possession of the family for some generations, the learned Marco himself, being neither a Hebraist nor an art-critic, may have believed in its noble history. One knows how easily heirlooms and ancestors become "invested by family tradition with a dim and dusky grandeur," as Nathaniel Hawthorne has said.
>
> Thus, there is hardly any reason to cast aspersions on the moral character of the good friar of Montescudo. At a time when the interest in local antiquities and parochial patriotism had grown to enormous proportions in the "underprivileged" artistic centers of Italy, he merely furnished evidence for what he honestly believed to be the truth. Firmly convinced of his little volume's connection with Gotio Battaglia, Galeotto de' Malatesti, Pope Benedict XII, Maimonides, and Giotto, he labored only for the glory of God and of the Patria Ariminese. His beatified spirit must have rejoiced when the result befooled the Librarian to the Earl of Ashburnham and, perhaps, the mighty Bernard Quaritch; may he forgive the present writer for a belated exposure!

It is amazing that for years this binding was accepted as a fourteenth-century original, despite the naïveté of the forgery.

Intarsia bindings simply were not made before the eighteenth century! But I suppose that most binding forgeries are such combinations of less-than-evil intentions: attempts to bind a book in a style befitting what is thought to be its origins; mis-attributions by collectors, curators, and dealers blinded by rumor, partial provenance, or wishful thinking. This is why it is so important to consider all the evidence, the technical as well as the historical, the structural as well as the decorative.

The other side of the coin is the tendency today to doubt the authenticity of everything. Many wary young curators come to a fine binding with the prejudice that it must be an intentional forgery. But anyone skilled enough to produce a truly convincing

Baptista Mantuanus, Omnia opera *(Bologna: Benedictus Hectoris, 1502).*

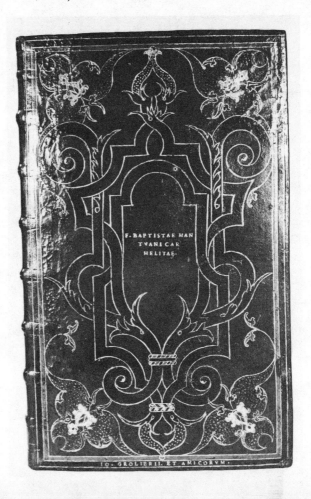

forgery, with each structural and decorative element properly in place, could probably command equal financial reward for his own contemporary fine binding work.

One fine binding at Princeton had been questioned as a possible forgery. I have chosen to accept it as authentic, however, at least for the time being. I refer to the Grolier binding on the *Omnia opera* of Baptista Spagnuoli Mantuanus (Bologna, 1502). The binding was questioned on the basis of its tooling, which is extremely shallow. It was suggested to me that indeed it had never been tooled at all, but only painted with a Grolieresque design and with Grolier's motto. After having noted that this binding was worked in calfskin rather than morocco, I did some experiments with gold-tooling on calfskin and concluded that when the leather has been dampened or stored in a damp place for any period of time, the tooling will tend to lift. The possibility that the design and lettering had been painted onto the binding seemed remote to me, simply because it would be more difficult to paint such a design, including the very small regular lettering, than to reproduce Grolier-style tools and tool a forgery. The binding itself seems convincingly sixteenth-century, and the tooling seems quite comfortable here. Indeed, the overall quality of the binding, the success of the design, and the sculptural beauty of the book were the most compelling reasons for continuing to regard it as the work of a master binder. And comparison of such details as shape and treatment of the spine, assemblage of endpapers, and so forth, with known Grolier bindings seemed further to substantiate the attribution.

The binding of Robert Taylor's copy of Richard Allestree's *The Gentleman's Calling* (London, 1676) had been attributed to Samuel Mearne. Later reconsidered, it was reattributed to the Devotional Binder. I went back to the earlier attribution, basing my decision on the fact that none of the examples of the Devotional Binder's work that I have seen in this country in any way resembles this particular binding, while that on another Allestree volume, *The Ladies Calling* (Oxford, 1676), attributed to

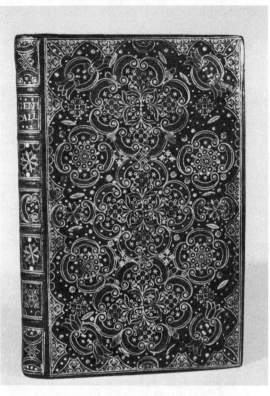

Allestree, Gentleman's Calling *(London: Paulet, 1676).*

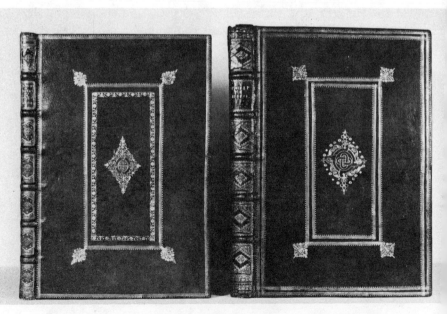

Two seventeenth-century English bindings in the "rectangular style," both probably the work of the Mearne bindery (left to right): Isocrates *(Venice: Sons of Aldus, 1543);* Colonna, Hypnerotomachia *(Venice: Sons of Aldus, 1545).*

Mearne and pictured in Maggs Bros. Catalogue 489, appears almost certainly to be the work of the same binder. I have since been challenged on this attribution, and I readily admit that I may be wrong. But here again, one can only go on available evidence. Quite possibly both Allestree bindings are by someone other than Mearne, but I do suggest that they are the work of the same hand or shop. Moreover, no one knows who the Devotional Binder was. A positive attribution to him seems in many ways merely an admission that the binder is unidentified.

Another Princeton binding, that on *Isocrates nuper accurate recognitus, et auctus* (Venice, 1534), had been ascribed to Charles Mearne, the son of Samuel. It may have been the work of the son, but it seems closer to the panel bindings turned out by the Mearne bindery under the father's direction. The binding of Colonna's *La hypnerotomachia de Poliphilo* (Venice, 1545) had no previous attribution but was so similar in style, execution, and feeling to the *Isocrates* that I attribute it, as well, to the Mearne bindery.

It is much easier to identify two eighteenth-century Irish bindings as the work of the College Binder, whoever he may have been, simply because this is really an attribution to a workshop, like the Mearne workshop, rather than an attempt to identify the individual who did the tooling.

The uniqueness of the combination of tools on the eighteenth-century English binding of an Aldine *Virgil* (1501) led me to seek out its binder. After matching the tools used to build up the design with those shown in photographs of other contemporary bindings, I conclude that this was the work of Thomas Elliot, one of the binders at the Harleian Library.

Needless to say, no attribution is infallible. Signed bindings are easier to approach—here, it is a question of genuineness. But few early bindings were signed. The obvious exceptions are the panel bindings which included the binder's name and motto in the panel border; the Grolier and Mahieu bindings which featured the collector's name; and of course the armorial bindings

[151]

which identified the owner or his family. Other bindings can be identified only by first placing them technically and stylistically in a larger historical and artistic context, and then by comparison of details, narrowing in on a particular workshop or binder.

Once in a while a book is encountered that defies any logical categorization. One such volume is an embroidered binding on a manuscript written by John Metham, a treatise on palmistry, Amoryus and Cleopes, and a treatise on physiognomy (England, 1449). The book is covered with brown velvet, very worn, embroidered with a border and horseheads that resemble chess pieces. Silk fabric hangs from the inside edges of the boards for no apparent reason. Comparison of the book with the wrapper bindings at The Walters Art Gallery provided no real clues. This binding may be as early as the fifteenth or as late as the nineteenth century.

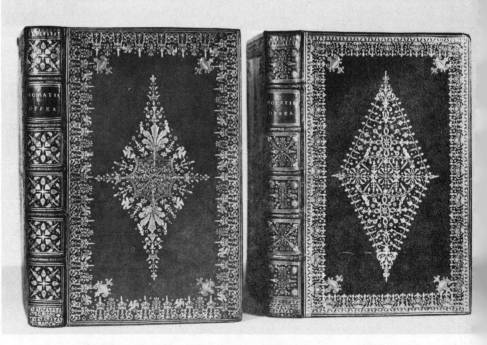

Eighteenth-century Irish bindings by the College Binder, both on copies of Horace *(Dublin: Typographia Academiae, 1745).*

Eighteenth-century English binding by Thomas Elliott on Virgil
(Venice: Aldus, 1501).

[153]

John Metham, A Treatise on Palmistry, Amoryus and Cleopes, and a Treatise on Physiognomy *(MS, England, 1449).*

The binding of a later fifteenth-century French book of hours is also unusual. It is decorated all over with concentric gold-tooled frames, with a small center panel tooled with leafy boughs, flowers, and an ellipse containing the initials *ML*. There is a penciled attribution in the book to Clovis Eve, which dates the binding ca. 1600. There is a similar binding at The Walters Art Gallery. It, too, decorates a late fifteenth-century book of hours. I was hoping that the provenance of each would suggest a connection, but life is never so simple. The provenance of the Walters volume goes back to a Thomas Dumesnil (1705); while that of the Princeton book of hours can be traced to Sir Edward Musgrave of Scaleby and Hayton Castle, created baronet in 1630. It was unfortunate that provenance did not link the two, but there is still a possibility that their similarity was no coincidence.

[154]

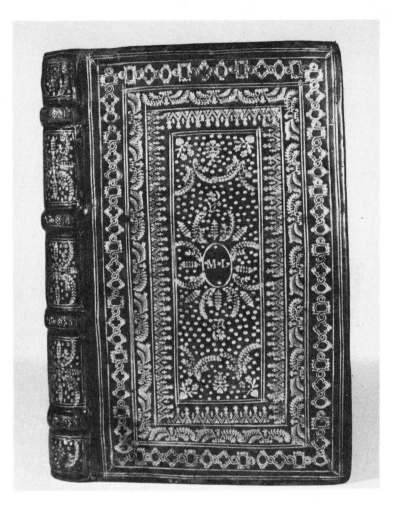

Late 16th-century French binding in the style of Clovis Ève, on a Book of Hours (MS, France, ca. 1490).

The overall history of fine bookbinding is largely unwritten. What we do have is an accumulation of clues, insights, separate and shifting identifications, and random technical expertise. Each fine binding presents a mystery to be solved, a piece to be assembled someday perhaps into a larger picture. Yet the danger of a piecemeal, book by book, approach to the subject is that it will just remain so.

[155]

The scholar who concentrates on tool identification performs a great service, but one that would be all the greater illuminated by a broad knowledge of, for example, engraving techniques, tool casting facilities, and the decorative arts in general. I am amazed by the amount of research still attempted by means of rubbings taken from fine bindings. It seems to me that such second-hand information cannot suffice to establish the identity of a bookbinding. Consider the many variables in the long process of binding a book; obviously it is unfair to judge a binding by any single element.

One binder using one tool can create many different effects, according to the leather he uses, the humidity of the air on the day he tools, how steady his hand happens to be, his patience and perseverance. The historian must be capable of allowing for such variations. For this reason, he should know how the binder works, the processes involved, and the elements that may affect the quality of the work.

The historian is further burdened by the requirements of his own discipline to trace the relationship of the individual binder to contemporary artistic and cultural movements. The relationship itself is interesting to consider: Does bookbinding precede or follow stylistic movements in the other arts? Does it relate more intimately to the architectural or the sculptural arts?

The task of identifying fine bookbindings is overwhelming if performed in isolation. It can be enlightening when pursued with a knowledge of technical possibilities and in relation to a broad cultural milieu.

BIBLIOGRAPHY

William Loring Andrews, *Roger Payne and His Art* (New York: De Vinne Press, 1892).

Book Bindings: Historical & Decorative (London: Maggs Cat. 489, 1927).

Bookbindings in Great Britain 16th–20th Century (London: Maggs Cat. 966, 1975).

Maurice Craig, *Irish Bookbindings* (London: Cassell, 1954).

[156]

E. Ph. Goldschmidt, *Gothic and Renaissance Bookbinding* (London: Benn, 1928).

Bernard Middleton, *A History of English Craft Bookbinding Technique* (London: Holland Press, 1978).

——, *The Restoration of Leather Bindings* (Chicago: American Library Association LTP Publication No. 18, 1972).

Dorothy Miner, *The History of Bookbinding 525–1950 A. D.* (Baltimore: Walters Art Gallery, 1957).

Howard M. Nixon, *Sixteenth-Century Gold-Tooled Bookbindings in The Pierpont Morgan Library* (New York: Pierpont Morgan Library, 1971).

J. Basil Oldham, *Blind Panels of English Binders* (Cambridge: Cambridge University Press, 1958).

——, *Shrewsbury School Library Bindings* (Oxford: Clarendon Press, 1943).

S. T. Prideaux, *Bookbinders and Their Craft* (New York: Scribner, 1903).

PHILIP SPERLING, *a retired executive from the corporate business world, has been an avid reader and bibliophile as far back as he can remember. In addition to his constant pursuit of William Pickering (as both bookseller and publisher), he also collects books in the field of American fine printing, circa 1900.*

Looking for
Mr. Pickering

Philip Sperling

A ND WHO, might you say, is Mr. Pickering? I refer, of
course, to William Pickering, bookseller and publisher,
once located at 177 Piccadilly, London, and now long since gone
to his rest. William Pickering was one of the men who published
books for English readers at the beginning of the third decade of
the nineteenth century, who made attractive books of both
classical authors and contemporary ones available at cheap prices
and in a format easy to handle in pocket and in hand. He was
the publisher of The Modern Library of his times. Updike states
in his prodigious *Printing Types: Their History, Forms, and Use*
(Cambridge, 1966) that the Chiswick Press is famous in the
annals of English typography and its best books were printed for
William Pickering. The series of 16mo volumes which he published have not been surpassed for beauty and utility in modern
times. It was Pickering and Whittingham of the Chiswick Press
who were responsible for the revival of Caslon, and since then

its popularity has never dimished. After Pickering's time, we find the bookseller separating from the publisher and the designer separating from both. Today we are all specialists, but we all owe a debt to William Pickering for showing us the way.

With all the thousands of books published since his death and with the many more constantly coming off the presses, it is indeed surprising that no one has written a full-length biography of this most eminent figure in the English bookworld. Admirable as they are, the only two books to treat the man at some length are: *The Charles Whittingham Printers* by Arthur Warren, published in a limited edition of 385 copies on hand-made paper and 3 copies on vellum by The Grolier Club of New York in 1896, and *William Pickering, Publisher: A Memoir and a Check-List of His Publications* by Geoffrey Keynes. The first edition of this work was published in an edition of 350 copies by *The Fleuron*, London, in 1924. Forty-five years later, a revised edition of this work was issued by the Galahad Press. Sir Geoffrey (an honor bestowed upon him in the years between) not only revised and extended this memoir, but also added titles to his check-list. One hundred copies of this revised edition were signed by the author. No collector of this English pupil of Aldus should be without a copy of both these books to guide him or her along the way looking for Mr. Pickering's books.

William Pickering was born on 2 April 1796, and in as dramatic and scandalous a situation as could whet the appetite. Keynes suggests that, though of illegitimate birth, he was not thrust out into the world unthought of, or uncared for. After a nurtured childhood, young William was placed as an apprentice with a firm that operated as both booksellers and publishers, a very usual combination in those days. How informative it would be if we knew the details of his early childhood, his schooling, his reading habits, the pleasures he indulged in both good and bad. After all, that old and worn cliché ''the child is father to the man'' still holds. Why was he directed into the book world? Was there something in this means of livelihood, a cut above the usual tradesman or laborer, more in keeping with someone related, properly or not, to his relatives, the nobility? Certainly many publishers considered themselves a minor sort of nobility— witness John Murray. In any event, after an apprenticeship of about ten years, Pickering started on his own at the age of twenty-four as a bookseller at 31 Lincoln's Inn Fields. With (perhaps parental) capital and native intelligence he soon was on his way to success. Keynes says that

> the fact that some of the earliest books afterwards published by Pickering, beginning with the Diamond Classics edition of Virgil, 1821, have on their title pages the coat of arms of Earl Spencer (second earl, 1758–1834), followed by a dedication to him, is perhaps sufficient indication of the source of both his life and fortune. In December 1822 an advertisement printed on the wrapper of *The Gentleman's Magazine* even referred to the classical authors printed in diamond type as "the Spencer Classics."

William Pickering is very frequently considered a Victorian publisher, and so he was to a degree; but when he first entered the field, probably in 1820–21, George III was still on the throne of England, long since famous as the king who had lost the American colonies. Two other monarchs, George IV and William IV, were to precede Victoria before she became queen in 1837 and ushered in what later became the Victorian Age, and by that time half of William Pickering's career was gone. There remained only another seventeen years. Pickering's career begins in 1820 and it is for the books published between 1820 and 1854 that I have long been looking. He began his first venture as a publisher by issuing between 1820 and 1831 reprints of classical authors in a series of miniature volumes in 48mo or 32mo. The series was known as the Diamond Classics and the authors included Horace, Virgil, Terence, Catullus, Cicero, Dante, Tasso, Petrarch, Walton, Milton, and Shakespeare. Later Pickering also added, in an admired diamond Greek text, the New Testament and the works of Homer. Those volumes which appeared

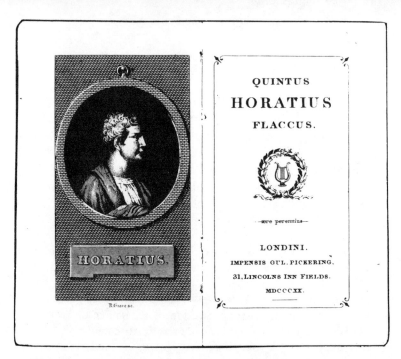

Rare proof impression of the title page and frontispiece of the Diamond Classics Horace *(1820).*

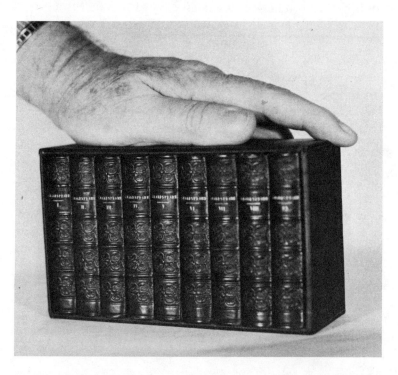

The Plays *by William Shakespeare (Diamond Classics, 1825). This set is embellished with a portrait and 37 engraved plates after Stothard.*

before 1829 were printed by Charles Whittingham the elder, at the Chiswick Press. These fascinating miniature books, which required the use of a magnifying glass to be read, were really an advertising gimmick of Pickering's to call attention to his new publishing company. To a degree he never escaped this association with preciosity, although by far the greater majority of the books he published were of quarto size.

I could give many reasons why these lovely books delight me and why I collect them, but I shall be content to say that their physical features please my eye (and I like to think that it is a critical one), my hands encompass them pleasantly, and almost always I find the contents enjoyable to read because I am a collector who must read his books—no unopened pages for me. A. N. L. Munby in one of his delightful essays ("Some Caricatures of Book Collectors: An Essay"; Privately printed, 1948) settled, I think, the question of book collecting very well:

> For cold print and reasoned argument are not the media through which to communicate the evanescent excitements which the pursuit of rare books entails: it is largely an affair of the heart, and like most such affairs, does not look its best when dismembered and placed under the analyst's microscope: and, in any case, the would-be apologist is wasting his time. Between the sceptic and the initiate there is a well nigh unbridgeable gulf fixed, and one might as well discourse upon port vintages to a confirmed teetotaller.

Nevertheless I know why I like William Pickering's books, and it is very nice indeed to have my opinions reinforced by men whose statements carry more force and weight than mine; this was a discovery I made many years after I began my collection. The men I refer to—they are three in number—are Theodore Low De Vinne, Francis Meynell, and Joseph Blumenthal.

Theodore Low De Vinne (1828–1914) was the American printer most held in esteem at the turn of the century. His work was quite meticulous, if not original and inspired, but perhaps even

[163]

more important was his ability to put his thoughts down on paper. In a very illuminating book, *Title Pages As Seen by a Printer*, published in 1901 in a handsome, limited edition by The Grolier Club (De Vinne was one of the founding members of that bibliophilic organization), De Vinne had many commendatory remarks to say about William Pickering and devoted a chapter, if a very brief one, to "The Pickering Title." He wrote that

> A title in the Pickering style is not so easily composed as the ordinary displayed title. To select, group and arrange the words of a title in a few sizes of roman letter calls for more intelligence and discretion.... Pickering did not neglect ornament, but he made it keep its place. It usually appeared on the title in the form of a border, preferably architectural, and generally in the old Italian outline style. The border decorated but did not suppress the type; the lettering always had a fair presentation.

From speaking to printers, and reading their books and manuals, I know that the creation of a title page demands great art. It requires the ability to combine the most suitable type face and size with an attractive relief of white space in order to achieve readibility at a glance. For me, this art William Pickering has to a great degree.

Sir Francis Meynell (1891–1977), one of the founders in London of the famous Nonesuch Press and author, has written a most entertaining and informative monograph on *The Design of Books: Function and Fashion* (New York, 1966). For him a book should be legible and properly illuminated, and by this term Meynell means the decoration or (as he puts it) "enhancement" of the work printed. Undoubtedly Meynell thinks highly of Pickering and his aims and achievements. "I go back a little over a hundred years, to William Pickering. He called himself the English Disciple of Aldus; and in the Aldine fashion he made books handsome but also handy. He applied to books a classical tradition—like that of the brothers Adam in house decoration."

 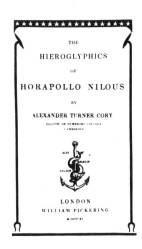

A very unusual Pickering title page from 1840.

Joseph Blumenthal (born 1897), the founder and guiding hand of The Spiral Press, planned a major exhibition at The Pierpont Morgan Library on The Art of the Printed Book, 1455–1955 (11 September–2 December 1973). Not only have books of surpassing beauty been printed by Mr. Blumenthal at his Spiral Press, but he has that fine ability to put his thoughts in clear, concise prose. There is, for example, the catalogue written by Mr. Blumenthal and published by the library for the exhibition, as well as his highly recommended study, "The Great Printers and Their Books." In this exhibition two of the better known Pickering books were shown: *The Complete Angler* of Izaak Walton, 1836 (two volumes), and *The Book of Common Prayer*, 1844. Of our subject, Mr. Blumenthal writes that

> William Pickering, a publisher—not a printer—was responsible for the design and execution of a notable program of excellent books. He was, moreover, the first conspicuous figure in the

[165]

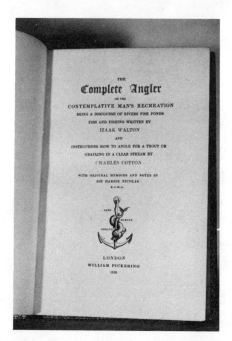

Title page of The Complete Angler *(1836).*

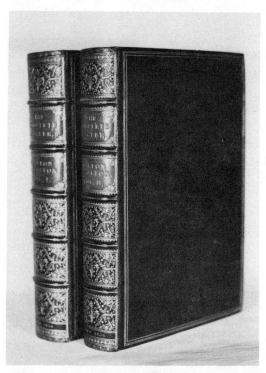

The Complete Angler *of Izaak Walton (1836), in two volumes.*

Crown Octavo, with Ninety Wood Cuts, Price One Guinea,

ICONES VETERIS TESTAMENTI;

ILLUSTRATIONS OF THE OLD TESTAMENT, ENGRAVED ON WOOD, FROM DESIGNS BY HANS HOLBEIN.

Dr. Dibdin has given five specimens of the wood cuts in his Bibliographical Decameron, vol. i. 174—180, where will be found a copious account of this work. He observes, " The pencil of Holbein throws a charm and an interest about this volume, which I have rarely felt in any other similar production."

" We are not aware of any more successful efforts in this department than the copies in Ottley and Singer, from the ' Dance of Death.' Among those who have entitled themselves to celebrity for their able management of this branch of decoration, Hans Holbein is one of the foremost. His designs for the spirited and monitory series just mentioned, are of admirable invention and expression : and, although his ICONES VETERIS TESTAMENTI are less elaborately finished, they may be reckoned among the best things of the kind. We are happy to speak highly in praise of the enterprise, and its execution. There is skill in grouping, able management of subject, simplicity and distinctness in the mode of telling the story, knowledge of what to attempt and what to put aside ;—all these are set off by the free and resolute handling of a ready and practised hand. The texts to which the different subjects refer are printed in English, Latin, Italian, French, and Spanish."—*Eclectic Review*, April 1830.

A beautiful Pickering prospectus from 1830.

emerging separation of book design from printing and publishing.... Pickering might well be considered an early ancestor of the men and women who design books in today's publishing houses.

In building my collection, I can no longer count the letters I have sent out to the booksellers of the world (well, at least to those in the United States, Canada, and Great Britain, and a smaller number in The Netherlands, France, and Italy), saying that I am interested in the imprints of William Pickering, 1821 through 1854, and that I would appreciate their kind favor in helping me to find copies of his books in fine condition. I prefer, of course, volumes in the original cloth, boards, or wrappers as issued, next in a Hayday leather binding, and finally in some other contemporary binding. (To digress here, for a bit: James Hayday is a name not familiar to many in the book world. I have drawn stares, blank looks, and questions in most places where I have spoken the name, but some scholar some day will give him his proper due. I probably have not researched thoroughly enough, but even in the many works on English binders, I have seen very little on James Hayday [1796–1872]. In his pleasant, discursive *Gossip About Book-Collecting* [New York, 1900], William Loring Andrews tells us that "William Pickering, bookseller, of 57 Chancery Lane, gave him the benefit of his long experience and introduced him to many wealthy patrons.") In assessing the work of William Pickering, "binding" is a key element, for it was Pickering who is generally given credit for introducing the use of cloth to commercial publishing in the early 1820s—the date not yet definitively set, nor the title of the first book so bound, although there are several strong candidates.

The year 1829 is an important one in the career of Pickering, for it was in this year that he began his long association with the Whittinghams of the Chiswick Press, who became the chief printers employed by Pickering. In 1838, Charles Whittingham, the nephew (with whom Pickering developed a lasting friendship), assumed from his uncle of the same name practical control of

[168]

the press. It was about 1830 that the entwined anchor and dolphin made its first appearance as Pickering's beautiful press mark, which he adapted from the books of that most famous Venetian, Aldus Manutius (ca. 1449–1515). Pickering used many other devices for decorating the title pages of his books, and a substantial essay could be written on that aspect of his work alone. Keynes's book shows many sizes and variants of the anchor and dolphin, in addition to other devices.

Today, book-collectors are advised to specialize early, to focus their collecting on a single author, a theme, or some special subject to give the collection direction, comprehension, and unity. I have met collectors who specialize in the imprints of William Pickering, although only in two categories—the Diamond Classics and the color-plate books of Henry Shaw. Pickering's series in the Diamond Classics provides a field day for the collector of miniature books, and the number of volumes in the series is large with both the regular editions and the large-paper and vellum copies included, plus the inevitable variants. Many collectors have William Pickering books on their shelves, but not because they are Pickerings *per se*. These books have that wonderful aspect of being sought after for many reasons, and that has made the hunt so much more difficult and exciting for me and others of my collecting persuasion.

Looking for Pickering books are collectors of imprints demonstrating the revived use of Caslon old-face type. The credit for this revival belongs to William Pickering and his friend Charles Whittingham (in about the year 1844), although the exact date has not been finally established. After collectors of typography may come those of fore-edge paintings, an aspect of book decoration at the height of its fashion during the end of the eighteenth and the beginning of the nineteenth centuries. Many of Pickering's books were selected for this treatment. Our list of collectors might then include those searching for books printed on large paper or on vellum, collectors of books on religious subjects and prayer books, of medical books, and—certainly not the least

[169]

important—books in the first-edition category. William Pickering has the distinction of being the publisher to introduce to the world (if not in their very first appearance in print, then in some new aspect) such authors as T. L. Beddoes, William Blake, Samuel Taylor Coleridge, Edward Fitzgerald, N. H. Nicholas, Coventry Patmore, and others.

What books should a well-rounded Pickering collection contain? What is important? On what books or series of books does his fame rest? Questions like these will always be answered in different ways by different people, and it is impossible to achieve complete objectivity. Since the Diamond Classics were among the first books Pickering published (and for many other reasons as well), the collection should contain examples from this series in both the regular editions and the large-paper format. Then at least a goodly selection of first printings from the most famous of all Pickering series, the Aldine Poets (1830–1853), if not the entire set comprising fifty-three volumes. The Aldine Poets represent William Pickering at his very best. Not only are the individual volumes delightful to handle and to read, but they are especially well-edited for their day. The title page of each volume in the Aldine Poets series carries the entwined dolphin and anchor, surrounded by the motto *Aldi Discip. Anglus.* It is through these lovely books of poetry that Pickering has primarily become known to both booklovers and booksellers, and these are the books which show up most frequently in antiquarian book shops. Incidentally, it is interesting to note that the prospectus of 1830 announcing this series is entitled The Aldine Edition of the British Poets, and it is only on page 2 that we find the phrase now in such common use, Pickering's Aldine Poets. In his bibliography, Keynes mentions two designs for the prospectus. With apologies to Sir Geoffrey, I am also showing the 1830 prospectus of this famous publishing event as it cannot have too wide an audience. I have in my collection a third design, however, undescribed by Keynes, which was bound into Volume III of a copy of *The Bibliographer's Manual of English Literature* by William Thomas Lowndes, 1834.

WORKS PUBLISHED BY WILLIAM PICKERING.

CHRISTOPHER MARLOWE'S WORKS,

Three volumes, 1l. 7s. boards.

" Kit Marlowe is beyond comparison the finest of the neglected dramatists."—*Literary Gazette.*

CHAUCER'S CANTERBURY TALES,

With an Essay on his Language and Versification, an Introductory Discourse, Glossary, and Notes, by TYRWHITT. This edition contains a portrait of Chaucer, and a reduced engraving of the celebrated Canterbury Pilgrimage, by Stothard, 5 volumes, 2l. 12s. 6d. boards.

JOHNSON AND WALKER'S DICTIONARY.

A Dictionary of the English Language by SAMUEL JOHNSON and JOHN WALKER, with the pronunciation greatly simplified, and on an entirely new plan; revised, corrected, and enlarged, with the addition of several thousand words, by R. S. JAMESON, Esq. 8vo. price 14s.

In this Dictionary the labours of Johnson and Walker are combined. The accentuation is greatly simplified by the adoption of points instead of figures, the typographical beauty of which will be immediately perceived.

This edition supersedes the necessity hitherto felt of having more than one Dictionary for the ordinary purposes of the English student.

Preparing for Publication.

THE WORKS OF THOMAS GRAY,

A new edition in crown octavo: containing the whole of his English and Latin Poetry, his Letters, as printed from the original MSS. (the text of Mason being rejected as not authentic) with the addition of his Correspondence with Mr. Chute and others, and his Journal as kept by him when at Rome, consisting of Criticisms on the Statues, Pictures, and Architecture in that City, hitherto unpublished, with Notes, and an essay on his Poetry. By the Rev. J. MITFORD.

MARSTON'S
DRAMATIC AND OTHER POETICAL WORKS,
Four Volumes.

PROSPECTUS OF

THE ALDINE EDITION

OF THE BRITISH

POETS.

LONDON:
WILLIAM PICKERING.
1830.

PICKERING'S ALDINE POETS,

PUBLISHING IN MONTHLY VOLUMES, IN CLOTH, PRICE FIVE SHILLINGS, TO RANGE WITH THE FAMILY LIBRARY, THE WAVERLEY NOVELS, AND THE CABINET CYCLOPÆDIA.

PROSPECTUS.

IT is the characteristic of the present age, to place science and literature within the reach of every class of society, by the publication of standard and popular works in a form to combine the advantages of cheapness, convenience, and beauty. The success which has attended this plan is not greater than might be expected from an arrangement so well calculated to meet the unprecedented desire for knowledge by which the world is actuated; and there is reason to believe that, in a few years, every work of reputation will be printed to range with these new and judicious editions of British authors.

Under these circumstances, it is presumed that a similar edition of THE POETS of our country will be favourably received; for if it be desirable that the Prose Writers should be thus brought before the public, it must be more important that those productions of genius, which are connected with our earliest associations, and which exercise so powerful an influence over the heart, should be printed in the same beautiful manner, and with the same attention to economy and convenience; thus supplying the most interesting branch of a series of publications, which will soon become " The Library of the People."

With this view the ALDINE EDITION OF THE BRITISH POETS is undertaken. It will comprise all the popular and standard Poets, and the early volumes will be appropriated to those of the last century. The text of each author will be carefully formed from the best editions; and an original Memoir and a Portrait will be prefixed.

Volume II. which will complete the " POEMS OF BURNS," will appear on the First of June: and from the arrangements already made, One Volume will be punctually delivered on the First of each succeeding Month.

WILLIAM PICKERING, CHANCERY
LANE, LONDON.

The title page and text of the 1830 prospectus for Pickering's Aldine Poets.

A third variant of the 1830 prospectus.

In addition to the Diamond Classics and Aldine Poets, a representative Pickering collection should contain some books edited and written by N. H. Nicholas, and of course some Shaw color-plate books. Henry Shaw (1800–1873) was a wealthy artist and antiquarian who, with a great driving passion for medieval books and ornaments, worked closely with Pickering for a number of years. Of the Shaw books published under the aegis of Pickering my own favorites are: *Illuminated Ornaments*, 1833, *Encyclo-*

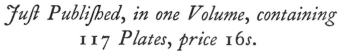

Juſt Publiſhed, in one Volume, containing
117 *Plates, price* 16s.

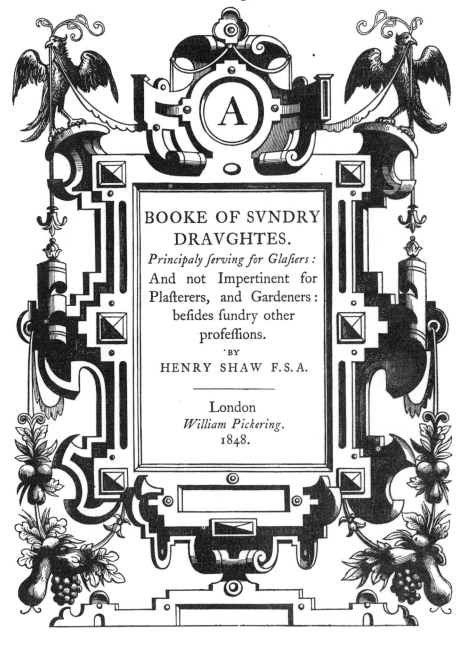

A

BOOKE OF SVNDRY
DRAVGHTES.

Principaly ſerving for Glaſiers :
And not Impertinent for
Plaſterers, and Gardeners :
beſides ſundry other
profeſſions.

·BY

HENRY SHAW F.S.A.

London
William Pickering.
1848.

Prospectus for A Booke of Sundry Draughtes *(1848)*.

paedia of Ornament, 1842, and *Dresses and Decorations of the Middle Ages*, 2 volumes, 1843. For a good account of the fascinating publication history of these books I refer the reader to Ruari McLean's *Victorian Book Design and Colour Printing* (Berkeley, 1972).

Then there are books of poetry and drama including *Chaucer: The Canterbury Tales*, 5 volumes, 1822 and another edition in 1830; *The Dramatic Works and Poems of Robert Greene*, 2 volumes, 1831; *The Works of Christopher Marlowe*, 3 volumes in 1826 and again in a much better version in 1850; and *The Works of George Peele*, 1829–1839, also in 3 volumes.

Our collection should include some books on heraldry, and some books on scientific topics—perhaps the set entitled *The Bridgewater Treatises*. We would also want some of the annuals and gift books which the Victorians were so fond of exchanging. It would be especially challenging to be able to put together the three volumes of *The Bijou* that were issued in 1828, 1829, and 1830. Here again there are many variants for which the collector must be on the alert.

Pickering, with the assistance of Whittingham, published many outstanding liturgical books. Very special is William Keeling's *Liturgiae Britannicae*, 1842. This quarto of liturgies of the Church of England is set two columns to the page, so that the open volume presents four to the eyes of the reader. Printed throughout in black and red, this book is a masterpiece of clarity, beauty, and the printer's art. Other important religious books issued by Pickering are two by William Maskell: *The Ancient Liturgy of the Church of England*, 1844, and the *Monumenta Ritualia Ecclesiae Anglicanae* in three volumes, 1846–1847. But the greatest liturgical works ever to appear under the Pickering imprint were seven magnificent black-letter folio editions of the Prayer Book, published in 1844. Six of the books were historic reprints, and the last was for contemporary service. They are, in order: The First Book of Edward VI, 1549; The Second Book of Edward VI, 1552; The First Book of Queen Elizabeth, 1559;

[174]

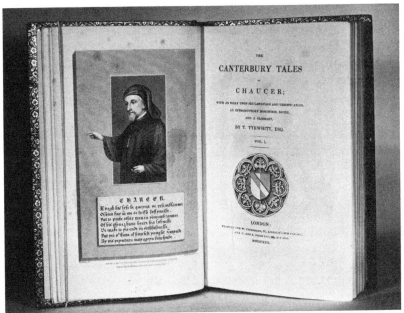

Title page of the Chaucer *of 1822 (in five volumes).*

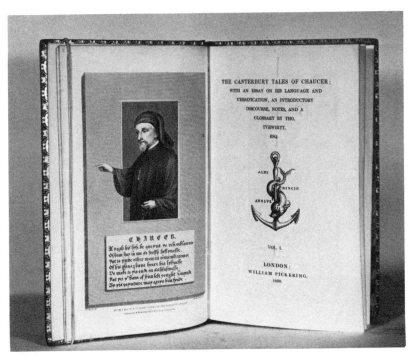

Title page of the Chaucer *of 1830 (in five volumes).*

The Bijou *(1828). As issued in decorated boards and morocco back.*

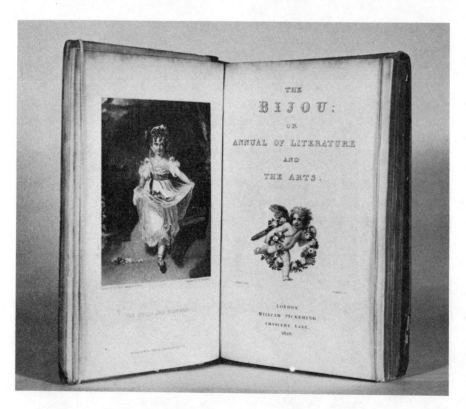

The Bijou *(1828). Title page with engraved frontispiece.*

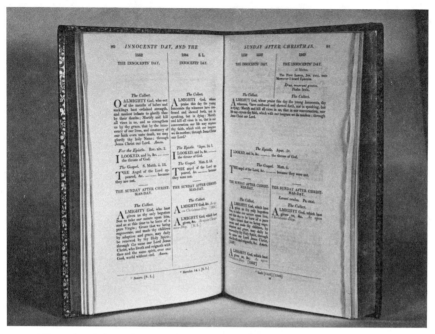

Liturgiae Britannicae *(1842). A typical page spread (printed in red and black) showing the four-column format.*

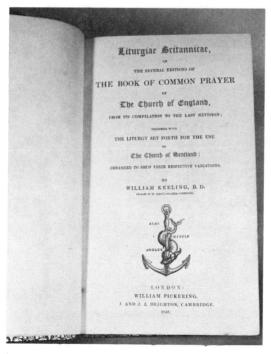

Liturgiae Britannicae *(1842). Title page printed in red and black.*

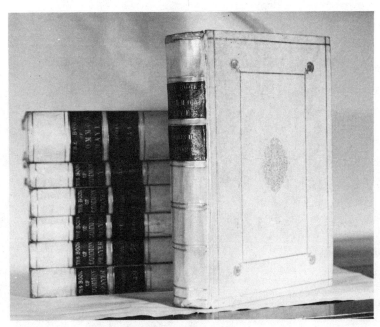

The Book of Common Prayer *(1844)*. *A complete set of all seven volumes, bound as issued in parchment gilt.*

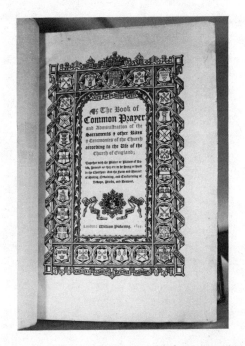

The Book of Common Prayer *(1844)*. *Title page printed in red and black.*

King James's Book, called the Hampton Court Book, 1604; The Scotch Book of Charles I, 1637; King Charles II's Book, 1662; and, the final volume, (Queen Victoria) *The Book of Common Prayer Together with the Psalter*, 1844. All seven of these volumes were printed in black and red on Pouncy's hand-made paper and bound in parchment gilt. Many exhibitions have included one or more of these prayer books as exemplars of fine printing and typographic design.

Of the very little we know about William Pickering, it is certain that he was an ardent fisherman, and so books having to do with this sport and recreation must have been close to his heart. In this category, Pickering published many volumes for sale and at least one book for private distribution. Early in the Pickering annals (1827) appeared Dame Juliana Berners' *The Treatyse of Fysshynge wyth an Angle*. This charming little book was once thought to have been printed with the types of the great English printer John Baskerville (1706–1775), but recent scholarship has disclosed that it was printed from a font cut in imitation or improvement of Baskerville's type. No matter—it is very beautiful and sought after. Walton and Cotton make expected appearances in the Diamond Classics. Some other related books are: *The True Enjoyment of Angling* by Henry Phillips, 1843; *The River Dove—With Some Quiet Thoughts on the Happy Practice of Angling*, 1847 (by J. L. Anderdon); *Piscatorial Reminiscences and Gleanings by an Old Angler and Bibliopolist*, 1835 (the author of this work was Thomas Boosey). Added to this last volume, as noted on the title page, is a catalogue of books on angling entitled ''Bibliotheca Piscatoria.'' Fortunate is the collector who finds this catalogue as issued, apart from the book, in wrappers. It was in the year 1836, however, that Pickering published his most important work in this field—the two sumptuous volumes of *The Complete Angler*. There have been many descriptions of these two books, but I particularly like the one given in a rare American auction catalogue, the *Auction Sale Catalogue of the Library of William P. Fowle*, Sold by Leonard

[179]

A scarce Pickering catalogue, separately issued in wrappers.

and Company, Boston, Massachusetts, December 20–21, 1864. William P. Fowle was, in America, the most avid of Pickering collectors:

Item 754. Walton and Cotton: The Complete Angler, or the Contemplative Man's Recreation; being a Discourse of Rivers, Fish Ponds, Fish, and Fishing; written by Izaak Walton; and Instructions how to Angle for a Trout or Grayling in a Clear Stream, by Charles Cotton. With Original Memoirs and Notes by Sir Harris Nicholas. Portraits. Views and plates of Fish. Rubricated titles. 2 vols. Imperial 8vo., elegantly bound by Hayday in green Levant morocco, super extra, edges gilt in the round. Splendid Copy. W. Pickering London 1836. This copy contains an ADDITIONAL set of the plates, printed upon plate paper separate from the text, in ARTIST'S PROOF state upon INDIA PAPER. Very few were issued in this manner. In 1829 Mr. Pickering announced that "a few copies would be printed upon LARGE PAPER for the purpose of illustration." Such an edition never appeared.

Another item (one which I have never seen) listed in this catalogue is also mentioned by Keynes for its beauty and rarity:

> Item 759. Walton and Cotton Club. Rules and Regulations of. Small 4to. W. Pickering London 1840. PRIVATELY PRINTED: and only 50 copies. Illustrated with cuts of fish. Very beautifully printed within carmine borders by Whittingham.

As a kind of postscript to the books just described, I would like to call attention to the fact that before *The Complete Angler* made its formal appearance in two volumes, Pickering issued it in parts over a number of years (1832–1836). The complete set of twelve parts is now excessively rare (there is a handsome set in the Beinecke Library at Yale University), and seldom appears on the antiquarian book market; this is also true for the other Pickering books issued in parts, and especially so for the Henry Shaw volumes. For additional bibliographical details on Pickering's editions of Walton, Bernard S. Horne's *The Compleat Angler: A New Bibliography* (Pittsburgh, 1970) will be very helpful.

Finally, the following titles would certainly find a place in any representative Pickering collection, not merely as superb typographic specimens, but also because each possesses some outstanding literary or artistic attribute. I list them chronologically by publication date: *Robert Herrick: The Poetical Works*, 1825; Bishop Joseph Hall, *Virgidemiarum*, 1825; Thomas Stothard, *The Alphabet*, 1830; Francis Douce, *The Dance of Death*, 1833; William Pickering, *Catalogue of Biblical, Classical and Historical Manuscripts and of Rare and Curious Books on Sale*, 1834; W. T. T. Lowndes, *The Bibliographer's Manual of English Literature*, 1834; Thomas Wright, *The Tale of the Basyn and the Frere and the Bow. Two Early Tales / The Nutbrowne Maid / Songs and Carols printed from a MS in the Sloane Collection in the British Museum / The Turnament of Totenham and the Feest. Two Early Ballads* (4 small volumes printed in Caslon gothic letter, 1836); *Master Wace: His Chronicle of the Norman Conquest from the Roman de Rou*, 1837 (especially beautiful are the copies on large paper with the illustrations colored by hand); William Blake, *Songs of Innocence and of Experience*, 1839 (printed in association with W. Newbery on Whatman paper dated that year, this is the first appearance in type of the verse of this great English poet); Oliver Byrne, *Euclid*, 1847 (a brainstorm perhaps, but surely a triumph of color printing); Edward Fitzgerald, *Polonius: A Collection of Wise Saws and*

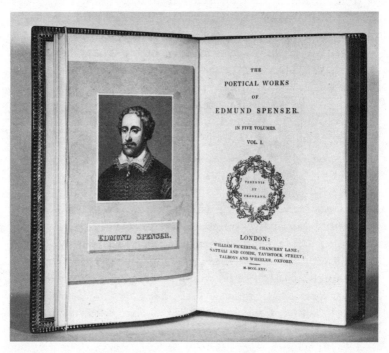

The Pickering Spenser *(wreath edition of 1825).*

[182]

Modern Instances, 1852; and *The Book of Common Prayer*,
1853 (with fabulous woodcut borders on every page after Holbein,
Dürer, and other artists).

In place of a coda, I should like to touch very briefly on two
aspects of Pickering's career. One has been treated at length by
James J. Barnes (*Free Trade in Books: A Study of the London
Book Trade Since 1800* [Oxford, 1964]), and the other not at
all. The first is Pickering's fight on behalf of the reading public
of his time, and the second is his American audience.

Book publishing and bookselling in the eighteenth and early
decades of the nineteenth centuries combined into a very special
world where one trod with great precaution. There were organizations and combines (the Booksellers' Committee) of one sort
or another which wanted things—basically prices and profits—
their way. William Pickering, like the pupil of Aldus Manutius
he declared himself to be, wanted to produce the best books at
the most economical prices. In 1832, Pickering published two
pamphlets that brought the conditions in the book world to
public attention: *Booksellers' Monopoly* and *Cases Showing the
Arbitrary and Oppressive Conduct of the Committee of Booksellers*. Both these pamphlets are excessively rare.

That Pickering had an American audience there is no question,
but regarding how it came about, there is. Bound in at the back
of Volume II of my 1834 edition of Lowndes' *The Bibliographer's
Manual* is William Pickering's Catalogue of Historical and Antiquarian Works, Including the early Poets and Dramatists, with
Others of Standard Reputation, sold by Thomas Wardle, Philadelphia. Henry Walcott Boynton (*Annals of American
Bookselling, 1638–1850* [New York, 1932]) describes him as
"Thomas Wardle of Philadelphia, by all odds the leading im-
porter of English and foreign books for the American market."
Perhaps there is extant somewhere correspondence between
these two bookmen which, if ever discovered, will reveal the
magnitude of Pickering's transatlantic business. In 1835 there
was published in the United States *The Poetical Works of S. T.*

Coleridge in three volumes, 16mo. Below the entwined dolphin and anchor the title page reads, London: W. Pickering (2 lines) Boston: Hilliard, Gray & Co. (2 lines) 1835. The printer's name on the verso of the title is J. D. Freeman. I am unaware of any other title so issued under this joint imprint. I do, however, have a trade catalogue put out by this same Boston firm, in buff-colored wrappers and dated 1837. This catalogue lists many Pickering books, some specifically so designated and others not. Most interesting is the description of the edition of Coleridge mentioned above, which appears on pages 59–60 of this piece of advertising:

> Beautifully printed to match in size the edition of the British Poets now publishing by W. Pickering, London. The text made use of was that of Mr. Pickering, being the last edition prepared by the Author and printed under his superintendence a few months previously to his death.
>
> This edition contains upwards of 40 pages of additional Poems, which have since been published in the Literary Remains of Coleridge, edited by his nephew.

The only other American imprint, again a dual one, with which I am familiar is on an edition of the works of John Milton, in eight volumes (two for poetry and six for the prose). The title page carries device No. 16 (see Keynes) printed in black and red, and under it: William Pickering London (printed in caps on one line) followed by (on three lines and in a smaller type size, but also in caps): Charles C. Little and James Brown / Boston, United States / 1851. How interesting to see so early in its career the beginning of what was to become a famous and long-lived American publishing house—Little, Brown and Company. But even more intriguing is the relationship of Charles Little and James Brown to William Pickering and his books. In *The Book in America*, Hellmut Lehmann-Haupt wrote that

> The first half of the nineteenth century saw the revival for a short period of the eminence of Boston as a publishing center.

A SELECT

CATALOGUE OF BOOKS,

CHIEFLY PUBLISHED OR IMPORTED BY

HILLIARD, GRAY, AND CO.

𝔓𝔲𝔟𝔩𝔦𝔰𝔥𝔢𝔡 𝔄𝔫𝔫𝔲𝔞𝔩𝔩𝔶.

BOSTON.
112 WASHINGTON STREET.

1837.

An American book catalogue listing many Pickering volumes.

In 1821 Charles Coffin Little entered the bookstore of Carter, Hilliard and Co., an organization which, through its several proprietors, traced to the eighteenth century, and in 1827 he became a member of the firm, then reorganized as *Hilliard, Gray & Co.* [the italics are mine]. He became senior member and soon thereafter formed an association with James Brown. The firm of Little, Brown & Co., so called since 1837, thus is to be regarded as one of the few which carry back to the eighteenth century.

According to record, James Brown had charge of the foreign importations, but no doubt both partners were in agreement that William Pickering was good for America.

* * *

PICKERING's career, like any other in the precarious business of publishing, no doubt had its ups and downs, its good times and bad. On the whole, however, it rolled along successfully to the early years of the 1850s. He died, 58 years of age, on 27 April 1854.

The search for Pickering books has gone on a long time. I know it will continue, for something new always seems to crop up—something to read with pleasure, and something from which to learn: in short, something to make the reader realize that William Pickering, late of 177 Piccadilly, London, is as responsible a man as any for the way the contemporary book looks.

BIBLIOGRAPHY

Daniel Berkeley Updike, *Printing Types: Their History, Forms, and Use* (Cambridge: Harvard University Press, 1966).

Theodore Low De Vinne, *The Practice of Typography* (New York: Century Company, 1900–1904), 4 vols.

——, *Title-Pages as Seen by a Printer* (New York: Grolier Club, 1901).

Sir Francis Meynell, *The Design of Books: Function and Fashion* (New York: Rockefeller University *Review*, May–June 1966).

William Loring Andrews, *Gossip About Book-Collecting* (New York: Dodd, Mead, 1900).

Carl J. Weber, *A Thousand One Fore-Edge Paintings* (Waterville, Maine: Colby College Press, 1949).

Ruari McLean, *Victorian Book Design and Colour Printing* (Berkeley and Los Angeles: University of California Press, 1972).

Frederick W. Faxon, *Literary Annuals and Gift Books* (British Private Libraries Association, 1973—reprinted with supplementary essays by Eleanore Jamieson and Ian Bain).

Bernard S. Horne, *Free Trade in Books—A Study of the London Book Trade since 1800* (Oxford: Clarendon Press, 1964).

Joseph Blumenthal, *Art of the Printed Book, 1455–1955* (New York: Pierpont Morgan Library, 1973).

Colin Clair, *A History of Printing in Britain* (New York: Oxford University Press, 1966).

Norma Levarie, *The Art and History of Books* (New York: Heineman, 1968).

Henry Stevens, *Who Spoils Our New English Books* (London: Henry Newton Stevens, Christmas 1884).

Paul Johnston, *Biblio-Typographia—A Survey of Contemporary Fine Printing Style* (New York: Covici–Friede, 1930).

BARBARA J. KLINE *is the Head of Cataloging at New York University's Bobst Library. She is also the Assistant Editor of the American Printing History Association newsletter, and is currently studying the role of the novelist Edith Wharton in American printing history, as well as printing activity in American utopian communities. Her collecting interests include twentieth-century feminist literature and protest literature from the United States' military involvement in Vietnam.*

The Author
as Book Designer

Barbara J. Kline

THE HISTORY OF THE AUTHOR AS BOOK DESIGNER must be told as a part of the history of authorship itself. In England and the United States, the author's role in the book-making process evolved in relation to the changing role of the publisher and the growing importance of the reading public. Within the dynamics of these relationships lies the key for understanding where the responsibility for design has rested, and how much power the author has over the way in which his work is packaged. Many authors have, of course, printed their own works or collaborated with a private press owner in order to achieve the desired effect. Authors of children's books have always shown concern over matters of appearance, and publishers have probably been, as a rule, more sensitive to their suggestions. But the authors to be discussed here are those whose design aesthetic, particularly as it relates to typography and binding, was carried out in commercially published books, primarily for adults. For as soon as the status of authorship gained a certain amount of recognition as an economic and creative factor in the bookmaking process, some authors began to negotiate with their publishers on such matters.

For the purposes of our discussion, the millennia before Gutenberg and the first centuries after he worked his miracle are not germane. But the changes become apparent with the early modern period. The eighteenth century was crucial to the history of the author as book designer, especially in the English-speaking world. The major event was the Copyright Act of 1709, effective April 1710, which finally gave the author control over his writing. His raw material was now his property to sell. Property rights were increasingly perceived as individual rights, not as corporate privilege alone. The author was given copyright for twenty-one years for already printed material, and fourteen years, renewable once, for unpublished materials. The author could now begin to replace the publisher as the prime producer in the bookmaking process. The Copyright Act of 1709 was, in fact, an acknowledgment of the diversification in the printing process as it attempted to strike a balance for all involved in bookmaking: writer, printer, publisher, and reader. Modern publishing thus dates from this time when the author/publisher relationship takes the shape with which we are familiar today. Jacob Tonson is often called the "father of modern publishing" as he secured a list of authors, including Addison, Steele, Dryden, and Milton, whose *Paradise Lost* was one of Tonson's greatest publishing successes. The patronage system began to die as the booksellers, publishers, and authors gained power. From April 1710 on, an author had property as a bargaining device. The bookseller, in turn, knew that that value depended increasingly on public taste. While the booksellers' monopoly had some negative aspects, it did make possible collaboration, or congers, for producing such expensive books as Dr. Johnson's *Dictionary*.

While there is little evidence that eighteenth-century authors were deeply concerned with book design, the century did produce two of the most outstanding type designers of all time, as Caslon and Baskerville introduced their influential typefaces. Their work was particularly important to the future of book design because both men felt that typography was just as important as illustrations and binding in achieving a fine book.

Thus, although the author as book designer had not yet emerged, the activities of printers, type designers, authors, publishers, and readers in the eighteenth century laid vital groundwork for William Morris' revival in the nineteenth. Morris' work could not have been accomplished without the author's gain in stature in the eighteenth century; his writing was now his property to sell. The reading public was clamoring for his service, so he could negotiate with a publisher willing to risk capital on his behalf. The author's creativity was, of course, given freer rein in an environment of such favorable competition.

But though the author entered the nineteenth century in a better bargaining position, the readership expanded so fast that design was the victim. Victorian books are, for the most part, lacking in fine design and typography. The major focus of the Victorian book world was the search for a way to distribute to the vast, growing reading public. J. A. Sutherland's recent *Victorian Novelists and Publishers* (Chicago: University of Chicago Press, 1976) is informative in this area. George Eliot, for example, became popular enough with her reading public that she could, to a limited extent, negotiate with publisher John Blackwood. But the publishers were having their own problems because novel publishing was almost monopolized by circulating libraries and serialization in part-issues. Eliot and others would first be printed in a three-decker, then a two-volume reprint, then a six-shilling issue at the end of the publisher's term of copyright. Blackwood finally was forced to confront the problem with the publication of *Middlemarch*. It was going to be too long to fit into the three-decker format, and Eliot detested the serial format. G. H. Lewes, her husband, suggested that this would be the chance to entice the public to buy, not borrow, the novel. It

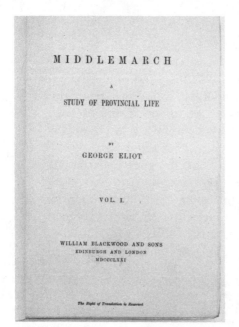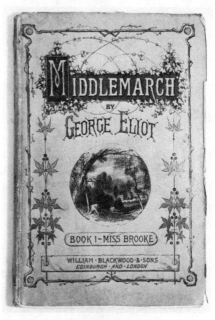

The wrapper design and title page of Middlemarch *by George Eliot, published in eight parts between December 1871 and December 1872.*

could be published in parts at two-month intervals, but with stiffer covers and more narrative unity than a serialization. And it was calculated that such a publication could be affordable and typographically attractive at the same time. *Middlemarch* was published in eight volumes from December 1871 to December 1872. Publisher William Tinsley noted in his *The Random Recollections of an Old Publisher* (London, 1900; pp. 54–55):

> ... And even though the original editions of George Eliot's (Miss Evans') books are mostly in crown octavo, they are beautifully printed, in good readable types, and on good paper. There is no huddling the type and matter together, and making the pages a conglomeration of almost invisible lines hard to decipher.

The wrapper, however, was not universally admired. Eliot chose and insisted upon a garbled design of vines, foliage, scrolls, and a circular vignette on a yellow-green paper. After the appearance of Book I, her friend Barbara Bodichon and others expressed disappointment that the cover was not worthy of her writing. As Gordon Haight's definitive *George Eliot: A Biography* (New York: Oxford University Press, 1968) indicates, book design was not Eliot's prime concern, but her powerful position in negotiations with her publisher is significant. While the primary objective of publisher and author was finding a profitable format, here was an attempt to produce an attractive book the general public could afford.

* * *

CHARLES DICKENS was also in a position to assert his power as an author, and constantly took an interest in the design, format, and illustration of his books. In the matter of illustrations, Dickens

The "Fireside" plate done by George Cruikshank for Oliver Twist. *Upon seeing this design in the first copies of the book delivered to him, Dickens immediately required the artist to draw and etch another plate to substitute for this one.*

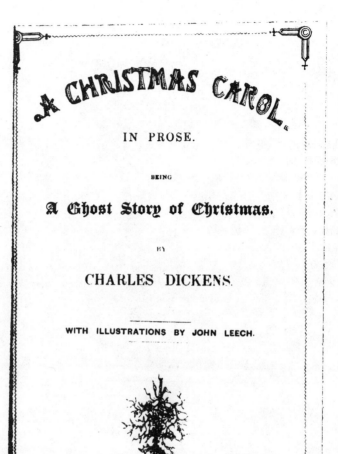

The title page of the first edition of A Christmas Carol *(1843).*

was the sole ultimate arbiter of what would and would not do. He required artists to redraw their designs in accordance with his instructions and, even as a young man, forced the renowned George Cruikshank to substitute a totally new design for the last plate in Volume III of *Oliver Twist* for no greater reason than that Mr. Dickens did not like the original. The production arrangements for *A Christmas Carol* were completely controlled by Dickens; under his peculiar arrangement with Chapman & Hall for the publication of this book, Dickens was to pay all the costs and in return receive all the profits. The book did not make as much money for its author as expected, primarily because Dickens insisted that the little volume be handsomely got up, with gilt edges, a two-color title page, and hand-colored plates. With the author also insisting that despite the deluxe format the book be priced at five shillings, it is no wonder that the profits were considerably less than expected.

* * *

LEWIS CARROLL (Charles Dodgson) was another Victorian concerned with the illustration of his books. While he was not terribly interested in typography, his active participation in the book-making process deserves mention. When Carroll decided to have *Alice's Adventures in Wonderland* published in 1863, he wanted to have it printed at his own expense so that he could retain some control. His correspondence with Macmillan, his publisher, is quite interesting. Carroll insisted that the color of the binding be red, a color popular with children. He tried to get Macmillan to agree to a special quarto format, with double columns, and even provided a specimen page. Eventually, he was convinced to leave it at octavo size. Carroll attempted the illustrations, and even prepared a half-length of Alice on a woodblock. Even though he could envision what he wanted, he could not reproduce it successfully on paper. His friends eventually dissuaded him; he paid to have John Tenniel's illustrations printed, and employed Macmillan to publish them on a commission basis. In the *Aspects of Alice* anthology (New York: Vanguard, 1971;

[195]

pp. 4–15), Roger Green traces the chronology. The Clarendon Press printed the galleys, which were sent to Macmillan in December 1864, and proofs of the illustrations were checked by Tenniel in June 1865. When he saw the quality of reproduction in the published work, however, Tenniel was dissatisfied and Carroll withdrew it from circulation by means of a letter to those friends who had received the initial forty-eight bound from the 2,000-copy run. Thirty-four were retrieved and sent to children's hospitals; the survivors are now among the most valuable books of the nineteenth century. The remaining unbound sheets went to New York's Appleton, who issued 1,000 with an 1866 title page printed at Oxford, thus creating the second issue of the first edition. The remaining copies had title pages printed in the United States—hence the third issue of the first edition. When Macmillan of London published the second edition in December 1865, Tenniel approved of the quality of reproduction.

The title and a page of text from the extremely rare first London edition of Alice's Adventures in Wonderland *(1865), which was suppressed by the author due to the artist's dissatisfaction with the quality of the reproduction of his illustrations.*

ALICE'S

ADVENTURES IN WONDERLAND.

BY

LEWIS CARROLL.

WITH FORTY-TWO ILLUSTRATIONS

BY

JOHN TENNIEL.

London

MACMILLAN AND CO.

1865.

[The right of translation is reserved.]

110   A MAD TEA-PARTY.

"Really, now you ask me," said Alice, very much confused, "I don't think——"

"Then you shouldn't talk," said the Hatter.

This piece of rudeness was more than Alice could bear: she got up in great disgust, and walked off: the Dormouse fell asleep instantly, and neither of the others took the least notice of her going, though she looked back once or twice, half hoping that they would call after her: the last time she saw them, they were trying to put the Dormouse into the teapot.

ADVERTISEMENT.

For over 25 years, I have made it my chief object,
with regard to my books, that they should be of the
best workmanship attainable for the price. And I
am deeply annoyed to find that the last issue of
" Through the Looking-Glass," consisting of the
Sixtieth Thousand, has been put on sale without its
being noticed that most of the pictures have failed
so much, in the printing, as to make the book not
worth buying. I request all holders of copies to
send them to Messrs. Macmillan & Co., 29 Bedford
Street, Covent Garden, with their names and
addresses ; and copies of the next issue shall be
sent them in exchange.

Instead, however, of destroying the unsold copies,
I propose to utilise them by giving them away, to
Mechanics' Institutes, Village Reading-Rooms, and
similar institutions, where the means for purchasing
such books are scanty. Accordingly I invite applications for such gifts, addressed to me, " care of
Messrs. Macmillan." Every such application should
be signed by some responsible person, and should
state how far they are able to buy books for themselves, and what is the average number of readers.

I take this opportunity of announcing that, if
at any future time I should wish to communicate
anything to my Readers, I will do so by advertising,
in the ' Agony' Column of some of the Daily Papers,
on the first Tuesday in the month.

LEWIS CARROLL.

Christmas, 1893.

A notice which Lewis Carroll caused to be printed in copies of his
Sylvie and Bruno Concluded *(1893), in which he indicates his
dissatisfaction with the printing of the illustrations in an issue of*
Through the Looking-Glass.

Carroll continued his vigilance. In *Sylvie and Bruno Concluded*,
he inserted an announcement relinquishing royalties to *Through
the Looking Glass* because of the poorly reproduced illustrations.
Again he asked that people send copies back to Macmillan and
that unsold copies go to orphanages and hospitals. For the
binding of *Through the Looking Glass* (1872), he requested that

[197]

fifty be bound in red, twenty in blue, two in vellum, one with uncut edges, one with primrose edges, and one with a piece of mirror in the cover. In a letter dated December 17, 1871 (*Letters to Macmillan* [London: Macmillan, 1967], p. 74), Carroll expressed concern that in their hurry to get the book in the shops before Christmas, Macmillan had allowed shortcuts in the paper-making process and hence a loss of "brilliance of effect" in the illustrations:

> My decision is, we must have *no more hurry*: and *no more sheets must be pressed under blank paper*. It is my *particular desire* that all the sheets shall in the future be "stacked" and let to dry naturally. The result of this may possibly be that the 6000 will not be ready for sale till the end of January or even later. Very well: then fix that date in your advertisement: say that, "Owing to the delay necessary to give the pictures their full artistic effect, no more copies can be delivered until the end of January."

Thus, while Carroll did not dabble in typographical aesthetics, he is worth mention because he did make special arrangements with his publisher, as did Shaw later on, to control the appearance of his books. There was, then, some concern being shown in the Victorian era for the look of books. William Morris took the essence of these various undercurrents and amplified it into a working aesthetic. Indeed, Morris was inspired by earlier printers who were alarmed at the state of the art. One such was publisher William Pickering, whose collaboration with Charles Whittingham of the Chiswick Press produced many attractive volumes.

* * *

JOHN RUSKIN should be mentioned here because his aesthetic philosophy inspired Morris and because he himself was interested in the typography of his books. As demonstrated by his praise for Samuel Rogers' *Italy* (1830), which was beautifully illustrated with J. M. W. Turner vignettes, Ruskin was fascinated by book design as early as age thirteen. Avoiding the uniformity characteristic of the machine society, Ruskin requested the printers of his own books to design them in accord with the books' specific requirements. Further, Ruskin encouraged fine printing produced by craftsmen who found pleasure in their work. Prolific as he was, Ruskin never specifically set down his typographic philosophy, though in *Seven Lamps of Architecture* (1849) he employs the analogy of a book to explain beautiful architecture. He received William Morris' admiration for the "Nature of Gothic" chapter in *The Stones of Venice* (1851–53). Ruskin hearkens back to the kind of society that could produce Gothic architecture—a society in which the individual workman could express himself creatively and take pride in the roughness of handmade or amateur work. He despises the separation of the artist from the tools of his craft: "The printer should grind his own colours; the architect work in the mason's yard with his men" (New York: Wiley, 1860; p. 187). Morris was excited by this as he set up the Kelmscott Press so that he could participate in the entire bookmaking process.

James Dearden recently wrote a brief essay on Ruskin's typography in his *Facets of Ruskin* (London: Skilton, 1970; pp. 103–109), and notes that W. H. Harrison was Ruskin's literary editor in later years. For *Modern Painters*, little effort was made to create books of consistent design. The second volume was larger than the first so that it would match the third, which was larger in order to accommodate a large plate. Volume One was increased in size for the third edition, with Harrison seeing it through the press. Thus not only are the margins of early editions of Volume One quite large, since the text was not reset, but the typeface differs between the first and second volumes. Ruskin was actually more concerned with obtaining plates from good engravers. As indicated in his preface to *The Stones of Venice*, he is concerned with the problem of keeping the book small enough for the reader's comfort and the plates large enough for detail. Part of Ruskin's motivation for taking charge of the publication of his own books in 1871, however, was his political

[199]

attitude regarding booksellers' pricing methods. Whether concern for book design was another factor in this decision is an area needing further study.

In the same anthology (pp. 110–17) Dearden also recounts collaboration between Pre-Raphaelite Edward Burne-Jones and Ruskin on several projects which, unfortunately, were never realized. In 1863 Ruskin decided to issue his *Fraser's Magazine* pieces in book form. He explains in a December 10, 1863 letter to Burne-Jones:

> I want you to do me a set of simple line illustrations of mythology and figurative creatures, to be engraved and to make a lovely book of my four Political Economy papers in *Fraser*, with a bit I'm just adding. I want to print it beautifully, and make a book everybody *must* have. And I want a Ceres for it, and a Proserpine, and a Plutus, and a Pluto, and a Circe for it, and an Helen, and a Tisiphone ... and ever so many people more, and I'll have them all engraved so beautifully, you can't think—and then I'll cut up my text into little bits, and put it all about them, so that people must swallow at once, and it will do them so much good....

The project was never completed as envisioned; when the essays were published as *Munera Pulveris* nine years later, there were no embellishments. The only surviving design probably intended for the binding or frontispiece was later adapted by W. G. Collingwood for an 1895 Ruskin publication. The original design featured "Justitia" repeated seven times in a scrolled design set amidst flowers. In the Collingwood adaptation, the seven scrolls were replaced by two, reading "Studies in both arts" and "John Ruskin."

Two of Ruskin's most famous lectures were published in book form as *Sesame and Lilies* (1865). Once again, a Burne-Jones title page was designed but not used until later for Volume XVIII of the much acclaimed Library Edition of Ruskin (1903–11).

Finally, there was the Burne-Jones design for the proposed *Bibliotheca Pastorum* series. In the 1870s, Ruskin became interested in publishing a library of classical authors for the homes of men in the Guild of St. George, a group of Englishmen who would buy land with the agreement that they would not build on it, but cultivate it themselves. In 1875, Ruskin asked Burne-Jones to prepare a design, with a shield, dragon, and English oak. But Ruskin could not reach agreement with Burne-Jones on this design. After several redrawings and much correspondence ("We mustn't have English oak looking like a seaweed"), the design was finished and the block was cut by Arthur Burgess. Ruskin was still dissatisfied, and by this time publication could no longer be delayed. Once again a Burne-Jones design went unused. In the first book of the series, *The Economist of Xenophon* (1876), a slip was issued with early copies: "I have spoiled the engraving of Mr. Jones's design by my interference with it...."

* * *

WILLIAM MORRIS was well aware of these efforts which culminated in the Arts and Crafts Movement and the revival of fine printing in the late nineteenth century. This essay will not treat Morris' own books in depth because in printing his own he did not have to negotiate with an outside publisher. Yet his influence on twentieth-century fine printing is vast and must be mentioned. His friendship with Emery Walker led to a cooperative printing venture at the Kelmscott Press. Morris believed that a book must have unity—of type, ink, and paper. He evaluated this unity by looking at an open book, not at a single page. He used bold, black type, often "gothic"; very blackened, solid pages, and handmade laid paper. Thus, in addition to the printing of books, William Morris' important contribution was showing us how to look at a book as a whole unit with parts which can relate through design.

Morris profoundly influenced such private presses as Doves, Ashendene, and Vale. But what is less documented is his influence on mass-produced books. By the 1920s, Knopf, Chatto and Windus, Jonathan Cape, and others in England and the United States began to think seriously about design standards.

[201]

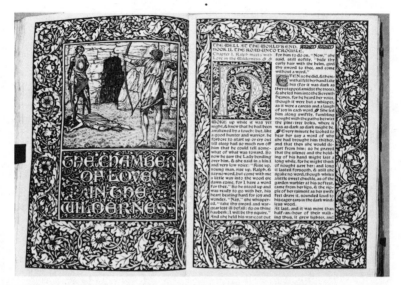

Typical William Morris typography, from the Kelmscott Press edition of his own The Well at the World's End *(1896).*

Warren Chappell is an example of the kind of designer increasingly employed by publishers. When the firm of Alfred A. Knopf was founded in 1915, they set out to establish a distinguished design staff. Chappell later studied in Germany at Rudolf Koch's workshop, and he became an artist, illustrator, and graphic designer for Knopf for many years.

It is important to remember that the United States was affected by the Morris movement. While American printing had tended toward the utilitarian, the late nineteenth century saw a rise in interest in the production of books by artists, whose interest in publishing began to extend beyond illustration to the book as an entity. The American Society of Arts and Crafts was founded by Ruskin's admirer, Charles Eliot Norton, in 1897. American printers influenced by Morris, some of them only for a time, include Ray Nash, Fred Day, Herbert Copeland, Elbert Hubbard, Herbert Stone, and Hannibal Kimball. Even printers such as

Daniel Berkeley Updike and Theodore Low De Vinne, whose work as a whole was not patterned after Morris, admired his demanding specifications for high-quality materials and fine craftsmanship.

*   *   *

AT the turn of the century, it is significant that the responsibility for design passed from printer to publisher, and that within publishing houses the profession of book designer became a distinctive role. Ruari McLean notes in his *Modern Book Design* (London: Faber & Faber, 1958) that it is often hard to tell whether publisher or printer was responsible for design during this period. Bruce Rogers, considered by many as the first book designer by profession, began as an illustrator and during his work at the Riverside Press in Cambridge expanded his interests to typography and design. He reminisces that in the early twentieth century, design was too often done in consultation in the publishing office over specimen pages modeled on a previously published volume. But publishers began to hire professional book designers to meet the demands of the reading public and the authors whose consciousness had been raised by Morris' Arts and Crafts Movement. In his *Authors and Publishers* (London: Dent, 1932) Sadleir describes this situation, in which the author had gained a certain amount of power and knowledge of book design, and the book designer had been hired by the publisher to arrange a book both attractive and profitable.

We have all heard of cases where authors are unrealistic, or publishers inflexible; this conflict is documented in almost every major publishing memoir. The result was that some authors of stature wanting to control the design of their works made special arrangements with their publishers. It is interesting, but also unfortunate, that the last major essay devoted to this subject is Holbrook Jackson's *The Printing of Books* (London: Cassell, 1947), in which he includes Dibdin, Edward Fitzgerald, Ruskin, Whistler, Robert Bridges, George Moore, Bernard Shaw, E. G. Craig, Eric Gill, and Francis Meynell. The survey is a fine one,

[203]

but needs updating. Further, Jackson's contention that the majority of authors' apathy toward fine printing is a matter of egotism—the obsession to see one's work in print overpowers the aesthetic considerations—is questionable. I submit that for many years authors *were* more concerned with "simply" getting into print because it was, indeed, a difficult enough task. But as the author's status grew, he gained more power to determine the look of his work.

* * *

GEORGE BERNARD SHAW is an early key figure in understanding the author as book designer, since he transformed Morris' ideas into his own needs in arrangements with his publishers. He became extremely close to the Morris family, visited the Kelmscott Press, and reported in a letter to Ruari McLean (*Modern Book Design*, p. 33):

> My acquaintance with Morris led me to look at the page of a book as a picture, and a book as an ornament. This led to a certain connoisseurship in types and typesetting. I chose old face Caslon as the best after Jenson. I discarded apostrophes whenever possible ... and banished mutton quads between sentences because they made "rivers" of white in the black rectangle of print....

One gets from this correspondence a sense of Shaw's specifications. Like Morris, he was concerned with margins—widest at the bottom, narrowest at the inner margin, the top a bit wider, and the outer margin still wider though narrower than the bottom one. These principles are stated in Shaw's "On Modern Composition," in *Caxton Magazine* (1902). He liked an even, unruled block of color. What is particularly interesting is his concern for finding a typographical solution to the hard-to-read dialogue format of plays. *Plays Pleasant and Unpleasant*, published by Grant Richards and printed by R. & R. Clark in 1898, offers a good example. He used small capitals for the *dramatis personae* and italics within square brackets for stage directions. As Dunlap

[204]

*dressed, and clean-shaven except for a moustache, with an eager,
susceptible face and very amiable and considerate manners.
He has silky black hair, with waves of grey and white in it.
His eyebrows are white, his moustache black. He seems not
certain of his way. He looks over the paling; takes stock
of the place; and sees the young lady.*

THE GENTLEMAN [*taking off his hat*] I beg your pardon.
Can you direct me to Hindhead View — Mrs Alison's?

THE YOUNG LADY [*glancing up from her book*] This is
Mrs Alison's. [*She resumes her work*].

THE GENTLEMAN. Indeed! Perhaps — may I ask are you
Miss Vivie Warren?

THE YOUNG LADY [*sharply, as she turns on her elbow to get
a good look at him*] Yes.

THE GENTLEMAN [*daunted and conciliatory*] I'm afraid I
appear intrusive. My name is Praed. [*Vivie at once
throws her books upon the chair, and gets out of the hammock*].
Oh, pray dont let me disturb you.

VIVIE [*striding to the gate and opening it for him*] Come
in, Mr Praed. [*He comes in*]. Glad to see you. [*She
proffers her hand and takes his with a resolute and hearty grip.
She is an attractive specimen of the sensible, able, highly-edu-
cated young middle-class Englishwoman. Age 22. Prompt,
strong, confident, self-possessed. Plain, business-like dress,
but not dowdy. She wears a chatelaine at her belt, with a
fountain pen and a paper knife among its pendants*].

PRAED. Very kind of you indeed, Miss Warren. [*She
shuts the gate with a vigorous slam: he passes in to the middle
of the garden, exercising his fingers, which are slightly numbed
by her greeting*]. Has your mother arrived?

VIVIE [*quickly, evidently scenting aggression*] Is she
coming?

PRAED [*surprised*] Didnt you expect us?

VIVIE. No.

PRAED. Now, goodness me, I hope Ive not mistaken
the day. That would be just like me, you know. Your

mother arranged that she was to come down from London
and that I was to come over from Horsham to be introduced to you.

VIVIE [*not at all pleased*] Did she? Hm! My mother
has rather a trick of taking me by surprise — to see how
I behave myself when she's away, I suppose. I fancy I
shall take my mother very much by surprise one of these
days, if she makes arrangements that concern me without
consulting me beforehand. She hasnt come.

PRAED [*embarrassed*] I'm really very sorry.

VIVIE [*throwing off her displeasure*] It's not your fault,
Mr Praed, is it? And I'm very glad youve come, believe me. You are the only one of my mother's friends I
have asked her to bring to see me.

PRAED [*relieved and delighted*] Oh, now this is really
very good of you, Miss Warren!

VIVIE. Will you come indoors; or would you rather sit
out here whilst we talk?

PRAED. It will be nicer out here, dont you think?

VIVIE. Then I'll go and get you a chair. [*She goes to the
porch for a garden chair*].

PRAED [*following her*] Oh, pray, pray! Allow me. [*He
lays hands on the chair*].

VIVIE [*letting him take it*] Take care of your fingers:
theyre rather dodgy things, those chairs. [*She goes across
to the chair with the books on it; pitches them into the hammock;
and brings the chair forward with one swing*].

PRAED [*who has just unfolded his chair*] Oh, now do let
me take that hard chair! I like hard chairs.

VIVIE. So do I. [*She sits down*]. Sit down, Mr Praed.
[*This invitation she gives with genial peremptoriness, his anxiety
to please her clearly striking her as a sign of weakness of character
on his part*].

PRAED. By the way, though, hadnt we better go to the
station to meet your mother?

VIVIE [*coolly*] Why? She knows the way. [*Praed hesi-
tates, and then sits down in the garden chair, rather discon-*

VOL. I   M

A two-page spread from Shaw's Plays Pleasant and Unpleasant
(1898), showing typical Shavian typography.

points out in his 1961 articles in *The Shavian*, this practice distinguishes names, actions, and words with minimal breaking-up
of the page. Title pages were often in 24-point Caslon upper
and lower case, to a fixed measure, breaking words anywhere it
was convenient for achieving close spacing; as Shaw himself
states in "Notes on the Clarendon Press Rules for Compositors
and Readers" (in *On Language* [New York: Philosophical Library,
1963], p. 27), "evenness of the color…is far more important
than the philological pedantries of word division." Shand recounts a story of Shaw's dealing with printer Edward Clark on
the spacing of words and letters in his essay on Shaw in *Books
and Printing* (Cleveland: World, 1951; pp. 381–401):

Edward Clark doubtless also got much entertainment from his
dealings with a teetotal, non-smoking, vegetarian, Socialist of an
author. There is a story that, on one specimen, Shaw's instructions

for close and mechanically-equal spacing between words were so precisely followed by the pragmatical Scots, that at the end of some closely spaced lines the definite article "the" was divided "t-" and "he" turned over, and the indefinite article "a-" with "n" turned over. Shaw's comment when returning the specimen, as Maxwell tells the story, was, "Excellent; but please do not go so far as to prove the author is really a damn fool." Shaw denies the story; nevertheless, true or untrue, it has a Shavian flavour.

The binding was usually pale green with gold lettering. Because Shaw wanted to avoid straggling lines in a printed play, he was known to rewrite to make an exchange look better on the page. For word emphasis he preferred utilizing extra space between letters, in the German manner. Dunlap notes that while Shaw sometimes used italic, he preferred this other method, which he may have seen and read about in William Archer's translation of Ibsen. Shaw continues in "Notes" that "To the good printer the occurrence of two different founts on the same page is at best an unavoidable evil" (p. 28).

To achieve the look he required, Shaw arranged to buy his own printing and binding. Then the publishers received the complete book to market, and accounted to the author for the proceeds. One gets a sense of Shaw's strict requirements in a famous letter to William Orcutt, the book designer at the University Press in Cambridge, Massachusetts, who had been requested to prepare an American copyright edition of *Man and Superman*. Orcutt had difficulties because the instructions he received were based on the Edinburgh edition, in which the type faces differed from the American in width. He did the best he could, but received a letter from Shaw in 1903. The author was angered by the apostrophes, the quads at ends of sentences, the tasteless use of leaf ornaments, the narrow letters, and the margins:

> I am only too painfully aware that when all is done that can be done, a play, with its broken lines of dialogue, its mixture of

roman and italic, and its spaced out words for emphasis, can never enable a printer to do full justice to himself.... You can hardly imagine how atrocious you could make that play look by simply leading the page and putting large initial capitals to the names of the speakers . . . [*Bernard Shaw: Collected Letters, 1898–1910*, ed. Dan Laurence (New York: Dodd, Mead, 1972), p. 355].

Also of great interest is Shaw's tirade against the Roycrofters Shop, Elbert Hubbard's East Aurora, New York, printing concern based on the Arts and Crafts Movement. Shaw felt it to be a cheap imitation at best. Well-meaning friends kept sending him copies of a particular book Hubbard had printed, *This is the Preachment on Going to Church* (1896). His January 1900 reply to Mrs. Richard Mansfield is enlightening:

> What is this!—a Roycroft book!
> The fact is, the creature does not know the ABC of good printing. I gave him so precise an account of his ignorances in that letter that he has made some attempt to correct those which admitted of correction by mechanical instruction.... He no longer sticks two or three fly leaves of dirty brown felt at the end.... He has discarded his sham "Kelmscott Capitals." ... Look at a page of a Morris book, and you see the block of letter-press constituting the printed page, as a piece of rich black on white. There are no bars of white between the lines—no rivers of white trickling down between irregularly spaced words like drops of rain down a window pane on a wet day....

Shaw was not without his critics—those who felt that his Caslon was too tiny, those who disapproved of his disregard for hypens and apostrophes, and those who thought he was being misinterpreted. Shaw himself relaxed his standards somewhat. For his 1931–32 Standard Edition, he went to a larger type face which was easier to keep clean. And he finally accepted Linotype and Monotype, which he had resisted for years because they could not justify as well as hand-set type, when printer William Maxwell submitted two specimen pages, one handset and one in

Monotype Caslon, and Shaw preferred the latter! The interest in Shaw continues, as witnessed in a review of a Shaw exhibition catalogue prepared by Dan H. Laurence for the Humanities Research Center at Austin, Texas. Laurence styled the catalogue's design to conform to Shaw's views. This attempt received a mixed review in *The Library* (33 [March 1978], 71–72):

> I did not find that the catalogue gave a very strong impression of Shaw-the-typographer. The asymmetric style of page arrangement, which attracts me, is hardly Shavian, and the spotty manner in which many exhibit numbers of illustrations are placed does not give a particularly clean effect.

Shaw would have enjoyed both the catalogue and the review.

* * *

HENRY JAMES's New York Edition is a fine example of an author's aesthetic sensibility reflected in the authorized collected edition, with the total cooperation of the publisher. At the invitation of Scribner, James chose those works he wished to survive, revised them extensively, added the now famous theoretical prefaces which outline his theory of fiction, and commissioned photographic frontispieces by Coburn. It was published volume by volume between December 14, 1907 and July 31, 1909. The total is twenty-four volumes in octavo, with russet covers. (James tried to squeeze it into twenty-three, in imitation of Balzac's collected works.) Two volumes were issued posthumously, but the frontispieces are not Coburn's.

James felt very strongly that illustration should have no direct bearing on a writer's words. In the preface to *The Golden Bowl*, Volume I (New York: Scribner, 1909), he explains:

> ... Anything that relieves responsible prose of the duty of being, while placed before us, good enough, interesting enough, and, if the question be of picture, pictorial enough, above all *in itself*, does it the worst of services, and may well inspire in the lover of literature certain lively questions as to the future of that institution [pp. ix–x].

[208]

He decided to use photography, an art which he felt could provide the subtle suggestion of mood desired. He chose Alvin Langdon Coburn, greatly admired by George Bernard Shaw, and sent him out to photograph scenes:

> ... Nothing in fact could more have amused the author than the opportunity of a hunt for a series of reproducible subjects— such moreover as might best consort with photography—the reference of which to Novel or Tale should exactly be *not* competitive and obvious, should on the contrary plead its case with some shyness, that of images always confessing themselves mere optical symbols or echoes, expressions of no particular thing in the text, but only of the type or idea of this or that thing. They were to remain at the most small pictures of our "set" stage with the actors left out; and what was above all interesting was that they were first to be constituted [pp. x–xi].

Thus, the frontispiece for Volume I of *The Golden Bowl* is "The Curiosity Shop" where, in the story, the bowl is first seen. James wanted, and got, a "shop of the mind ... not 'taken from' a particular establishment anywhere, only an image distilled and intensified ..." (p. xii). The cost, incidentally, was underwritten by Scribner. James was pleased with the original photographs, and only moderately disappointed with the reproductions, which were slightly reduced.

Interestingly, the New York Edition, now extremely valuable, was a financial failure. James's friend Edith Wharton, whose own interest in books will be discussed next, arranged with Scribner for $8,000 to be diverted from her royalties to the New York Edition earnings, so that James could add another novel to the definitive edition if he desired.

* * *

EDITH WHARTON herself is another extremely important author/ book designer who has only recently received attention. Her role as author and her typographical specifications are worthy of study beyond the scope of this essay. She had a great influence on the spread of tasteful commercial printing in the United States.

[209]

Wharton was one of the few women writers who negotiated directly with their publishers. Earlier authors such as George Eliot used their husbands as agents to handle their literary concerns. Thus Wharton set a positive precedent for the woman author. Her view of the relation of the author's words and book's design was, to my mind, more balanced than T. E. Lawrence's, which will be discussed later. My research has turned up no evidence that Wharton ever changed her words to fit the printed page. Her writing had an integrity of its own, but she also wanted it printed well. Happily, R. W. B. Lewis documents her interest in fine printing in his critically acclaimed *Edith Wharton: A Biography* (New York: Harper & Row, 1975).

Wharton had met Daniel Berkeley Updike socially and was aware of the world of fine printing. She called him "Upsie" and thought him somewhat provincial, but she felt that his Merrymount Press in Boston was becoming the best commercial printing house in the United States. He would eventually print six of Wharton's volumes. Updike himself acknowledges her importance: "Nothing could have helped the Press more, just then, than the Scribner connection ... for it showed we were not amateur but could hold our own with larger printing houses" (quoted in Joseph Blumenthal's *The Printed Book in America* (Boston: Godine, 1977; p. 60). Updike designed the title page for her *The Decoration of Houses* (1897), a study of the features of an upper-class private city dwelling. Scribner's terms of royalty were rather low, because they did not think it would sell. But Wharton was concerned more with the quality of the book than with the earnings. William Crary Brownell, a senior literary consultant at Scribner's, worked closely with her and was sensitive to her specifications. She negotiated with Brownell on binding and front cover lettering, the design and type style for the title page, and the number of illustrations, which Brownell reluctantly, at her insistence, increased from thirty-two to fifty-six.

For her first work of fiction, *The Greater Inclination* (1899), Wharton insisted that Updike do the printing. There is much

The title page of Edith Wharton's The Decoration of Houses
(1897), designed by D. B. Updike.

The binding design for Edith Wharton's The Greater Inclination
(1899), printed by D. B. Updike.

interesting research yet to be done on Wharton's relationship and correspondence with Scribner and Updike.

* * *

ONE of the truly fascinating figures in the history of the author as book designer is the controversial T. E. Lawrence (of Arabia). Though Lawrence was extremely particular about the printing of his work for private distribution, he was also concerned, albeit to a lesser extent, with the trade editions based on the original. *Seven Pillars of Wisdom* is a good example of a book in which the very wording was altered by Lawrence to achieve an attractive appearance on the page. And when the Cape trade edition came out, many of his ideas on book design were continued in the same spirit as the private printings.

In March 1922 Lawrence met Sydney Cockerell for lunch and they discussed, among other things, typography. Cockerell introduced Lawrence to G. B. Shaw that day, and in August Lawrence asked Shaw if he would be interested in reading a "Private" printing of *Seven Pillars of Wisdom*, done at the *Oxford Times* office in 1922: "I have very little money and do not wish to publish it: however it had to be printed, so I got it done on a lino. press, in a newspaper office. That means it's beastly to look at ..." (*Letters of T. E. Lawrence* [London: Spring Books, 1964], p. 356).

The book was likely to create a scandal, but Lawrence was finally convinced that it must be published. This endeavor became the 1926 Manning Pike edition. For this, he received help from Shaw. Typographically they agreed on most issues, though Lawrence was not unalterably opposed to leading. But, like Shaw, he disapproved of too much white space. Lawrence was quick to alter his text to achieve a particular appearance on the page. His directions to printer Manning Pike were to set thirty-seven lines per page, each page beginning with a new paragraph. Ideally, Lawrence wanted most pages to begin with an ornamental capital, and the last line of each page was to be solid. To avoid white space, he specified that the last lines of paragraphs should run beyond the middle of the line.

[212]

The following arrangement was set up. Lawrence sent his writing to Pike who, in turn, sent proofs back. Lawrence reworked sections so that his typographical standards could be met, and sent them back to Pike. One interesting sidelight is Lawrence's acknowledgment of Shaw's assistance in the 1926 preface to the Pike edition of *Seven Pillars*, in which he mentions his distress over the semicolons. He was surprised that Shaw had permitted them in the proofs, since both men disapproved, in theory, of semicolons on the printed page. Vyvyan Richards reflected that such typographical purity did not harm the work: "But there is almost no trace of these Procrustean games in the actual text—he had an amazing command of word and phrase. The most careful reader of the later popular edition, where, of course, all

A summary
22. III. 17

HAD now been eight days lying in this remote tent, keeping my ideas general,* till my brain, sick of unsupported thinking, had to be dragged to its work by an effort of will, and went off into a doze whenever that effort was relaxed. The fever passed: my dysentery ceased; and with restored strength the present again became actual to me. Facts concrete and pertinent thrust themselves into my reveries; and my inconstant wit bore aside towards all these roads of escape. So I hurried into line my shadowy principles, to have have them once precise before my power to evoke them faded.

It seemed to me proven that our rebellion had an unassailable base, guarded not only from attack, but from the fear of attack. It had a sophisticated alien enemy, disposed as an army of occupation in an area greater than could be dominated effectively from fortified posts. It had a friendly population, of which some two in the hundred were active, and the rest quietly sympathetic to the point of not betraying the movements of the minority. The active rebels had the virtues of secrecy and self-control, and the qualities of speed, endurance and independence of arteries of supply. They had technical equipment enough to paralyse the enemy's communications. A province would be won when we had taught the civilians in it to die for our ideal of freedom. The presence of the enemy was secondary. Final victory seemed certain, if the war lasted long enough for us to work it out.

* Not perhaps as successfully as here. I thought out my problems mainly in terms of Hejaz, illustrated by what I knew of its men and its geography. These would have been too long if written down; and the argument has been compressed into an abstract form in which it smells more of the lamp than of the field. All military writing does, worse luck.

176

BVIOUSLY I was well again, and I remembered the reason of my journey to Wadi Ais. The Turks meant to march out of Medina, and Sir Archibald Murray wanted us to attack them in professional form. It was irksome that he should come butting in to our show from Egypt, asking from us alien activities. Yet the British were the bigger; and the Arabs lived only by grace of their shadow. We were yoked to Sir Archibald Murray, and must work with him, to the point of sacrificing our non-essential interests for his, if they would not be reconciled. At the same time we could not possibly act alike. Feisal might be a free gas: Sir Archibald's army, probably the most cumbrous in the world, had to be laboriously pushed forward on its belly. It was ridiculous to suppose it could keep pace with ethical conceptions as nimble as the Arab Movement: doubtful even if it would understand them. However, perhaps by hindering the railway we could frighten the Turks off their plan to evacuate Medina, and give them reason to remain in the town on the defensive: a conclusion highly serviceable to both Arabs and English, though possibly neither would see it, yet.

Accordingly, I wandered into Abdulla's tent, announcing my complete recovery and an ambition to do something to the Hejaz railway. Here were men, guns, machine guns, explosives and automatic mines: enough for a main effort. But Abdulla was apathetic. He wanted to talk about the Royal families of Europe, or the Battle of the Somme: the slow march of his own war bored him. However, Sherif Shakir, his cousin and second in command, was fired to enthusiasm, and secured us license to do our worst. Shakir loved the Ateiba, and swore they were the best tribe on earth; so we settled to take mostly Ateiba with us. Then we thought we might have a mountain gun, one of the Egyptian Army Krupp veterans, which had been sent by Feisal to Abdulla from Wejh as a present.

177

Two pages from the privately printed edition of T. E. Lawrence's Seven Pillars of Wisdom *(1926).*

[213]

this typographical precision is dropped, would never suspect that the text had been so forced" (Stanley Weintraub, *Private and Public Shaw* [New York: Braziller, 1963], pp. 88–92). He distributed the subscription copies in November 1926.

Jonathan Cape, publisher and friend of T. E. Lawrence, was interested in a trade edition of *Seven Pillars* as early as the 1920s. The fascinating story is recounted in Michael Howard's *Jonathan Cape, Publisher* (London: Cape, 1971). Lawrence did not feel that a quality job could be done by a fledgling publishing house; Cape, however, was willing to invest in this venture. Negotiations had gone back and forth, canceled not by Cape, but by Lawrence, always wary of publicity. He finally had it printed privately, as we have seen, and Cape published an abridgment, *Revolt in the Desert*, in 1927.

In 1935 Lawrence died. Much of Cape's concern regarding libel was now not a problem. And A. W. Lawrence demanded that Cape honor his dead brother's wish that no more abridgments be published. The Cape edition of *Seven Pillars* does not follow Lawrence's typographical strictures as closely as the Pike edition, but it is a fine book. G. Wren Howard, book designer and partner to Cape, took charge of this new edition. Howard gave much of Cape's printing to the Alden Press, who followed his typographical formulas carefully. He went to John Dickinson to supervise the paper quality. Howard was known to be a shrewd businessman who cut corners in some areas of the manufacturing process so that he could afford fine paper and binding. He followed the "golden rectangle" theory of page proportion, and avoided distracting ornamentation and italic.

The final work was published July 29, 1935, in an edition of 750 numbered copies on rag, and 30,000 for general sale. By the end of September, there were 100,000 copies in print. It is a quarto volume of 672 pages, with three folding maps and about forty illustrations. Interestingly, Howard used the proceeds of *Seven Pillars* to buy the Bain Bindery in 1936, evidence of his concern for the total look of the book.

* * *

AND what of the contemporary author as book designer? There are many authors who do care about the look of their books, and who go to private presses to fulfill their requirements. Those who go to commercial publishers often play an active role with the design staff in planning the book. Julia Child's relationship to Knopf is an interesting example of an author's concern that the book design combine readability and beauty. A cookbook, after all, must have both these features. In the introduction to the 1975 *From Julia Child's Kitchen*, she exclaims:

> What a beautiful looking book this is! My editor, and the designers and technical people at Knopf are responsible for that. I love the headings, the use of space, the way the titles and ingredients are set off from the text. It is a stylish and distinguished example of the bookmaker's art, I think, and one that is easy and pleasant to use, as well [p. xvi].

John Updike has, in his relations with the Knopf staff, consistently shown an interest in the typographical look of his books.

A jacket and slipcase designed by John Updike for one of his own books.

(It is interesting that the main character of *Rabbit Redux* is a linotypist!) The appearance of his novels has remained basically unchanged. He is concerned that when his works stand unjacketed on the shelf, there be a uniformity of author name and book title, which is placed between two rules. On one of his works, *Buchanan Dying* (1974), the spine-binding die was off approximately one-quarter inch, and when the book was reprinted Updike requested that the printing on the spine be readjusted.

Updike prefers a smaller-size book, both aesthetically and because an oversize, "blown-up" book is uncomfortable to hold. On the other hand, type that is too small is unreadable. Updike has consistently used Janson in a readable size. He is also concerned about the typographical look of his chapter headings. Thus, when he hands in a manuscript, he marks out the pattern the chapters will take. If he has ideas about book jackets, which he often does, he sketches them out. These sketches and the proof pages for the novel travel back and forth between him and Knopf.

Within one month, *The New York Times* has noted two books in which the authors took great care in design specifications. Novelist Doris Grumbach's *Chamber Music* (New York: Dutton, 1979) was rewritten four times, and even then she did not let go. In an April 6, 1979 article she states that "There is a discontinuity between the time an author finishes a book and its appearance.... The writer has no sense of being in his book once it is out of his hands." She insisted that Dutton use Garamond typeface and match the end-papers with the boards.

Peter Jenkins' *A Walk Across America* (New York: Morrow, 1979) is an account of his own travels. A holder of a degree in fine arts, Jenkins states in the April 8, 1979 *New York Times Book Review* that he chose Morrow as his publisher because they respected his concern that the book be beautiful. The book includes photographs and maps of the journey. Editors at Morrow report that he was particularly vigilant about the use of the maps as a unifying device. The general map is the frontispiece, used

[216]

to coordinate the smaller maps at the beginning of each chapter.

Other less famous but important authors who have recently played a key role in the design of their works are William Kotzwinkle, Thom Gunn, and John Gardner. And it is likely that authors will be increasingly aware of design. In a *Heritage of the Graphic Arts* lecture (New York: Bowker, 1972; pp. 3–17), Hermann Zapf predicts that the responsibility of the book designer, too, will be larger, because his design concept for a particular work will be computerized to be used for both inexpensive and fine editions of the same work. In another lecture in the same series, Hugh Williamson adds that because designers know little about machines, design may end up as the printer's responsibility, as it was in the earliest days of printing (pp. 255–65). The author's role in design, especially the legal implications, will be interesting to follow. Copyright lawyer Robert O'Neil has spoken recently of the absence in American copyright law of the "doctrine of moral right." In some European countries, for example, the author's "reputation" is recognized as a legal issue; he is more than an owner of property. A creator may thus object to the way in which, for example, his painting is displayed or book is edited. Could this recognition of the importance of the author's reputation be linked to quality of design? (*The Copyright Dilemma* [Chicago: American Library Association, 1978], pp. 119–31.) The Authors Guild, Inc., of New York City, has issued a recommended form of trade book contract as a guide to authors. It includes the following clause: "The format, style of composition, and price of the trade edition shall be determined by Publisher. Publisher will consult in advance with Author concerning the format and style of the trade edition, and concerning the text, graphic material and style of the dust jacket."

* * *

THE status of the author as book designer will depend, as always, on three elements: the author, the publisher/printer, and the reading public. Their interaction, tastes, and needs will determine the look of books in the future.

[217]

BIBLIOGRAPHY

Nicholas Barker, *The Oxford University Press and the Spread of Learning* (Oxford: Clarendon Press, 1978).

Joseph Blumenthal, *The Printed Book in America* (Boston: Godine, 1977).

A. S. Collins, *Authorship in the Days of Johnson* (London: Holden, 1927).

——, *The Profession of Letters* (London: Routledge, 1928; repr. 1973 by A. M. Kelley).

J. S. Dearden, *Facets of Ruskin: Some Sesquicentennial Studies* (London: Skilton, 1970).

Joseph Dunlap, "Typographical Emphasis," *The Shavian*, 2 (October 1961), 10.

——, "The Typographical Shaw," *The Shavian*, 2 (February 1961), 4–15.

Leon Edel, *A Bibliography of Henry James*, with Dan H. Laurence (London: Rupert Hart-Davis, 1961).

——, *Henry James, the Master: 1901–1916* (Philadelphia: Lippincott, 1972).

Jean Gattegno, *Lewis Carroll: Fragments of a Looking Glass* (New York: Crowell, 1974).

Roger Green, "Alice," in *Aspects of Alice*, ed. Robert Phillips (New York: Vanguard, 1971), pp. 4–15.

Gordon Haight, *George Eliot: A Biography* (New York: Oxford University Press, 1968).

Heritage of the Graphic Arts: A Selection of Lectures Delivered at Gallery 303, ed. Chandler Grannis (New York: Bowker, 1972).

Michael S. Howard, *Jonathan Cape, Publisher* (London: Cape, 1971).

Holbrook Jackson, *The Printing of Books*, 2d ed. (London: Cassell, 1947).

Edgar Johnson, *Charles Dickens: His Tragedy and Triumph* (New York: Simon and Schuster, 1952).

R. W. B. Lewis, *Edith Wharton: A Biography* (New York: Harper & Row, 1975).

Robert Patten, *Charles Dickens and His Publishers* (Oxford: Clarendon Press, 1978).

Bruce Rogers, *Paragraphs on Printing* (New York: Rudge, 1943).

James Shand, "Author and Printer: G. B. S. and R. & R. C.: 1898–1948," in *Books and Printing*, ed. Paul Bennett (Cleveland: World, 1951), pp. 381–401.

George Bernard Shaw, *Bernard Shaw: Collected Letters, 1898–1910*, ed. Dan H. Laurence (New York: Dodd, Mead, 1972).

S. H. Steinberg, *Five Hundred Years of Printing*, 3d ed. (Harmondsworth: Penguin Books, 1974).

J. A. Sutherland, *Victorian Novelists and Publishers* (Chicago: University of Chicago Press, 1976).

Susan Otis Thompson, *American Book Design and William Morris* (New York: Bowker, 1977).

OTTO PENZLER *leads a shady existence. Founder and president of The Mysterious Press, publisher of* The Armchair Detective, *and owner of The Mysterious Bookshop, he is a member of the Board of Directors of the Mystery Writers of America, the editor of the Gregg Press Mystery Fiction Series, a member of the advisory board of First Printings of American Authors, a contributing editor of* Contemporary Authors, *and a columnist for* Ellery Queen's Mystery Magazine. *He is also the author of* The Private Lives of Private Eyes, *co-author of the* Detectionary, *editor of* The Great Detectives, *and co-author of the* Encyclopedia of Mystery and Detection, *for which he won an Edgar Allan Poe Award from the Mystery Writers of America.*

Incunabular Detective Fiction

Otto Penzler

IN THE LONG HISTORY of book collecting, the era of detective fiction is little more than a wink. It was not until 1934 that the first catalogue devoted to the subject was issued (by George Bates). Entitled *Murder: Catalogue the Seventh of Rare and Interesting Books Illustrating the Development of the Detective Mystery Story*, this little-known and now rare item by the London bookseller was the first of three seminal events in that year which helped to legitimize the genre as a sphere of collecting.

The second was John Carter's attempt to educate the timid bibliophilic community with his prophetic *New Paths in Book-Collecting* (Constable, London). Among the previously untrodden avenues of acquisition which he suggested to courageous collectors was "Detective Fiction."

Carter was also responsible for the third event of that year in the elevation of detective fiction collecting. Scribner's Book

Store issued the second catalogue of the year exclusively devoted to mystery fiction (although it is generally assumed to be the first, the Bates list being more obscure). *Detective Fiction, a Collection of First and a Few Early Editions* was a breathtaking list of items primarily from Carter's own collection, begun in 1927.

In the early days of collecting detective fiction (that is, the 1930s), there were only occasional rivals for the abundant treasures being amassed by the few great collectors in the genre: E. T. (Ned) Guymon, whose extraordinary collection—the greatest ever assembled—is now housed at Occidental College in Pasadena, California; John Carter, whose volumes formed the core of the collection at the Lilly Library at the University of Indiana in Bloomington; Michael Sadleir, whose unrivalled collection of yellowbacks and three-deckers was acquired by the University of California at Los Angeles, which has more recently succeeded in putting together one of the world's most impressive pulp magazine archives; Vincent Starrett, whose personal misfortunes forced him to disburse more than one monumental collection of Sherlock Holmes items and detective fiction (which helps to explain the abundance of detective fiction first editions bearing the bookplate of the dean of Sherlockians); and Frederic Dannay (one half of the Ellery Queen collaboration), whose distinguished collection specialized in the short story and formed the basis for his two major reference books: *Queen's Quorum,* an annotated list of the 125 most important short story collections published in the mystery genre, and *The Detective Short Story*, a bibliography.

Queen's popularity and his ability to transmit his enthusiasm for the short form helped to make this one of the most collectible sub-genres of mystery fiction. In a field so diverse and so massive, with at least 60,000 titles published to date, only the foolhardy or the innocent would attempt to collect it all.

One of its extensions, Sherlock Holmes, has become the most avidly collected literary subject of this time, with more aficionados than Dickens, for example, or Shakespeare. Among the great collections of detective fiction with specialties in Sherlockiana are those formed by Marvin P. Epstein and Norman S. Nolan. Other collectors concentrate on Victorian mystery fiction, or the "hard-boiled" private eye stories of Dashiell Hammett, Raymond Chandler, Ross Macdonald, and their ilk, or books listed in the *Haycraft–Queen Definitive Library of Detective-Crime-Mystery Fiction: Two Centuries of Cornerstones, 1748–1948*, or books by a favorite author, or, probably, books in which the victim was left-handed.

One area of collecting in the mystery genre which remains largely virgin is the era before Edgar Allan Poe, that time in which no one yet realized that something which would later be termed "mystery fiction" existed. This period, in which elements of the genuine mystery story could be discovered in various works by the most popular writers of the day, has a modest number of works which can be legitimately regarded as part of the genre, but it is an exceptionally difficult area in which to collect.

Just as was true of later detective novels, this type of fiction was not purchased and set immaculately on the shelf to fill some need of ego or social acceptance. It was bought to be read and enjoyed and read again, and perhaps lent to a friend for his entertainment as well. And, since the best fiction holds up well through the years, the books were read again and again, with the consequent result that it is nearly impossible to find even acceptable collector's copies nowadays, not to speak of truly fine copies.

Several books will be discussed here, and they have common elements: all are significant in the history of the development of the mystery novel, and all are extremely scarce or rare today— particularly in fine collector's condition.

It was once reported by the leading bookseller in the mystery field that only two copies are known of the true first appearance of Voltaire's *Zadig*, which came out as a part of his larger work, *Memnon*. Even if that statement exaggerates its rarity (and I am not sure that it does), it serves to suggest that this is indeed an

[223]

exceedingly difficult title to obtain. Similarly, the first American edition of Vidocq's *Memoirs* had been neither recorded nor seen by Ellery Queen when he compiled his short story bibliography. All of Charles Brockden Brown's first editions are rare, and the only copy of *Richmond* I have ever seen is the one in my collection.

A checklist with publishing information appears at the end of this article, together with a short bibliography for further reading.

* * *

ALTHOUGH crime and the romance of its commission have been among the oldest themes in the world's literature, it is both customary and accurate to date the first detective story precisely at April 1841, with the publication of Edgar Allan Poe's historic "The Murders in the Rue Morgue" in *Graham's Magazine*.

Fully realized and the inspiration for countless thousands of succeeding tales, this is the first pure tale of ratiocination, of observation and deduction, of detection. Curiously, the first detective in literature, C. Auguste Dupin, was never called a detective since the word was not invented until 1843 or 1844, according to the *Oxford English Dictionary*. James Graham, then the British Home Secretary, hand-picked the most dependable and intelligent members of the London police force and created an elite department known as The Detective Police.

If the word itself did not exist, there was no shortage of crime-fighters, both official and unofficial, in real life and in fiction, who detected. The Bow Street Runners in England were the precursors of Scotland Yard and, while they were largely inefficient and often of dubious character, they ostensibly performed the functions of police. Relying inordinately much on informers, they nonetheless performed occasional feats of detection, which is to say, they discovered clues and attempted to solve crimes from their subsequent deductions.

Crimes and criminals had always existed, of course, and so had puzzles and riddles and mysteries. Literature reflected the intense fascination of man with those elements of his existence, but it remained for Poe to pull together the inherently related components of crime fiction and mystery fiction to produce a *bona fide* detective story. Today the most collected and most widely read type of fiction in the world, it did not exist as a definable genre until "The Murders in the Rue Morgue."

Several books, however, are very clearly marked paving stones on the road to that singular achievement. Largely forgotten or ignored because it is simpler and more convenient to have a firm birthdate (just as it is easier to identify Gutenberg baldly as the inventor of movable type, without bothering to acknowledge the contributions of his predecessors), these volumes of incunabular mysteries are highly collectible and of enormous historical significance in the development of detective fiction.

It is essential to distinguish between crime fiction and detective fiction although they are so closely allied that it is often impossible and frequently inadvisable to separate the two. In order to qualify as a genuine detective story, a fictional narrative must be about a crime or a threatened crime, involving a person whose principal function is to detect the method of that crime, its motive, or its perpetrator, and often all of these matters.

To assist us in establishing perspective, we should note that the first murder story occurs in the first part of the first book— the Bible. In the landmark tale of Cain and Abel, however, there is little opportunity or need for detection, so it may be eliminated from a discussion of the earliest detective stories.

If detection is being sought—that is, a series of logical deductions based on observation—it is again possible to turn to the first book for the history of the first great detective: Daniel.

In the history of Bel, Daniel stakes his life on his abilities as a detective. Assured in his mind that a clay and brass idol cannot consume the meat and wine given to it each night, he lays a trap for the seventy priests and their families whom he knows to be the thieves. Inside the temple, he strews ashes on every part of the floor and, when he returns with the king the following morning, they see the fresh footprints clearly visible, despite the locked door and unbroken seal of the entrance. Found out, the priests reveal a secret entrance but are nonetheless put to death for their chicanery.

In the history of Susanna, Daniel again establishes a technique which many years later became familiar. Via clever cross-examination, he outsmarts two elders to free an innocent suspect, much in the style of Perry Mason.

But both of Daniel's stories lack the primary component of a genuine detective story: the *raison d'être* of the tale must be a crime and its attempted solution. Whatever else a story may have, those other ingredients must be supplementary. Take away the crime, the person who seeks the criminal, or, at the very least, the explanation of the apparently criminal occurrence, and there is no detective story. Biblical tales exist primarily for a different reason—frequently to demonstrate the existence of God—and so cannot be legitimately regarded as part of the evolution of the detective story.

With that criterion firmly established as essential, it becomes satisfactory, if not outright mandatory, to eliminate from consideration such works as the myriad adventures of rogues and rascals which have constituted such a popular form of entertainment for many centuries. Rarely do mysteries appear, and never does a detective—who is detecting—appear. The ballads, folk tales, and stories of Robin Hood, Tom Jones, Gil Blas, and Jonathan Wild, such highwaymen as Dick Turpin and Jack Sheppard, and the picaresque Spanish rogues, recount their thefts and other crimes, but there are no elements of detection. Daniel Defoe's *Robinson Crusoe* and *The Leatherstocking Saga* of James Fenimore Cooper, both often advanced as examples of the prototypical detective story, feature excellent instances of observation and deduction (as when Crusoe reasons logically from the evidence of footprints in the sand and when Cooper's redmen observe and deduce from evidence in the forest which enables them to track their quarry), but crimes are not central to the themes of the novels.

Further tales of crime and murder abound in Oriental legend,

A Thousand Nights and a Night (*The Arabian Nights Entertainments*), parts of Giovanni Boccaccio's *Decameron,* Thomas Murner's *Adventures of Tyll Eulenspiegel,* and Geoffrey Chaucer's *Canterbury Tales,* of which "The Pardoner's Tale" is decidedly melodramatic and modern in concept.

In this forerunner of many similar stories, three men discover a treasure in the forest and, preparatory to dividing their chest of gold, they decide to buy food and drink in a nearby town, casting lots to see which will make the trip. The youngest is chosen and, while he is on the errand, decides to poison the other two so that he may have the entire fortune for himself. His friends, in the meantime, plot his assassination so that they will have to split the gold only two ways, instead of three. When he returns, they attack him with daggers and slay him. Sitting down to celebrate their act, they drink the poisoned wine and die in great agony.

Shakespeare, too, wrote frequently of revenge and murder. *Hamlet* and *Macbeth,* two of his greatest tragedies, could easily have been rewritten as first-rate thrillers. One would no longer have much drama if the crimes in these plays were eliminated, but Shakespeare had largely different objectives in mind when creating them; it was not his aim to tell a mystery story.

The master of satire, Voltaire, planted the most fruitful seeds in the still spare garden of pure detection with the publication of *Zadig; or, The Book of Fate* (1748). When his king's horse and queen's spaniel are reported missing, the philosopher Zadig attempts to aid in the search. As recounted in "Le chien et le cheval" ("The Dog and the Horse"), Zadig's description of the lost animals is so accurate that it is evident to all that he must have seen them, so he is thrown into prison as a thief, to be whipped first and then exiled to Siberia. He is permitted to explain his deductions from observations he had made and is saved when the queen's dog and the king's horse are found, but he is nonetheless fined four hundred pieces of gold for lying, since he must have seen the animals to have been able to describe

[227]

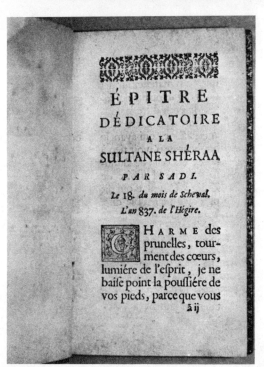

The opening chapter of Voltaire's Zadig *in the first separate edition of the work; it had previously appeared as part of Voltaire's rarest work,* Memnon.

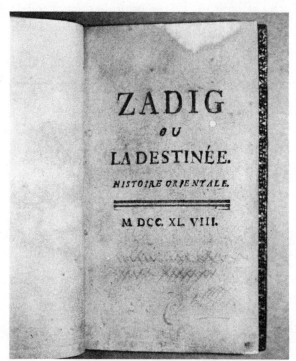

The title page of the first edition of the first separate edition of Voltaire's Zadig. *The type has faded badly on this copy and a previous owner darkened the lettering with pen-and-ink.*

them as accurately as he did, all the while insisting that he had not laid eyes upon them. Again permitted to plead his case, he brilliantly describes the process by which he logically deduced the appearance of the animals from their tracks and hairs left behind when they brushed against a bush. The explanation is worthy of Sherlock Holmes himself, and the king dismisses the case against him, although the court retains three hundred and ninety of the gold pieces to "defray the expenses of the Court."

From a different direction can be seen another arm of detective fiction: the Gothic novel. These atmospheric tales of murder and revenge, of dark castles and chilling landscapes, of madness and terror, flourished late in the eighteenth century and remained astonishingly popular and successful throughout the nineteenth century, their era ending with the most famous and most towering figure, Bram Stoker's *Dracula* (1897).

One of the first great giants of the genre, Ann Radcliffe, sufficiently shaped its form to deserve the appellation of the great-grandmother of detective fiction. During an eight-year span, beginning with *The Castles of Athlin and Dunbayne: A Highland Story* (1789), her novels were fabulously successful, and she earned enormous sums for her fiction. Then, with no further stories to tell, she abruptly quit writing and her vast readership believed rumors that she had gone insane and been committed to a lunatic asylum or that she had died. In fact, she merely shunned publicity and traveled quietly with her husband.

In her greatest success, *The Mysteries of Udolpho* (1794), Mrs. Radcliffe employs the familiar accoutrements of her novels and, indeed, of all Gothic novels: a mood of mounting terror and dread amidst unrelentingly bleak, brooding geography. Set in a castle that has hidden passageways behind secret sliding panels, it is a tale of a beautiful heroine persecuted by a series of abductions and threats of violent death and the torments of inexplicable terrors. The heroine ultimately escapes unharmed, and her torturers are vanquished, much like all Gothic fiction of the time.

[229]

While "Monk" Lewis and Horace Walpole and the other giants of the Gothic era permitted supernatural occurrences to permeate their work, or at the very least failed to explain apparently occult events in a rational way and thereby left implicit the presence of ghosts and other creatures of a darker world, *The Mysteries of Udolpho* broke away from this long-established precedent by carefully providing a natural explanation for the eeriest of events. Her other works, too, relied on rational explanations for seemingly inexplicable occurrences, most of which have befallen the heavily beleaguered heroines. While these explanations were often far-fetched, stretched credulity, or relied on coincidence or inspired guesswork, they were always the result of human intervention and deduction, thereby taking a huge step down the path toward the pure detective novel.

Another giant step taken by Mrs. Radcliffe is evident in *The Italian* (1797), in which the denouement of the mystery is presented in a dialogue between two people. The same device is used to advance the plot throughout the long story. Just as in the dialogue between Dupin and his chronicler, between Holmes and Watson, and between countless other detective teams, the more perceptive and intelligent person takes the time to explain the course of events to a slower, generally perplexed person, helping the reader to fathom the mysterious goings-on.

William Godwin's *Things as They Are; or, The Adventures of Caleb Williams* (1794) was published in the same year as *The Mysteries of Udolpho* and makes as great a stride in the direction of genuine detection as that book, albeit from a very different perspective. Mrs. Radcliffe was already involved in the tale of mystery and changed its format somewhat. Godwin wrote a political and social tract in the form of a novel, using it purely to make a philosophical point. Julian Symons and others often regard this as the first detective novel—an ironic situation since its viewpoint is diametrically opposite that of virtually every detective story which followed. In *Caleb Williams*, the law is depicted as an instrument of evil, the ultimate example of the in-

[230]

justice of any social system in which all men are not precisely equal.

In this novel, the kindly Ferdinando Falkland is accused of murdering his tyrannical neighbor. Although all suspicion is instantly directed at him, he is quickly acquitted when the murder weapon, a knife, is discovered to belong to another man, Hawkins, and his son. They are tried, found guilty, and executed summarily, after which Falkland's personality transmogrifies. Caleb Williams, his secretary, is convinced that his employer is the true murderer and he sets out to prove his theory. When Falkland falsely accuses him of theft and has him imprisoned, Williams is forced to escape and charges his employer with murder. His search for clues, his careful observation, the very rational deductions he elicits from the evidence, forces Falkland into a confession, giving weight to an argument for the acknowledgment of Williams as the first amateur detective in literature.

An interesting sidelight and probable precedent is that Godwin wrote the third book of this three-volume novel last, a popularly accepted method of creativity for detective fiction writers ever since.

Godwin had tremendous influence on the first American novelist whose sole profession was writing: Charles Brockden Brown. Most of Brown's novels are tales of mystery and terror but his major work is *Wieland; or, The Transformation* (1798), generally regarded as the first American Gothic novel. A man hears a strange voice commanding him to commit murder and, eventually, in the certain belief that the voice is the voice of God, he is driven to the act. In a denouement employed not infrequently by subsequent writers of mystery fiction, it is learned that the murder plot had been accomplished by a ventriloquist.

Another American, William Leggett, a friend and associate of William Cullen Bryant, produced a short story in 1827 which is as near as one can imagine to the pure detective story in form and intent. "The Rifle" was published prior to Christmas of 1827 (although it is dated 1828, as was the publishing custom of the day), anonymously as "by the author of *Leisure Hours at*

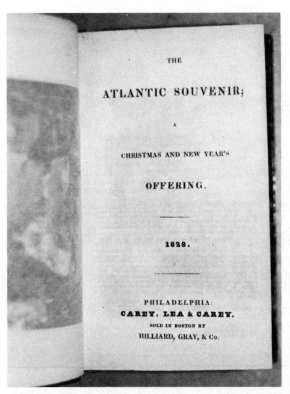

The title page of The Atlantic Souvenir; A Christmas and New Year's Offering *for 1828, in which William Leggett's anonymous story "The Rifle" first appeared.*

Sea'' in *The Atlantic Souvenir.* In this largely forgotten work, Dr. Charles Rivington is accused of murdering an old hunter, Mr. Silversight, and the evidence is overwhelmingly against him, so he is sentenced to be hanged. Another young hunter, Jim Buckhorn, decides to clear the accused man, partly as a method of winning the affections of a girl. He succeeds in breaking the alibi of the genuine killer and proves his guilt by intelligent deductions in ballistics.

The same year in which "The Rifle" was issued also produced

[232]

RICHMOND;

OR,

SCENES

IN THE

LIFE OF A BOW STREET OFFICER.

DRAWN UP FROM HIS PRIVATE MEMORANDA.

Some be'th of war, and some of woe,
And some of fun and fudge also,
Some of escapes, and guile, and death;
Also of love forsooth there be'th.

LE FRÈNE.

IN THREE VOLUMES.

VOL. I.

LONDON:

HENRY COLBURN, NEW BURLINGTON STREET.

1827.

Richmond; or, Scenes in the Life of a Bow Street Officer, Drawn Up from His Private Memoranda, *is one of the rarest titles in the mystery fiction world. The title page of the first edition gives no clue to the identity of the author.*

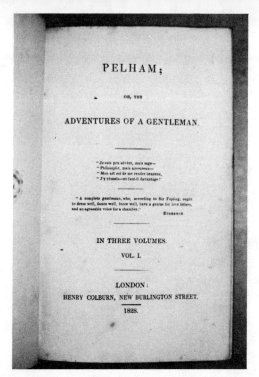

The title page of the first edition of Pelham *by Sir Edward Bulwer-Lytton.*

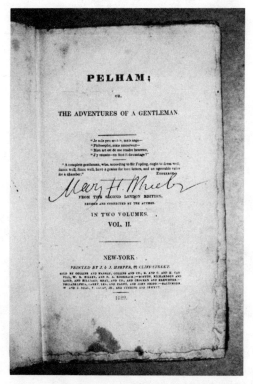

The title page of the first American edition of Pelham, *published a year later than the first English edition.*

a purportedly factual account of real-life crimes encountered by an officer in the precursor of Scotland Yard's force, the loosely held together Bow Street Runners. Nevertheless, it is impossible to believe the veracity of *Richmond; or, Scenes in the Life of a Bow Street Officer, Drawn Up from His Private Memoranda* (1827). The exaggerated feats of courage and intellect, the melodramatic narrative and absurd dialogue, are so obviously fictional that the work must be regarded as a further step in the development of the detective story. Published anonymously, it was attributed for many years to Thomas Gaspey, until E. F. Bleiler, in a scholarly introduction to a new edition published in 1976 by Dover, offered evidence to throw doubt on the authorship.

The next figure to participate significantly in the evolution of the detective novel is Sir Edward Bulwer-Lytton, whose most famous book is *The Last Days of Pompeii* but whose most important contribution to English literature is *Pelham; or, The Adventures of a Gentleman* (1828), which follows (or, rather, establishes) the classic lines of the modern detective novel in nearly every respect.

The hero is involved in a long series of exciting adventures, one of which is a murder mystery. When his friend is unjustly arrested for committing murder, Pelham requests and is granted two days to prove the innocence of the imprisoned man or to find the actual villain. In the time-honored tradition of such tales, he begins a systematic investigation and quickly learns that the true murderer is the head of a London criminal gang. Enlisting the aid of a gang member, he is taken to the scene of the crime, arranges to take possession of the murder weapon, and brings it to court, dramatically freeing his friend. Pelham, through a series of investigative procedures, has tracked down the murderer and brought him to justice, complete with incriminating evidence, making him in many ways the most complete detective hero in a novel to that time.

A later Bulwer-Lytton novel, *Eugene Aram* (1832), introduces

[235]

an amateur detective who seeks to solve the crime that was based on an actual murder mystery of the day. The real-life murderer and the fictional one had the same name—an unusual procedure even in those days before libel laws were as stringent as today.

The law was held in small regard by François Eugène Vidocq during his years as one of France's most notorious criminals. After serving a substantial jail term, he offered his services to Napoleon Bonaparte (chiefly as an informer), who made him the first head of the Paris police department, the Sûreté. He hired other criminals and ex-convicts for his staff and maintained a law enforcement agency of extremely questionable practice. His resignation was finally forced by his superior and he opened a private practice, continuing to use the same dubious methods and techniques with which he had operated the official police department. Harassed by the authorities, he was ultimately driven from practice and died impoverished.

In the meantime, however, he had produced his autobiography, *Mémoires de Vidocq* (1828–29), a ghost-written, highly sensationalized account of his years as a fighter of crime. So many of the cases were obviously of a fictional nature, and those which were true were magnified so greatly that it was impossible to determine where truth ended and fiction began, that the book is now accepted matter-of-factly as a work of fiction in all circles but the most gullible.

The character of Vidocq so appealed to Honoré de Balzac that he contrived to meet him, became his friend, and used him as a character in several novels, the criminal Vautrin.

Balzac ambitiously planned to write the complete social history of France as his enormous literary undertaking. He produced more than ninety novels and tales to which he gave the collective name *La Comédie Humaine* (*The Human Comedy*), and most of them dealt with crime and criminals and the underside of society. Like many other authors of his day, he used his literature as a platform for his philosophy, and twisted the social landscape so that criminals became the heroes and the sympathetic characters

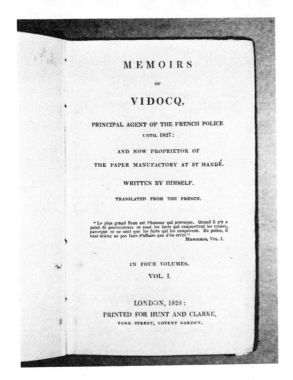

MEMOIRS

OF

VIDOCQ,

PRINCIPAL AGENT OF THE FRENCH POLICE
UNTIL 1827:

AND NOW PROPRIETOR OF
THE PAPER MANUFACTORY AT ST MANDÉ.

WRITTEN BY HIMSELF.

TRANSLATED FROM THE FRENCH.

" Le plus grand fléau est l'homme qui provoque. Quand il n'y a
point de provocateurs ce sont les forts qui commettent les crimes,
parceque ce ne sont que les forts qui les conçoivent. En police, il
vaut mieux ne pas faire d'affaire que d'en créer."
MÉMOIRES, VOL. I.

IN FOUR VOLUMES.
VOL. I.

LONDON, 1828:
PRINTED FOR HUNT AND CLARKE,
YORK STREET, COVENT GARDEN.

The first English edition of Vidocq's Memoirs, *in four volumes,*
in the original boards.

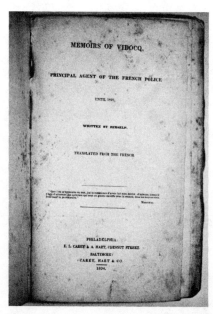

The title page of the very rare first American edition of Vidocq's Memoirs, *published in one large volume.*

while the police were depicted as villains. Unintentionally and ironically, the police officer who pursues and ultimately captures Vautrin, M. Gondureau, bears a remarkable similarity to the real-life Vidocq and has his title, Chef de Sûreté.

Balzac's best-known work in this style is *Le Père Goriot* (1834–35), translated variously as *Daddy Goriot, Father Goriot, Old Man Goriot*, which is largely devoted to the efforts of Gondureau to capture Vautrin, and the criminal's attempts to avoid imprisonment. The methods of modern police procedure are evident throughout, with such techniques as inductive reasoning, surveillance, and deducing significant information from apparently trivial clues. Like later detective novelists, Balzac displays no reluctance in having his detective stop in the middle of the action to deliver a lecture on a scientific or other esoteric subject in a demonstration of his erudition. Also, *Le Père Goriot* is a seminal work in that it is with this book that Balzac determined to have his characters appear in subsequent books with regularity, even rewriting sections of previous books so that their lives and characters would be woven entirely throughout *The Human Comedy*. This innovative concept has been followed to this day by writers of mysteries, whose detective heroes solve case after case in book after book. Even Poe immediately recognized the advantages of again using familiar characters who were successful in earlier works.

It is pehaps fitting that the last steps toward the creation of the pure detective story were taken by one of America's greatest literary figures, Nathaniel Hawthorne. Several stories in *Twice-Told Tales* (1837) are mystery and riddle puzzles, the most notable of which, "Mr. Higginbotham's Catastrophe," received ardent praise from Poe himself.

Mystery, crime, suspense, deduction are all factors in many of the greatest literary works of all time, and one or more of them are elements in virtually every well-turned story encountered in life, beginning with fairy tales (think for a moment of the murders, thefts, kidnappings, and other serious crimes in such tales as "Little Red Riding Hood," "Hansel and Gretel," and "Jack and the Beanstalk") and continuing through oral and written narratives of every kind. And their enduring attraction is the unending battle between the forces of Good and Evil, never more clearly defined than in the classic detective story.

Poe defined the genre, established its boundaries, and set a level of distinction for subsequent writers that has rarely been equalled. If "The Murders in the Rue Morgue" is not the most important piece of fiction ever published, it is worthy of the most extraordinary affection. As Dr. A. S. W. Rosenbach, the noted bibliophile, collector, and bookseller once wrote, "If I am found dead with a book in my pocket, I hope it will be the first edition of 'The Murders in the Rue Morgue.'"

APPENDIX

The ten most significant works in the development of detective fiction prior to the publication of Edgar Allan Poe's "The Murders in the Rue Morgue" in 1841.

1. Voltaire

A. First Edition: *Memnon, Histoire orientale.* Paris, 1747.

B. Second Edition: *Zadig; ou, La Destinée. Histoire orientale.* Nancy: Leseure, 1748.

C. First English Edition: *Zadig; or, The Book of Fate.* London: Brindley, 1749.

D. First American Edition: *Miscellanies* (third part). Philadelphia: Bell, 1778.

2. William Godwin

A. First Edition: *Things as They Are; or, The Adventures of Caleb Williams.* London: Crosby, 1794; 3 volumes.

B. First American Edition: (same title). Philadelphia: Rices, 1795; 2 volumes.

3. Ann Radcliffe

A. First Edition: *The Mysteries of Udolpho.* London: Wogan, 1794; 3 volumes.

B. First American Edition: (same title). Boston: Etheridge, printed for (several booksellers); 1785; 3 volumes.

4. Charles Brockden Brown

A. First Edition: *Wieland; or, The Transformation.* New York: Caritat, 1798.

B. First English Edition: (same title). London: Henry Colburn, 1811.

5. Anonymous

A. First Edition: *Richmond; or, Scenes in the Life of a Bow Street Officer, Drawn Up from His Private Memoranda.* London: Henry Colburn, 1827; 3 volumes.

B. First American Edition: (same title). New York: J. & J. Harper, 1827; 2 volumes.

6. William Leggett

A. First Edition: "The Rifle" contained in *The Atlantic Souvenir: A Christmas and New Year's Offering, 1828.* Philadelphia: Carey, Lea & Carey, 1828 (actually 1827).

B. Second Edition: "The Rifle" contained in *Tales and Sketches. By a Country Schoolmaster.* New York: J. & J. Harper, 1829.

7. Sir Edward Bulwer-Lytton

A. First Edition: *Pelham; or, The Adventures of a Gentleman.* London: Henry Colburn, 1828; 3 volumes.

B. First American Edition: (same title). New York: J. & J. Harper, 1829; 2 volumes.

8. François Eugène Vidocq

A. First Edition: *Mémoires de Vidocq, Chef de la Police de Sûreté jusqu'en 1827.* Paris: Tenon, 1828–29; 4 volumes.

B. First English Edition: *Memoirs of Vidocq, Principal Agent of the French Police Until 1827.* London: Hunt & Clarke, 1828 (first volume); London: Whittaker, Treacher & Arnot, 1829 (volumes 2–4): 4 volumes.

C. First American Edition: (same title). Philadelphia: E. L. Carey and A. Hart; Baltimore: Carey & Hart, 1834.

9. Honoré de Balzac

A. First Edition: *Le Père Goriot.* Paris, 1834–35.

B. First English Edition: *Daddy Goriot; or, Unrequited Affection.* London: Ward & Lock, 1860.

C. First American Edition: *Father Goriot; or, Scenes of Life in Paris.* New York: J. Winchester, n.d.

10. Nathaniel Hawthorne

A. First Edition: *Twice-Told Tales.* Boston: American Stationers Co., John B. Russell, 1837.

BIBLIOGRAPHY

Frank W. Chandler, *The Literature of Roguery* (Boston: Houghton, Mifflin, 1907); 2 volumes.

Allen J. Hubin, *The Bibliography of Crime Fiction, 1749–1975* (Del Mar, Calif.: Publisher's Inc., 1978).

A. E. Murch, *The Development of the Detective Novel* (London: Peter Owen, revised edition, 1968).

Ellery Queen, *The Detective Short Story* (Boston: Little, Brown, 1942).

——, *Queen's Quorum* (Boston: Little, Brown, 1951).

Chris Steinbrunner and Otto Penzler, *Encyclopedia of Mystery and Detection* (New York: McGraw-Hill, 1975).

Julian Symons, *Bloody Murder* (London: Faber & Faber, 1972).

ROGER N. MOHOVICH *is the Newspaper Librarian of The New-York Historical Society. In addition to newspapers, he collects posters, books, music, and other materials relating to the home front of World Wars I and II.*

Early American Newspapers: A Brief Guide to the First One-hundred Seventy-five Years

Roger N. Mohovich

UNLIKE BOOKS, PAMPHLETS, AND OTHER PRINTED MATERIALS, the American newspaper gives the scholar and collector a direct, undiluted link to the past. No other printed artifact lends such a sense of immediacy and reality to the study of those once current events now called history. In addition to providing the modern reader with a wealth of historical minutiae, it gives him a delightful way to learn and understand the day-to-day existence of those so far removed from us in time and temperament. Clarence Brigham, the bibliographer and historian of journalism, once said: "If all the printed sources of history for a certain century or decade had to be destroyed save one, that which could be chosen with the greatest value to posterity would be a file of an important newspaper.''

The importance of newspapers to scholarship is readily recognized and many institutions have actively acquired newspapers for many decades. As early as 1812, the year of the founding of The American Antiquarian Society, newspapers were considered an integral part of the collections and were avidly collected by Isaiah Thomas, the founder of the Society and himself an important figure in early American journalism. Other institutions which have assembled important collections include The New-York Historical Society, Library of Congress, New York Public Library, Harvard University, and the State Historical Society of Wisconsin.

Newspapers have fared less well, however, as desired objects of pursuit by serious private collectors. While most of the great collections of Americana did include some newspapers, these were included because they were printed documents of great historic interest, and their format as newspapers was incidental.

Within the last several years there has been what one might call a great re-evaluation and discovery of all aspects of our printed past. Newspapers have ceased to be dismissed as merely ephemera, and have begun to be recognized by the dealer and collector as meriting serious study and consideration.

THE ANCESTRAL BEGINNINGS

THE first true newspapers—that is, publications containing relatively current and topical information and appearing on a more or less regular basis—originated in the early part of the seventeenth century in Germany, Holland, and Antwerp. What is thought to be the first was the *Nieuwe Tijdinghen* published in Antwerp in 1605. It apparently grew from a commercial bulletin which circulated among merchants. Merchants and traders were the chief subscribers to these early newspapers, which flourished in centers of commerce such as Venice and Amsterdam. Other newspapers first began in Germany (1609), Switzerland (1610), Austria (1620), France (1631), and Italy (1636).

The early newspapers were published by and for the mercantile classes and contained commercial and political news of interest to them. These papers contained almost nothing that was not of economic interest, and the closest modern equivalents in content and readership would be business newspapers such as *The Wall Street Journal* and, more closely, the various trade newsletters published for the exclusive use of industry such as *Oil Week* and *Electronic News*.

The first English newspaper appeared in 1621 and was printed by a London stationer, Thomas Archer. It was an unauthorized publication and Archer was imprisoned. Nathaniel Butter was given a license later in the year to print translations of Dutch "corantos" (currents of news), and he is regarded as the father of English journalism. His paper was entitled *Corante, or newes from Italy, Germany, Hungarie, Spaine and France* (1621). In 1622 he also published a series called *Weekly Newes* which, although numbered and dated, appeared only irregularly as it had to rely for its news on the boats from Europe which arrived unpredictably. These early newspapers were highly censored, particularly with respect to the domestic news they were allowed to print. An apparent partiality by these early English papers toward the anti-imperial forces during the Thirty Years War displeased Charles I and they were consequently banned by decree of Star Chamber from October 1632 to December 1638.

With the abolition of the Star Chamber in 1641, newspapers began to appear again and domestic news became a regular feature. They took on a more modern format by the elimination of the bookish title page and blank verso. Now the news appeared under the title on the first page, and these papers were issued with greater regularity. New titles flourished, although most were "occasionals" printed to report the Civil War. There were also many propaganda newspapers published during this time.

[245]

Under Cromwell only two official papers were permitted, *Mercurius Politicus* and the *Publick Intelligencer* (Milton briefly edited the former). With the coming of the Restoration, other official papers took their place, eventually succeeded by the *London Gazette* (1665) which continues to this day, although now it contains only official announcements and appointments.

In the 1690s other newspapers began, including the first provincial paper, the *Worcester Post Man* (1690), and *Lloyd's News* (1696), a single-sheet paper containing shipping news which later grew into *Lloyd's List and Shipping Gazette*. This still exists and is London's oldest newspaper. Scotland also started a newspaper, the *Edinburgh Gazette* (1699). About this time improvements in the postal system created a steady supply of news and the first dailies were started. The first was *The Daily Courant* (1702) which appeared in London. It consisted largely of reports extracted from foreign journals. Daniel Defoe began a triweekly *Review* (1704) which contained opinions on political topics, thus beginning the practice of publishing editorials. Two other journals of this period, *The Tatler* (1709) and *The Spectator* (1711), published respectively by Sir Richard Steele and by Steele and Joseph Addison, contained social and artistic news.

THE COLONIAL PERIOD

THE first American newspaper was entitled *Publick Occurences Both Foreign and Domestic*. It was published by Benjamin Harris in Boston on September 25, 1690 and promptly suppressed by the Royal Governor and Council of Massachusetts. They held that it had been published "Without the least Privity or countenance of Authority," in addition to containing "Reflections of a very high nature; as also sundry doubtful and uncertain Reports." Doubtless the reflections which caused annoyance to the government were passages which contained gossip about the immoralities of the King of France and those which questioned the barbarous way the Indian allies of the English had treated some French captives.

[246]

Benjamin Harris was a London bookseller and publisher who had come to Boston in 1686. In London he was a Whig publisher and had played a prominent part in publicizing Titus Oates' allegations in the Popish Plot. Harris' newspaper, the (London) *Domestick Intelligence*, "exposed" the so-called plot and helped lead the persecution of the supposed incendiarists. Harris was later arrested for printing a seditious pamphlet and was sentenced to the pillory and prison. He fled England a few years after his release, taking with him wife, children, and a stock of books with which he began a bookstore and coffeehouse in Boston. He prospered by printing almanacs and one of America's first best-sellers, *The New England Primer*. Harris returned to England four years after *Publick Occurences* and started several other newspapers, but his wealth and fame diminished. It is not known when he died.

Only one original issue of *Publick Occurences* is known to exist. It is now in the British Public Records Office. The original consisted of three pages, 6 × 9½ inches. The fourth page was left blank to permit items to be added by hand when the paper was sent to distant friends. It was unusual among all the early American newspapers in that it contained more local stories and "hard news" than those which followed it.

It was not until fourteen years after *Publick Occurences* that another newspaper was attempted. *The Boston News-Letter* began publishing on April 24, 1704 and became the first continuous American newspaper. It was published by John Campbell, a postmaster and bookseller who had gained experience in gathering and disseminating news by writing manuscript newsletters and sending them to the governors and important merchants of the other colonies. The printed *News-Letter* was issued weekly, numbered and dated, and although its page size was slightly larger than *Publick Occurences* it contained only two pages. Campbell advertised that those who wished might subscribe to a copy on a full sheet of writing paper which would result in a newspaper with two additional blank pages for personal correspondence.

[247]

The first issue of the first continuous American newspaper.

The news contained in an average issue was taken largely from London newspapers or from the items reported by the captains of the ships which arrived in Boston Harbor. Campbell occasionally received letters from correspondents but these were irregular communications. Most of the news was about England and important items from Europe. English political developments and court news were of interest to the American reader. Occasionally there were brief items on political appointments, Indian affairs, ship arrivals, and major disasters. Maritime news was always an important feature in most of the newspapers in the coastal cities for the next hundred years, after which they tended to specialize either along commercial or political lines. Campbell achieved a circulation for his newspaper of about 250 to 300. An issue cost two pence a copy, or twelve shillings a year, delivered.

On December 21, 1719, a third Boston newspaper was begun, *The Boston Gazette.* It was started by William Brooker, who succeeded Campbell as postmaster of Boston. Brooker apparently

[248]

regarded the publication of the *News-Letter* as the function and domain of the postmaster, but when Campbell left the postmastership he took the paper with him and Brooker began his own. The *Gazette* continued to be edited by the next five postmasters of Boston.

A day after *The Boston Gazette* was first published, Andrew Bradford began publishing *The American Weekly Mercury* in Philadelphia, thus beginning the first newspaper outside of Boston and the third continuously published in America. Newspapers appeared in the other colonies slowly over the next forty years: New York (1725); Maryland (1727); South Carolina (1732); Virginia (1736); North Carolina (1751); Connecticut (1755); New Hampshire (1756); Rhode Island (1762); and Georgia (1763). By 1765, the year of the Stamp Act and the end of the era of newspaper innocence, twenty-three newspapers were being published in all the colonies. Almost as many were started but did not survive.

The typical newspaper of the larger cities during this early period consisted of four pages, each measuring about 10 × 15 inches. Occasionally an additional two or four pages were issued

Two typically elaborate "carriers' addresses" dating from the middle of the nineteenth century.

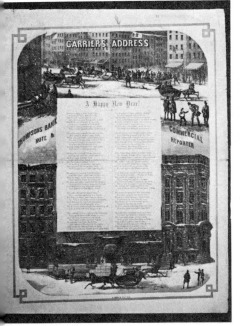

A group of colonial newspapers representing over half the colonies.
The Connecticut Courant *continues to this day as* The Hartford
Courant.

to accommodate extra advertising. Most of the materials used in the production of the newspapers—paper, ink, type, and presses—were imported from England. The paper was usually a rough, coarse rag stock which tended to act as a blotter, thus imparting a crude look and feel to most of the newspapers. This rag paper has proved to be far more durable than the newsprint in use today.

The average circulation at this time was usually a few hundred. The journalism historian Frank Luther Mott suggests that five per cent of the white families in the colonies in 1765 received a newspaper weekly, but it must be remembered that each newspaper may have been read in coffee houses and other public places by dozens of people and then sent to distant friends. Occasionally one comes across a colonial newspaper which has been folded, handled, and read to illegibility. The paper was distributed in town by a carrier, probably the printer's apprentice. On New Year's Day the carrier was allowed to plead for favors on his route by delivering to his patrons a broadside known as a "carrier's address." These addresses, written in doggerel, recounted the news of the year just past and invariably ended with a plea for a gift. Carriers' addresses continued to be published yearly by virtually every newspaper until the late nineteenth century. Many, particularly those of the big city giants, became a printer's *tour de force* embellished with every conceivable ornament.

Postriders carried the newspapers out of town, occasionally delivering issues to subscribers along the way. Printers in other cities freely borrowed material from out-of-town newspapers for use in their own papers, usually without attribution, this being another practice which continued until well into the nineteenth century.

During the period 1765–1783, from the Stamp Act to the end of the Revolution, American newspapers became for the first time highly politicized, and newspaper proprietors began to shift their news and opinions to either pro- or anti-English sentiments. News from London, still a staple feature of most papers, began to share the page with articles dealing with growing anti-British feeling. The Stamp Act was passed by Parliament in March 1765, and was to take effect the following November. It stated that all newspapers as well as books, legal documents, etc., were to be printed on special stamped paper which carried a special tax. The tax for newspapers was a half penny for a two-page paper and a full penny for four pages. In addition there was a tax of two shillings for each advertisement. It was outrageously high, almost fifty per cent of the price of some papers, and the colonies for the first time were united in opposition, less against the tax itself than against their lack of representation in Parliament.

The colonial printers, having at their disposal the means to express their feelings, did so. Newspapers reprinted in full accounts of meetings of colonial legislatures and lesser bodies to protest against the Act. Letters to the editor and other anti-tax statements were widely distributed. The papers also printed the names of the tax collectors and then gleefully reported stories of their harassment. When the stamped paper arrived there were several stories, widely reprinted, of mobs destroying it. Not one newspaper printed on stamped papers when the act went into effect on November 1st. Several printed defiantly as before, others explained that they were justified in using unstamped paper out of fear for life and property. *The Pennsylvania Journal* and *The Pennsylvania Gazette* printed their last issues before the tax in mourning for themselves, saying that they would have to suspend publication "in order to deliberate, whether any Methods can be found to elude the chains forged for us." These methods were soon found and the papers resumed on November 21, 1765.

A few papers evaded the requirements of the Stamp Act by changing their titles or by removing their serial numbering. This changed their status to broadsides. The most famous of these, *The New-York Mercury*, became the "No Stamped Paper to be Had." Some papers suspended for varying periods. The Stamp Act, thus rendered impotent, was repealed the following March. The first battle of the War for Independence had been won in part by the colonial press.

Two colonial reactions to the Stamp Act: the New-York Gazette *in mourning, and the former* New-York Mercury.

Leading this and ensuing assaults was *The Boston Gazette*, published by two radicals, Benjamin Edes and John Gill. Their newspaper contained the most vitriolic attacks on the Stamp Act as well as the Townshend Acts that followed. There were hundreds of letters, essays, and other contributions written (usually over a pen name) by Samuel and John Adams, John Hancock, James Otis, and others, who formed what was known as the Caucus Club in the office of the *Gazette*. Editorial policy of the newspaper was apparently decided by these men, particularly Sam Adams, and by 1768 the *Gazette* was broaching the subject of independence. Even the possibility of warfare was discussed in its columns by 1772. Tradition has it that the members of the Boston Tea-Party put on their Indian disguises in the office of the *Gazette*.

Following the outbreak of hostilities several newspapers had a very difficult time and were under assault either by occupying

[253]

British forces or outraged townspeople of both factions. Upon the occupation of New York, for instance, three of the four newspapers then publishing fled to outlying regions to publish, and one shut down completely. One paper, *The New-York Journal*, removed to Kingston, New York, after being chased around Connecticut for a few months. It was published there for fifteen weeks until the British captured Kingston. The paper then fled to Poughkeepsie where it published erratically due to lack of supplies. It returned again to New York in 1783. The most famous of the newspapers that supported the Royalist cause was published by James Rivington, a New York bookseller, and called *Rivington's New-York Gazetteer, or the Connecticut, New Jersey, Hudson's River, and Quebec Weekly Advertiser.* It was a handsome, large, and well-printed newspaper and it circulated in all the colonies, the West Indies, and the British Isles. Its Tory arguments irritated many patriots, however, and in April 1775 Rivington was hanged in effigy in New Brunswick. Rivington published a woodcut of the hanging along with a declaration denouncing "certain demagogues" who would not permit opposing viewpoints to be published. Twice that year his office was mobbed. During the second time the plant was destroyed and the paper was suspended. Rivington was later arrested by the patriots and forced to sign a loyalty oath to the Continental Congress, but he soon fled to England. He returned to New York during the occupation where he published a Royal Gazette under various titles. Unfortunately these journals were more propaganda sheets than newspapers, and were known commonly as "Rivington's Lying Gazette." He remained in New York after the end of the war and ran a bookstore.

AFTER THE REVOLUTION

FOLLOWING the close of the Revolution two developments occurred which changed the role of newspapers greatly: the focusing of a newspaper's outlook along political, mercantile, or other areas of special interest; and the rise of the daily paper.

The political turmoil of the Revolution divided printers into pro- or anti-British camps. The use of a newspaper as a constant vehicle of opinion had begun. Printers, ever aware of the effects of the printed word, now became aware of the power they could exercise. Even more significant was the realization that a newspaper did not have to be the vehicle of just one man but could become the chief organ of an entire interest group.

There were several major issues which had to be discussed by the young nation. Most important was the new Constitution. The first public printing appeared in the *Pennsylvania Packet and Daily Advertiser* for September 19, 1787.

The ensuing debate created the first major ideological division in the country. The Federalists fought for ratification and the Anti-Federalists fought against.

The most eloquent arguments for ratification were those first printed in *The Independent New York Journal*, and then throughout the country, written by Hamilton, Madison, and Jay, under the title of "The Federalist." One of the most important pieces of political writing in American history, its appearance first in a newspaper attests the growing importance of newspapers as a forum for rapid communication. There were less eloquent statements during the debate. At least one anti-ratification press, that of Thomas Greenleaf's *The New York Journal*, was destroyed. A rare newspaper cartoon of the period showed the nation as a Grecian edifice being propped up by pillars representing each state as they one by one ratified the Constitution.

Other major issues which were exhaustively discussed in the press were this nation's relationships with France and England, and the assumption by the federal government of the debt incurred by the states during the Revolution. Fortunately for the tender nation the election of the first President was never the subject of debate. Washington's selection was done by electors with the whole-hearted support of the press and people. It was not until the elections of 1796 and 1800 that not only ideas but people and personalities were at issue. Newspapers began to have names which expressed their political leanings. Titles with words like "Republican" and "Federalist" were common.

The American editorial, as such, began in the late 1790s in Noah Webster's *American Minerva* (New York, 1793). Before that, opinions were expressed as letters signed by pen names, or in comments placed after a news story, or by reprinting letters from other papers. Now, on an inside page under the heading of the paper's name there were a few paragraphs or columns of comment by the editor.

The second great development of this period is the rise of the daily newspaper in America (London had its first in 1702). Once again it was the mercantilists who created the demand. The traders and merchants of the eastern cities no longer traded primarily with a mother country. Their markets were now the entire world. The rapidly expanding trade possibilities created a demand for a constant update of shipping news, notices of newly arrived goods, etc. The daily paper filled that need.

The New-York Daily Advertiser (1785) was New York's first successful daily newspaper. Of its four 14" × 20" pages, three were nothing but advertisements, mostly of goods just arrived from abroad or other American cities. There was a column or two of shipping news so that traders would know if the ships upon which they had placed their cargo had reached their destinations, and a column or so of general news with a usual dose of editorial opinion. Its price, six cents a copy, limited its readership to the wealthy traders, but it was, after all, founded and printed for them. The political dailies which began later in the '90s were cheaper. By 1810 there were six dailies in New York, five in Baltimore, and six in Philadelphia, each one providing a constant source of opinion and information, and each day increasing the power of the newspaper as an institutional force in American life.

By the early 1830s several developments had occurred in the newspaper industry which combined to revolutionize completely the entire concept of news and its delivery. Improvements in paper-making reduced the price of newsprint considerably, and

[256]

steam-powered presses enabled a printer to produce a large quantity of newspapers cheaply and quickly. The chief beneficiary of these technological achievements was a new type of newspaper: flippant, brash, and, relative to the established papers, exceedingly common—the penny daily.

The first successful penny daily in America was *The Sun* which began publishing in New York on September 3, 1833. It was created (largely for profit) by Benjamin H. Day, a printer and journalist who had learned the newspaper trade while working in Massachusetts for *The Springfield Republican*. It was an instant success, achieving circulations of 5,000 in four months, 10,000 in a little over a year, and 15,000 within two years, at that time the highest in America and the third highest in the world. Its immediate popularity was caused by a combination of cheap price, a breezy and entertaining style of writing, and the heavy

Two cents' worth of penny dailies.

reporting of stories about crime, sex, local events, and human interest. Never before had an American newspaper successfully been able to appeal to the less exalted interests of the average reader, and it created dozens of imitators in every city.

The first issue of *The Sun* was four pages, each measuring about 8 × 11 inches and containing three columns. It greatly increased in size over the next few years but its contents did not alter. A major portion of each edition was crime news and police-court reports which were presented to the reader virtually as theater. Other local news also tended to emphasize the bizarre and the sensational. For the first time it became the business of news to amuse. This was a great revolution in American newspapers. Theretofore only matters which had obvious importance and significance were considered news. Now, anything was news if it elicited a smirk, a sneer, or, most important, a penny.

Not only did these newspapers speak to the common man, they spoke for him as well. The first "working-man's" newspapers appeared during this time and these began to add their powerful voice to the cause of labor reform. They had such names as *The Man* (New York, 1834), *Workingman's Advocate* (Rochester, 1840), and the *Workingman's Friend* (Boston, 1840). Although the daily and weekly mercantilist and political newspapers still were the most powerful and influential in this pre–Civil War period, the labor-oriented press helped to identify the needs and aspirations of the lower economic classes. The political ramifications were not to be felt until much later, but a solid foundation of communication and expression had been laid.

Other groups too began to be heard through the press. The first newspaper published by and for blacks was the *Freedom's Journal* (New York, 1827). It was devoted to abolition, as were all of the black papers including the famous *The North Star* (Rochester, 1847), published by Frederic Douglass, the noted abolitionist. The growing numbers of immigrants required many newspapers printed in foreign languages, and although the first were printed by Benjamin Franklin and others in Pennsylvania in the 1730s for the large German-speaking populations there,

A representative sampling of the early American foreign-language press.

it was in the first half of the nineteenth century that the foreign-language press really began. By 1860 there were American newspapers printed in many languages, including German, French, Italian, Spanish, Welsh, Czech, and several others. The first newspaper in America printed in Chinese appeared as early as 1854 in San Francisco. Even English-speaking immigrants had their own newspapers with titles like *Scottish American Journal*, *Irish-American*, etc. In all of these immigrant papers news from the home country naturally played a prominent part.

Westward expansion and settlement was also responsible for a great increase in the number of new newspapers. It seemed that a newspaper appeared within weeks of the founding of a new town. There were economic and political motives for the rapid growth of the press. A new town needed a printed "booster" to be sent back East to keep the flow of settlers coming, and competing political interests had to be sure that new settlers in emerging states were given proper political information. It was not unusual for communities of only a few hundred to have at least two weekly newspapers of opposite political opinion.

Religious newspapers also contributed to the growth of the press. While they tended to stress the spiritual over the temporal in their choice of topics, some, like the famous Mormon paper, *The Deseret News* (Utah, 1850) were the first newspapers in many localities.

The first Sunday newspapers were weeklies, published either on Sunday or on Saturday for Sunday reading. Usually they contained miscellaneous short stories and other light reading suitable for a leisurely day of rest. There was little "hard news" in them. The first Sunday edition of a daily newspaper was attempted by James Gordon Bennett with the *Sunday Herald* in 1835. It was not accepted by the public and Bennett had to discontinue publication. After a few more attempts he succeeded in 1841 in establishing a regular Sunday edition of his *Morning Herald* which proved very successful, exceeding even the weekday circulations.

There were other reasons besides cheapness, simplicity, and the narrowed interests of newspapers to account for the great increase in readership in the twenty-five years prior to the Civil War. America's population almost tripled during this period, public education brought the rate of illiteracy down to about 10 per cent, and a new democratic tradition created a nation in which a man took his politics seriously. Newspapers were the main printed source of both political information and zeal. Women, too, formed a large part of the newspaper-reading public.

The two major news stories of this period were the Mexican War of 1846–47 and the intensifying debate on slavery. From a journalistic standpoint the Mexican War is important because modern war reporting began during this period. Possibly due to the appeal of war news to the penny daily reader, and also as the result of competition among the papers in any particular city for the earliest and best news, a few northern newspapers (from different cities, of course) combined to pay for express services to bring the news rapidly from the war zone itself or from the city closest to it, New Orleans. In a sense, New Orleans had the responsibility to report the Mexican War to the rest of the nation, as its newspapers were the ones expected to report it most thoroughly. The nine daily newspapers in New Orleans were fiercely competitive and each had at least one correspondent at the front. No longer would newspapers rely on letters from the battlefields or official dispatches for their war stories. It now became the duty of the newspaper to be an eyewitness observer of the actual events and to report them as quickly and accurately as possible.

A selection of black and abolitionist newspapers.

The anti-slavery crusade was advanced by several big-city newspapers, and these were led and influenced by the daily and weekly editions of Horace Greeley's *New York Tribune*. The *Tribune* was founded in 1841 on the premise that a penny daily need not be base and sensational in its stories or reporting. It was Greeley's desire, stated in his autobiography, to "lift the Laboring class, as such—not out of labor, by any means—but out of ignorance, inefficiency, dependence and want." It was directed to those who wanted a cheap but moral newspaper written on a relatively high plane and containing such things as serialized novels by Dickens, lectures, poetry, regular book reviews, as well as a good deal of social and moral crusading for such issues as prohibition of liquor, abolition of hanging, and a protective tariff, not necessarily for the benefit of the industrialist, but for the elevation and maintenance of the American working man.

Other outstanding anti-slavery newspapers were William Lloyd Garrison's *The Liberator* published in Boston; *The National Era* of Washington which included a serialization of *Uncle Tom's Cabin* in its columns; and a host of religious journals, local organs of the anti-slavery societies, and the several black newspapers.

THE CIVIL WAR

THE increasing debate over the slavery issue was a prime cause of the Civil War. The American newspaper, which had played a major role in reflecting and influencing the attitudes held by the populations of both North and South, responded to the war itself with its usual omniscient tone and printed millions of words of advice, encouragement, and censure on the conduct of the war on both sides. "Newspaper generalship thrived." Abraham Lincoln and Jefferson Davis were targets of the severest criticisms and most acid barbs. It is perhaps a tribute to the by now engrained traditions of democracy and free expression that there was no unanimity of press opinion on either side. The New York press, for instance, never a Lincoln stronghold, included several pro-Confederate newspapers in addition to those which generally disagreed with the Republican administration but were loyal to the northern cause.

What might be called the maturation of American newspaper reporting began with the Civil War. For the first time correspondents were widely employed by larger newspapers to report the war at first hand. The telegraph, though not as widespread as it was later to become, permitted many of the reports from the battlefield to be reported relatively quickly and accurately. There were of course many breakdowns and delays caused by wartime conditions, and rumors were always rife, causing newspapers to lead many of their stories with a line "IMPORTANT—IF TRUE." But by and large most of the major stories of the war were, in the large cities, reported within a day. Several newspapers, particularly the *New York Herald*, printed front-page maps of the various arenas of war and it was quite common for the entire front page and most of the news columns to be devoted to reports from the fronts. Personality cults developed around generals such as Grant and Sherman, and their movements were followed carefully. A discussion of certain specific newspapers printed during the Civil War follows in the section on collecting.

TYPES OF COLLECTIONS

AS one would expect, there are dozens of areas in which a newspaper collector can concentrate. The normal standards of personal interest, finances, and available space are unchanging. Undoubtedly the most popular collections are of those newspapers which chronicle the major events in American history. Newspapers which contain items of the American Revolution and the stirring events leading up to it, announcements of the Declaration of Independence and Constitution, the elections and inaugurations of presidents, war declarations and peace treaties, the deaths of the famous (particularly presidents), and major disasters are all avidly sought. A newspaper printed in the city in which the

[263]

The first public appearance of the Declaration of Independence, published July 6, 1776 in The Pennsylvania Evening Post.

The first public appearance of the proposed Constitution of the United States, published September 19, 1787 in The Pennsylvania Packet. *The printers of this newspaper were John Dunlap and David Claypoole. Dunlap was also the printer of the first printing (a broadside) of the Declaration of Independence.*

event occurred is usually the most desirable. This is particularly true if the event is closely associated with the city, such as the Boston Massacre or Chicago Fire.

Also extremely popular with collectors are newspapers printed during the American Civil War. There are several reasons for this. First is the enormous continuing interest of many people in the Civil War and Lincoln. No other period in our history and certainly no other president has left such legacies. Anything associated with Lincoln is desirable to thousands of collectors, and newspapers are no exception. Fortunately for these specialists there is a great supply of newspapers available. To fill the insatiable demand for war news, papers often greatly enlarged their press runs and the printing of several editions became a widespread

The end of the Civil War.

ately | country, there will be no brighter page than
men, | that which relates to THE BATTLES OF GETTYS-
id of | BURG.
e for | President Lincoln then delivered the follow-
how | ing dedicatory speech.
esent | "Four score and seven years ago our fathers
rati- | brought forth upon this continent a new nation,
hose | conceived in liberty and dedicated to the prop-
low- | osition that all men are created equal. (Ap-
bute | plause.) Now we are engaged in a great civil
t be | war, testing whether that nation, or any nation
sting | so conceived and so dedicated, can long endure.
g of | We are met on a great battle-field of that war;
| we are met to dedicate a portion of it as a final
s of | resting place of those who have given their lives
the | that that nation may live.
wing | It is altogether fitting and proper that we
rity, | should do this, but in a larger sense we cannot
stra- | dedicate, we cannot consecrate, we cannot hal-
| low this ground. The brave men living and
from | dead who struggled here have consecrated it far
nful | above our power to aid or detract. (Applause.)
lains | The world will not note or long remember what
the | we say here, but it can never forbid what they
to a | did here. (Applause.)

A typical contemporaneous report of the Gettysburg Address.

The Louisiana Democrat

VOLUME 19................NO. 24
ALEXANDRIA, LA.:

TUESDAY, MARCH.........15, 1864.

THE SITUATION.

Our Compendium, elsewhere, will show a rather, brighter prospect abroad, on the other side, than most of folks had a right to anticipate, and, certainly, more cheering and encouraging to our cause than the Yankees would will it. Let our readers peruse the article headed "The News" from the Chicago Tribune of the 29th, and they will certainly cast off some of their gloom. With us, we believe, when we hear full particulars from both sides, our successes will be found more complete than now known. In fact we have trustworthy intelligence through Capt. Cleveland, of Texas, who had and read the Mobile Register of the

War----'s effects at the North·   **Benefits**

War, in its tendencies, is always demoralizing. What multitudes ther We see this statement confirmed at the North in unmixed evil in war. the history of their diabolical crusade against the ing against it as the s Confederacy. The demoralization there is not all human miseries, as i confined to the soldier, but diffuses itself, like a unmixed disasters, a fearful epidemic, among all ranks and classes of could not educe great the people, giving birth to evils, political and so- All that is great and g cial and moral, which will continue to spread their luxuriantly from the se malignant influence long after the demon of war in its gory path, But fo has retired from the scenes of carnage. Whoever the world, every nation will read, with a careful eye, the occasional accounts bowing to-day under th of what is transpiring in the midst of our enemies, merciless despotism. will be astonished at the terrible disclosures which now engaged, will prov are continually brought to light. The whole frame disastrous as it has be work of society is manifestly tottering to its fall. When its trials all ov Law and order are made subservient to a misera- of Janus are ble expediency. Justice looks over her bandage; again with her scales are false. The church, which ought to from the deep stand forth " fair as the sun," is corrupt to the past a more g core. The pulpit, which was designed to be the world has great dispenser of sacred truth, has been converted the better for pruning— into a rostrum, from which to fulminate anathem as by passing through the

A Confederate publication printed on ledger paper.

practice. Newspapers were often saved by families of the men whose units were the subjects of reports. Issues describing great victories were also kept as souvenirs, just as a later generation saved D-Day announcements.

Most newspapers were quick to highlight the important battles and movements of the war, usually under relatively extravagant headlines a column wide and often extending in smaller type to the middle of the page. Other, more profound developments, were given less play. The dedication of the National Cemetery at Gettysburg, for instance, was reported in most of the northern newspapers, but few if any of them gave prominence to President Lincoln's dedicatory address delivered that day.

The most interesting newspapers to be published during the Civil War were those printed in the South on paper other than newsprint. Since most of the paper mills were in the North and the blockade effectively cut off any foreign supplies, newsprint became scarce or nonexistent in many parts of the South. Printers used whatever they could find, including brown wrapping paper, colored tissue paper, and lined ledger paper. Of greatest interest,

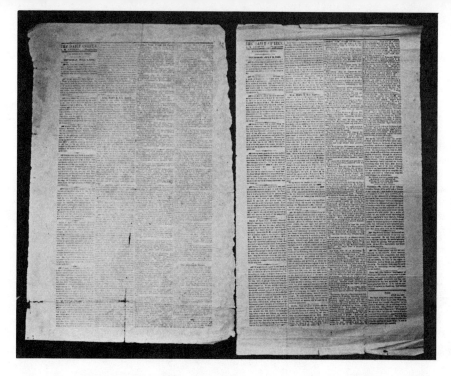

Two *issues* of The Daily Citizen *printed on different wallpaper patterns.*

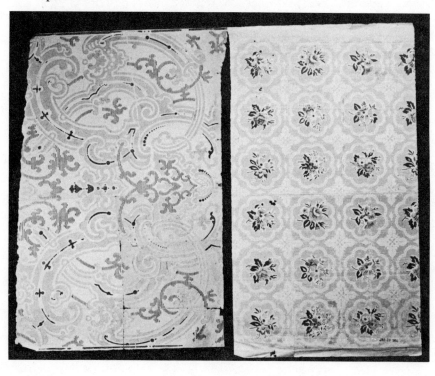

ry firing has | is 'dead'
broughout the

els made thei
day evening.
cavalry reached
this side of
all the sick in
a nt employe.
orses, seizing
force of rebel
y crossed ai
Refugees say
00, but pick
irthworks are
nd north sides
the chain of
being erected
om the high
thwarters or

NOTE.

JULY 4th, 1863.

Two days bring about great changes, The banner of the Union floats over Vicksburg. Gen. Grant has "caught the rabbit;" he has dined in Vicksburg, and he did bring his dinner with him. The "Citizen" lives to see it. For the last time it appears on "Wall-paper." No more will it eulogize the luxury of mule-meat and fricassed kitten—urge Southern warriors to such diet never more. This is the last wall-paper edition and is, excepting this note, from the types as we found them. It will be valuable hereafter as a curiosity

The famous Union addendum of July 4, 1863, added to the last (July 2) issue of the Confederate Daily Citizen.

however, several newspapers, particularly in Louisiana, printed for many weeks on nothing but the blank side of wallpaper.

The most famous of these wallpaper editions is *The* (Vicksburg, Mississippi) *Daily Citizen* for July 2, 1863. This paper was printed (on at least four different wallpaper patterns) just before the siege of Vicksburg ended and the capture of the newspaper office, apparently intact, by Grant's troops on July 4, 1863. The issue of July 2 was still set in type on the press and a victorious printer issued a second edition with the now-famous note dated July 4:

> NOTE. Two days bring about great changes. The banner of the Union floats over Vicksburg. Gen. Grant has "caught the rabbit;" he has dined in Vicksburg, and he did bring his dinner with him. The "Citizen" lives to see it. For the last time it appears on "Wall-paper." No more will it eulogize the luxury of mule-meat and fricassed kitten—urge Southern warriors to such diet never more. This is the last wall-paper edition, and is, excepting this note, from the types as we found them. It will be valuable hereafter as a curiosity.

[269]

The Daily Citizen is unquestionably one of the great curiosities in journalistic history and it has been reprinted often. A circular published by the Library of Congress enables one to distinguish an original from a reprint with relative ease.

Other newspapers published during this period which should be mentioned are the soldiers' newspapers published by the various regiments and units themselves. These were often hasty publications and were printed either on portable presses or, more often, on the commandeered press of an occupied town. Their titles indicate their usually irreverent nature—*Swamp Angel, Camp Kettle,* or *The Knapsack*—and the content of these papers is the usual stuff of unvarying interest to the soldier: camp gossip, news from home, jokes, satire, and complaints. Many of these papers found their way north enclosed in the letters sent home by the soldiers.

Newspapers reporting Lincoln's assassination and funeral are perhaps the most sought after of any reporting a single event.

A selection of "soldiers'" newspapers published during the Civil War.

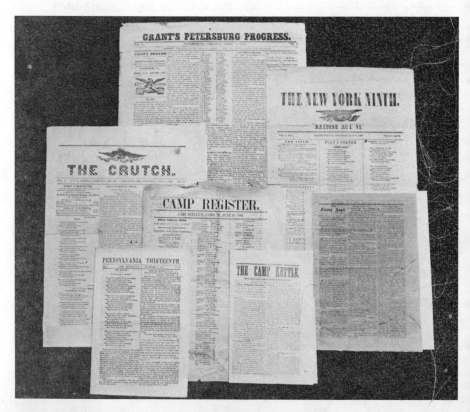

A rare example of a Civil War newspaper published by and for sailors, probably printed aboard The Black Hawk, *the flagship of Admiral David Dixon Porter.*

Many newspapers devoted almost their entire news space to reports of the assassination itself, the conspiracy, or the funeral. Heavy black mourning rules were used on every page for many days, particularly if Lincoln's cortège traveled through the paper's city. Several newspapers printed illustrations of Booth or the funeral bier to add to the drama and significance of their reports. Newspapers publishing first reports of the assassination were sold out immediately even though they appeared at two or three in the morning. Many of these issues were saved, just as many of us have saved the newspapers reporting the deaths of Roosevelt and Kennedy.

A collector might also concentrate on assembling newspapers from a certain city or area of the country, particularly if this location has an exceptional history. Widely collected, for example, are southern newspapers printed during the Confederacy, and

[271]

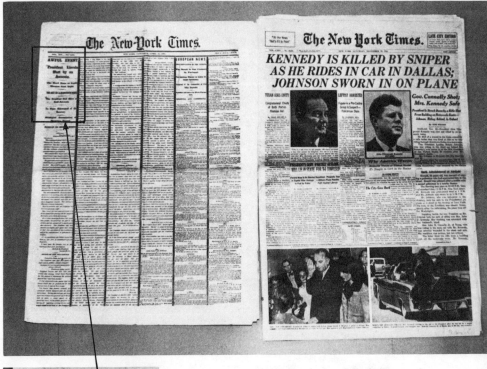

Changing standards in newspaper typography reflected in the coverage of two presidential assassinations.

California newspapers printed during the Gold Rush period, 1848–1860.

When gold was discovered at Sutter's Mill in January 1848, there were two tiny newspapers in San Francisco. By 1853 there were twelve daily newspapers and many more semi-weekly and weekly papers vying to meet the needs of thousands of men hungry for news from home. The great eastern newspapers, particularly the *New York Tribune*, *Herald*, and *Post*, published special California editions which were then sent on monthly steamers to the West Coast. As many as 10,000 copies of each edition were sent and were no doubt sold within minutes of their arrival in San Francisco. California newspapers also printed special steamer editions to be sent to the East Coast and throughout the world. Often the title of the ship upon which the newspaper would be sent was included in the masthead such as *The Alta California for the Steamers Columbus and Sara Sands* (June 15, 1850).

The turbulence of California society in these early years was reflected in its newspapers. The editorials and news articles were unmatched in vitriolic opinions directed against political enemies as well as competing papers. James King, who founded the *Daily Evening Bulletin* to fight lawlessness and the erratic government of San Francisco, was assassinated in 1856.

The phenomenal growth of the press in California was as remarkable as the growth of the state itself. By 1860 there were

Some early California papers published during the time of the Gold Rush.

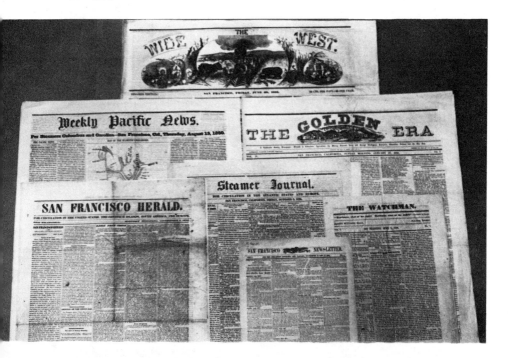

forty newspapers in San Francisco alone, of which fourteen were dailies. New York had only three more dailies. Early California imprints have always been eagerly sought after and are therefore highly valuable.

Other newspapers from the far west which have attracted the attention of collectors are the early territorial newspapers, particularly those which contain news of Indian disputes. Early Texas papers also have a ready market, no doubt reflecting the large number of Texan collectors and the less than muted enthusiasm of Texans for things Texan.

Other areas of collecting which should be briefly noted are newspapers reflecting developments and changes in journalism; newspapers from small towns; ethnic newspapers, particularly the black press; newspapers containing the early works of famous writers; and newspapers containing false or erroneous stories. This last group can contain some memorable headlines. *The Chicago Tribune*'s headline **DEWEY DEFEATS TRUMAN** is well known, and election stories are the source of many errors. But it was not an election that caused some of the greatest mistakes of all to appear in various forms on many front pages on Monday, April 15, 1912. The *Yonkers* (New York) *Daily News* version was **TITANIC IS IN TOW; ALL SAFE. New Liner Saved by Automatic Watertight Bulkheads.**

REPRINTS AND REPRODUCTIONS

BECAUSE of the relative ease with which a four page newspaper can be reprinted, many early American newspapers have been reproduced in facsimile, often in quantities of many, many thousands. It would be erroneous to call these reproductions "frauds," because there was usually no intent to deceive. Most of these reproductions were made to commemorate a birthday of the newspaper itself, or the county or state in which the original newspaper first appeared. Others were issued to commemorate the anniversary of an event described in the newspaper. These reproductions were either included as a souvenir supplement in the birthday issue of the newspaper or were sold or given away

TITANIC IS IN TOW; ALL SAFE

New Liner Saved by Automatic Water-Tight Bulkheads

(By United Press.)

New York, April 15.—Wireless dispatches from Captain H. J. Haddock of the White Star liner Olympic today said passengers had been transferred from the Titanic, which collided with an iceberg, by the Parisian of the Allan line and Cunard liner Carpathia.

The Parisian and Carpathia are standing by the Titanic and the Baltic was reported as approaching by the Olympic's captain.

This information came direct to the local offices of the White Star line and Vice President Franklin declared he personally had no doubt but that the Titanic would be safely towed to port.

Her passengers will this afternoon be transferred to the Baltic which will bring them here. They are due Thursday. The Baltic is the same liner that brought the passengers of the sunken liner Republic to this port.

The steel bow of the Titanic crumpled before the impact with the enormous iceberg. At the smash, however, the water tight compartment doors closed automatically. Immediately the wireless appeal for aid was sent out and the response was immediate. According to information the Titanic carried about $5,000,000 in bonds and diamonds. The White Star line officials today issued an official statement in which they stated that the Titanic was unsinkable and that there was no reason to believe she could founder.

The Titanic carried 1425 passengers and a crew of 860.

A somewhat less than accurate headline, demonstrating the dangers of assumption.

at fairs and celebrations. Other reproductions were used as advertisements either for the newspaper or for common items such as drugs and coffee. A list of reprints was published in the *Bulletin of the New York Public Library* for April 1931, compiled by Joseph Gavit. The list cites close to 150 different newspaper reproductions with several variants for many of them. The Civil War Centennial and the American Bicentennial have caused dozens of more titles to be added to this list.

Fortunately, most reproductions can be readily identified by anyone who has had even limited experience in handling newspapers. The first thing to examine is the newsprint. Virtually all reproductions have been printed since the introduction of cheap, wood-pulp paper and are quickly spotted by their usually deteriorated condition. This is one of the few cases in which a 200-year-old original can be in better shape than the 20-year-old copy. Most newspapers printed before 1870 which have not been exposed to extreme environments will still be soft, pliable, unchipped around the edges, and able to be folded without breaking. Most larger libraries have either information on reproductions or the original newspaper or newspapers from the period with which comparisons can be made. The Library of Congress has also published and has available several circulars describing the more common reproductions.

There are two papers which have been reproduced so many times and copies so widely dispersed that they deserve special mention. These are the (Kingston, N.Y.) *Ulster County Gazette* for January 4, 1800 and the *New York Herald* of April 15, 1865. They report the deaths of Washington and Lincoln respectively. Many librarians are convinced that no attic trunk in America is without at least one copy of either or both of these.

The *Ulster County Gazette* was one of the first newspapers to be reproduced. R. W. G. Vail, in two monographs on the subject of these famous reprints in the *Bulletin of the New York Public Library* for April 1930 and April 1931, suggests that the first reproduction may have been made as early as 1825 and was doubtless issued to commemorate the anniversary of the death.

Reproductions continued to be made for the rest of the century, and over 100 different variants have been noted. What is truly surprising is that until 1930, no original issue of this newspaper was known to exist.

Why the *Ulster County Gazette* and not another newspaper has come to be reproduced so many times is a mystery. Contrary to popular belief, it was certainly not the first newspaper to report the death of Washington. We must remember that before the telegraph, news traveled more or less radially from its point of origin. Thus Virginia and the District of Columbia newspapers were the first to report it. Indeed, the January 4 issue was not even the first issue of the *Ulster County Gazette* to report the death of Washington. The issue of December 28, 1799, now in The New-York Historical Society, contains the first announcement to appear in that newspaper, complete with mourning rules and appropriate solemnities. The *Gazette* was not a particularly influential or important newspaper. The paucity of extant issues for any date attests this. Kingston was a tiny city compared to Charleston, Boston, Philadelphia, or New York. Perhaps the only satisfactory explanation is that since we think that reproductions have existed since 1825, these early reproductions were probably the only "old" newspapers which, in later years, many people could find. It would therefore be a logical and convenient newspaper to reproduce again and again. Possibly most of the reproducers thought they were reproducing from an original. A genealogical table showing which issues were the basis for succeeding ones would be almost impossible but fascinating to compile.

There are two known originals, one each in The Library of Congress and The American Antiquarian Society. These were definitely proved to be genuine by careful comparison with other known originals of the *Gazette* of other dates. Precise similarities of watermarks, typography, etc. were conclusive. A quick and sure way to identify a reproduction is to check the first line of

[277]

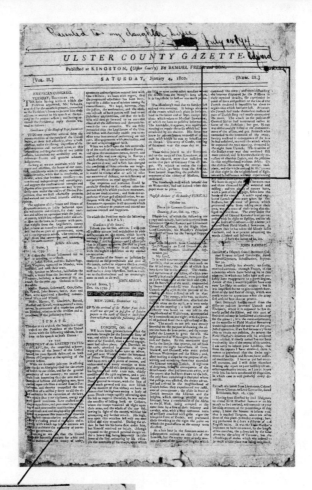

One of two known original issues of the Ulster County Gazette *for January 4, 1800. The test of a genuine example is found at the top of column four as shown here.*

column four of page one. Only the original contains the phrase "command the town; and not withstanding." If these words appear anywhere else the issue is a reproduction. Doubtless there is someone who collects reproductions of the *Ulster County Gazette*, but to the rest of us they are valueless curiosities.

The *New York Herald* of April 15, 1865 contains the early accounts of the assassination of Abraham Lincoln the night before. There was no "first" newspaper to report the calamity. The telegraph provided rapid communication to all points connected to it and many of the daily papers of this date printed at least one edition containing the news. The *Herald* was an important newspaper and its reportage of the Civil War was considered to be among the most thorough. To many later historians it is considered one of the newspapers of record of the Civil War.

There were five known editions of the *Herald* printed on the morning and afternoon of April 15, beginning at 2:00 A.M. and ending at 3:30 P.M. Fortunately for the collector it was a newspaper many people saved and originals turn up for sale periodically.

Of the half-dozen or so reprints of the *Herald,* the most common contain a portrait of Lincoln on the front page. The original had none. The inner pages of the reproductions are almost entirely devoted to advertising a single product such as Grain-O-Coffee, or Dr. Archambault's Paris Vital Sparks. Many of these ads contain testimonial letters dated in the 1870s and 1880s.

Other reprints encountered fairly frequently are the *Boston Gazette*, October 9, 1721; (Boston) *News-Letter*, April 24, 1704; (New York) *Gazette of the United States*, May 2, 1789 (Washington's Inauguration); (New York) *Sun*, September 3, 1833 (Vol. I, No. 1).

* * *

WHILE it cannot be within the scope of this essay to discuss prices or the value of certain newspapers, a few generalities might be appropriate. Prices for the same or similar newspapers vary greatly from dealer to dealer, largely because newspapers are not familiar territory to the average bookseller. He may either consider a newspaper too ephemeral to handle and get rid of it cheaply or he might think of it as so rare and unusual as to command a high price. Antique and second-hand stores also occasionally acquire newspapers along with other household goods, and their pricing system is equally erratic. It should be noted that the few dealers who handle newspapers exclusively tend to price their copies of average issues lower than the general rare-book dealer. An average issue would be one of the big city giants containing no major new stories.

The relative scarcity of a particular newspaper can usually be determined by consulting union lists and bibliographies. It is a general rule of thumb that the more libraries which have that issue or title, the greater was its circulation and importance. Usually the larger the circulation, the more copies still exist. We must remember, though, that a newspaper or periodical considered salacious, light-weight, or of transitory nature (such as a *Prices-Current*) would not, despite a large circulation, have found its way into many permanent archives. Indeed, how many libraries a century hence will have files of *TV Guide* or the weekly sensational checkout-stand newspapers (assuming, of course, they have not turned to dust)?

Clarence Brigham was undoubtedly correct when he asserted the immense importance of newspapers among all printed sources of history. The noblest contributions to modern civilization and the basest thoughts have appeared within their pages. The newspaper has been, since its inception, a continuing chronicle of the activities, thoughts, and customs of the American people. Fortunately, the opportunity to collect history itself, rather than just its scattered relics, is available to anyone who selects as his area of interest the early American newspaper.

BIBLIOGRAPHY

American Newspaper, 1821–1936: A Union List of Files Available in the United States and Canada, ed. Winifred Gregory for the Bibliographical Society of America (New York: H. W. Wilson, 1937).

J. Cutler Andrews, *The North Reports the Civil War* (Pittsburgh: University of Pittsburgh Press, 1955).

——, *The South Reports the Civil War* (Princeton: Princeton University Press, 1970).

Timothy Barnes, "Loyalist Newspapers of the American Revolution: 1763–1783," *Proceedings of the American Antiquarian Society*, 83 Part 2 (1974), 217–40.

Clarence S. Brigham, *Additions and Corrections to History and Bibliography of American Newspapers, 1690–1820* (Worcester: American Antiquarian Society, 1961).

——, *History and Bibliography of American Newspapers, 1690–1820* (Worcester: American Antiquarian Society, 1947), 2 Vols.

——, "Wall-paper Newspapers of the Civil War," in *Bibliographical Essays: A Tribute to Wilberforce Eames* (Cambridge: Harvard University Press, 1924), pp. 203–209.

Joseph Gavit, *A List of American Newspaper Reprints* (New York: New York Public Library, 1931: reprinted from the NYPL *Bulletin*, April 1931).

Edward Connery Lathem, *Chronological Tables of American Newspapers, 1690–1820* (Barre: American Antiquarian Society & Barre Publishers, 1972).

Earle Lutz, "Soldier Newspapers of the Civil War," in *The Papers of the Bibliographical Society of America*, 46, Fourth Quarter (1952), 373–86.

Stanley Morison, *The English Newspaper: Some Account of the Physical Development of Journals Printed in London Between 1622 and the Present Day* (Cambridge: Cambridge University Press, 1932).

Frank Luther Mott, *American Journalism: A History of Newspapers in the United States Through 260 Years 1690–1950* (New York: Macmillan, 1950).

Armistead Scott Pride, "A Register and History of Negro Newspapers in the United States 1827–1950" (Northwestern University Ph.D. diss., 1950).

Robert W. G. Vail, *The Ulster County Gazette and Its Illegitimate Offspring* (New York: New York Public Library, 1931: reprinted from the NYPL *Bulletin*, April 1930 and April 1931).

[281]

HARRY GEORGE FLETCHER III, *a confirmed city-dweller as a fifth-generation New Yorker, is an equally addicted bibliophile, and a member of The Grolier Club. He is the Director of Fordham University Press and, of course, the editor of this* Miscellany.

Over Against
Saint Paul's

H. George Fletcher

PUBLISHERS' NOTE: *The essay which follows is different from the others in this volume in that it is a strictly personal reminiscence about a book dealer who, unlike Rosenbach, Quaritch, and other famous colleagues, could never claim to be remembered for the important books he sold, or for the great and wealthy collectors who patronized his shop, or for the auction records he set, or for the magnificent and scholarly catalogues he issued. Dave Mendoza never regularly did sell great books to great collectors at great prices. Instead, he gave his time, encouragement, and friendship to those who entered his shop, regardless of the state of their solvency.*

    Dave Mendoza represents the sort of bookseller from whom most human collectors, as opposed to institutional ones, bought their first "fine" books and received their first guidance. It has traditionally been in shops like the one on Ann Street here described that persons who in later life became serious and sometimes famous collectors obtained, upon payment of only minimal tuition, that initial basic bibliographical education which all collectors must acquire.

The small dealer in "used and rare" books is not a likely candidate for memorialization in the literature of book collecting which, understandably so, focuses its attention primarily on booksellers, collectors, transactions, and volumes of magnitude. But we believe that some tribute, however modest, to those lesser-known dealers who give generously of their time and knowledge to young collectors possessing little money but much enthusiasm is appropriate and long overdue. Although Mr. Fletcher's essay is about one particular man, at its foundation lies the same sort of friendship which so many other collectors have developed toward so many other booksellers. Let this essay, then, be a token expression of the affectionate regard in which they all are held.

* * *

HOW I CAME TO GET THERE the first time I no longer recall. Ann Street, which starts at an awkward angle at Broadway and wanders three blocks to the east, has long since ceased to be either important or readily accessible. And the buildings at numbers 15, 17, and 19, even now of only qualified charm, were unremarkable for many years. Perhaps my father, who took me on Manhattan rambles with some regularity, knew of the old book shop at No. 15, or perhaps my aunt who worked on Wall Street for almost five decades knew and mentioned the place. Whatever the forgotten background, I reached the building for the first time not quite a quarter of a century ago. The why of it all is much easier to recall: fortunate in having a gifted English teacher at that stage in my schooling, I decided that an ancient copy of Shakespeare would be much preferable to the unimaginative modern one I was reading; so I set off to acquire something as close to the author's lifetime in its vintage as might be. The paucity of my means was surpassed only by my ignorance of what I was doing. Even so, I managed to buy what I wanted.

[284]

Fortunately for the future of my brand-new bibliophilia, and for the equanimity of the others involved then, an indifferent facsimile of the First Folio suited me down to the ground.

The others involved were the surviving active members of the bookselling Mendoza family, Aaron and David. They were also virtually the last unbroken connection with the days, generations before, when the antiquarian book trade was located in the Wall Street–City Hall area. The originator had been their father, Isaac—or better, Ike—who at the age of thirty opened for business in 1894 at No. 17. His photograph at the shop portrays him as a handsome man, with a mustache worthy of Imperial Germany. Family tradition spoke of Ike's influence upon and encouragement of the founders of Dawson's, in Los Angeles, and Goodspeed's, in Boston, during these early years. He moved one door to the west in 1901, and he and his three sons—Aaron, Mark, and David—spent their lives operating The Isaac Mendoza Book Company. Ike was long gone when I showed up just over half a century after the business had settled in as comfortably and seemingly immovably as only a book shop can do, at No. 15. Mark died in 1956, but I never met him, and Aaron died within a few years of my making his acquaintance; that left only Dave. Dave became my friend, guide, and benefactor; and it is around him that these reminiscences are principally formed.

* * *

THE immediate area in which the shop stands was once much-frequented and of no small importance. No. 19 is bordered on the east by Theatre Alley. Its name commemorates the Park Theatre, which opened in 1798 on Park Row and was for half a century America's premiere theater. Park Row, once the city's publishing center, is a near neighbor, City Hall Park is just to the northwest, and across Broadway is Saint Paul's Chapel of Trinity Church. With its handsome architecture and historic churchyard, Saint Paul's remains a most attractive piece of old New York, with unsevered ties to Revolutionary days, and its name is particularly appropriate for a bookish tale. It harks back to the location of the London publishing trade of so many years,

Nos. 15, 17, and 19 Ann Street as etched in 1899 by W. Wallace, two years before the Mendoza Book Company moved one door west to its present location.

and I confess that I have chosen the title of this slight piece self-consciously. But the church was and is a suitable complement to the shop at 15 Ann Street, which itself is a relic of Federal New York, and is reputed to date from 1820. Of six storeys, it must have been one of the tallest buildings in town when it was built, and it is good to be able to say that it remains largely unspoiled, since even the ground floor has not been improved to any extent which detracts from its somewhat battered appeal. Each storey reflects the building's period by being slightly shorter than the one next below. So the ground-floor windows are quite large, and those just below the roof are postage stamps. About half the place was full of books, floor to ceiling. The cellar was a long, narrow dustbin, holding odd volumes of broken sets, and similar debris. The second floor was crammed with extra stock, and the third floor less so. The top floors were unused for many years, and the roof leaked. (The Mendozas never could buy the place, and the landlord was a landlord.) Dave once told me that Walt

Whitman mentioned the building in the mid-1850s as the address of a bootmaker, but I have never found that source.

The main floor, relatively long and narrow, was entered through an enclosed porch piled high with more copies of *National Geographic* than one could hope to read. This floor was just books: in shelves around all the walls, down the middle in rows, around the rarely used rolltop desk in the rear, and into the eccentric back room with all its walls at irregular angles. Halfway along on the left was the cellar door, and in the space just next to that was the littered sloping desk over the cash drawer, all of this being on top of the old safe (security, of course, was nil). Nearby was the small wrapping table. The open spaces above some of the central bookcases were draped with an assortment of framed and unframed prints, documents, and maps, and a few of them were draped in turn with lint. Of course, the books spilled over onto the floor, especially in the many corners. The upper floors were reached perilously by means of a primeval staircase, rising from the left side of the front porch; the electric wiring was ancient and the lights increasingly scarce as one climbed, giving out entirely at the top.

The stock was just about everything, but there were areas of concentration. Always strongly represented, local history sold well. General history, biography, and literature were well represented, and there was always a brisk trade in reference books. Natural history did nicely, as did books in economics, and Dave kept quite a respectable section of books on books, which also did well. At this distant date, I suppose that I am not revealing a secret by mentioning the Mendoza code. Each bookseller has one, of course: often ten letters in a particular arrangement, perhaps spelling something, with no repeaters, each letter by simple transfer representing a number from 1 to 0. The family code was BLACK HORSE. So a book marked, for example, BLK/4.95 represented a gross margin of $3.70. But it seemed to be a rare day when a regular customer paid the entire marked price, because Dave had a habit of rounding off prices downward. The sales were mostly to people who dropped by; the purchases were usually accomplished by buying up entire collections or small libraries around town and in the countryside. On those occasions, Dave worked part of Sunday, too, when he could be sure of parking his car in front of the shop. The antiquarian and rare books to be found there will be apparent from my comments later on.

*　*　*

ONLY a few years ago New York was still crowded with old buildings filled with old books, but urban development and greedy landlords have destroyed most of them, and the replacements are for the most part beneath notice. What sometimes carries the sub-title of The Old Ann Street Book Store bulks large to survive as the oldest and perhaps one day the last of the old breed. When last I checked, and recently at that, the gaslights were still in place and working.

This was Dave's domain during the years I remember fondly. He was a big man, with an ebullient, extroverted personality, and he loved people. The brothers were apparently of quite differing temperaments, and Dave often spoke of his reluctance to get involved in the family business. His father had to tell him off, he remembered, to help one of his older brothers one day in the first decade of this century. They carried a large crate to Mr. Huntington, then stopping at a midtown club. He wondered years later whether he might not have carried the Huntington Gutenberg uptown that day (I have since been credibly informed that this could not have been possible). But Dave never quite learned what was in the crate, and at the time he cared not at all: it was just drudgery, and typified his early attitude toward the rare-book trade, even if he was only about ten years old. His older brothers eventually prevailed upon him to come in, however, and I for one am glad that he was persuaded. I am surely not alone in this feeling: the place was always busy, and friends and customers—the terms inevitably became interchangeable—dropped by constantly. As often as not, they just wanted to say hello, and, when the wind piped down narrow Ann Street in

David Mendoza, Christmas 1959, holding a copy of Sydney's Arcadia *(1651), once owned by the Brownings, whose signatures are at the top of the title-page.*

what Dave referred to as bourbon weather (the bourbon was kept in the rolltop desk), occasionally to chase out the chill.

The shop was in general pretty cold in winter. A constant visitor was the draft which the ill-fitting inside front door could not keep out—not that anything could, since the wind channeled itself through the groove worn in the floor by the feet of generations of booklovers. The main source of warmth was a single radiator of venerable age, and of an ancient pattern the likes of which I have never encountered elsewhere. Dave therefore spent his winters in tweed sport coats over heavy sweaters, and his usual position was taken in front of the radiator, with his hands behind his back. I would sometimes splash in on one of those New York rainy days when you are guaranteed a soaking from the knees down; my grousing about what a day it was was always countered, especially in his last years, by Dave's observation that any day was a great day to be alive. (There was another peripheral element to the cold weather: Dave always had a cigarette going—he usually clamped the filter between his front teeth—and in the winter his great beak of a nose dripped perpetually, thus extinguishing the cigarette. He must have run up a prodigious bill in tissues, since he persisted in using them over his wife's protests that she could easily and economically keep his supply of handkerchiefs up to the mark.)

* * *

OF Sephardic stock, the family emigrated from England in the nineteenth century and settled on the Lower East Side. Ike was born there, but Dave remembers that his grandfather preserved his habits from his native England, at least enough to pause for tea every afternoon. A forebear was the prizefighter Daniel Mendoza (1764–1836), a famous member of "the Fancy" in the late-eighteenth and early-nineteenth centuries. I remember Aaron as a quiet and studious gentleman, which seems to have been everyone's evaluation of him. Dave always thought of himself as a rascal, and I never saw any reason to dispute his judgment. I saw him with increasing frequency for nearly the last score of years of his life, and he was an absolute imp. He was addicted to puns, the ribald, and the outrageous. "What's de Worde, Wynkyn?" was an occasional groaner. I cannot recall the number of times I heard him inflict upon the uninitiated the following bit of Vaudeville flotsam: "You know about the two Sexes, don't you?—Sex Fifth Avenue and Sex Thirty-Fourth"

(I simply refuse to explain this encapsulation of old New York department-store history and fate to those who do not get the pun). He used to speak in disrespectful terms of his army service in World War I, and the only story of heroic events he related to me I am inclined to accept as absolute gospel. He was at a base somewhere as exotic as rural New Jersey, and they were camped out in large tents in the wintry cold and damp. Dave was a member of the National Army, of course, and he was waiting on the chow line one day, when another soldier broke in ahead of him, claiming pride of place as a regular. Dave replied by bashing him over the head with his mess kit; for that, he was banished to the mess tent for a long stint at peeling potatoes. He ever after reported his great enjoyment of the punishment, which had kept him in a warm kitchen while the other wretches were outside enduring the weather.

For some reason I never divined, his shop was frequented by women of all sorts who were interested in the sensational and totally unscientific interpretation of dreams. When one came in for the first time, her question, of course, was always "Have you any books on dreams?" And Dave's reply was invariably "Yes, Ma'am, wet or dry?" He always managed to bring this off by affecting an uncharacteristic mumble, so that the customer never quite heard all of the reply, but it still drove Dave's wife, Gilda (more familiarly, Gil), to justified distraction. The mumbling I have described as uncharacteristic because the lasting image before my mind's eye is of this big man with a grand smile on his face; he is clapping a friend heartily on the back, and he is rocketing forth what can only be described as great blasts of laughter which fill the old place and make newcomers start. His greeting to me, time out of mind, was "Well, you old stinker, how are you?" It was said in the fondest of tones, even to this reeking ancient half a hundred his junior. He was, of course, able to use most presentable terms when the situation demanded it or the visitor or caller was liable to be not amused. But everything proceeded in the most amiable, genuinely human way; malice was simply not in his make-up. He loved people, and for this reason could not stay away from the building. Except during the middle of the summer, he worked nearly a full day on Saturday, even though the financial district is notoriously empty from Friday evening until Monday morning. For a couple of weeks in July or August, he would put up his gone fishing sign and head off to the old country place he kept in Ballston Spa; especially the younger relatives loved it. Dave was always glad to get back, and find that the world had stayed reasonably intact on Ann Street while he had been away. Only a few years before his death he slipped on an icy sidewalk uptown, and the fall broke a hip. He got back into harness quite rapidly, and the main cause of this speedy recovery, Gil was convinced, was his impatience to be back with the regulars at the shop. It was not long before the Saturday work schedule resumed, too. I cannot imagine that he ever made a great deal of money out of the shop, since he was always obliging his customers; but he had a wonderful life, and his customers reciprocated his friendliness. Indeed, he was with them, and put in a regular workday, the last full day of his life.

The customers themselves were a representative selection of the human comedy. Many of them, of course, were from the financial district and the city governmental offices, and they seemed to come in to recharge their batteries at the same time as they regained some self-esteem by gathering up a new supply of intelligent reading to try to offset the daily rot which was surely turning their brains to mush. They always, to my observation, went away better than they had been when they came in. There was the improbable case of the man from Staten Island who made a substantial investment in several large folio volumes of an imposing incunabular edition of Nicholas of Lyra's Biblical commentaries; he presented them to his favorite college, which happened to be in New Jersey, and he never received so much as a written acknowledgment of their receipt, let alone thanks and an evaluation for an income-tax deduction. Then there was the man who eavesdropped (as who could not?) on a conversation about Thomas B. Mosher of mixed memory. I had made the inevitable comment about Mosher's methods of publishing by piracy, when our casual acquaintance—who may have collected Moshers, for all I knew—took considerable umbrage, butting in with "he made a lot of British authors in this country!" (Did I really get off the rejoinder that "he made them, all right: he made them mad"? Probably not; but I wish I had, and I sometimes believe that I did.) My mentioning Staten Island recalls the bit of Mendoza family history that Edwin Markham, who lived there across the inner harbor when his poetry was much in vogue, was not of entirely untarnished fame. It was reported that there had been a slight misunderstanding one day, decades before, about whether money had in fact changed hands for the book in his possession. Whatever the facts, his memory was kept green by the regular trade in autographed copies of various of his works which appeared on the shelves at 15 Ann Street not infrequently.

The customers had also included Samuel Clemens, Hetty Green, Gene Fowler, and A. A. Milne, but the one who outshines all others in Mendoza history was Christopher Morley. His aura still hangs about the place, his picture with its fond dedication "With love to the Mendoza Boys" has presided over the shop for decades, and he had a lot of direct and indirect connections with many events in the life of the store and its proprietors. He worked for years in the handsome *Evening Post* building on Vesey Street, looking over Saint Paul's churchyard. It was only a short trip across Broadway to the store, and Whyte's Restaurant was near at hand. What Chris liked to call the most civilized invention of the twentieth century, the Three Hours for Lunch Club, had some of its origins in Whyte's and the "club" convened there often, both before and after visits to 15 Ann. That most civilized invention still exists, in a way: it gave birth to the Baker Street Irregulars, which has met regularly, once a year, since 1934 (less organized gatherings, be it said, take place at much more frequent intervals to keep the "club" going in a suitably haphazard way).

[293]

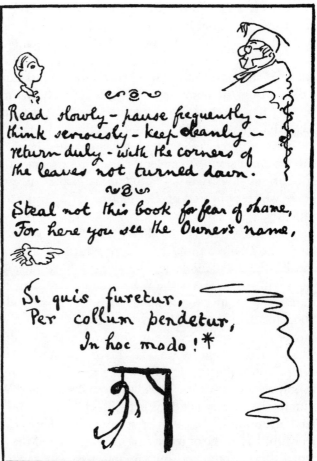

Read slowly – pause frequently –
think seriously – keep cleanly –
return duly – with the corners of
the leaves not turned down.

Steal not this book for fear of shame,
For here you see the Owner's name,

Si quis furetur,
Per collum pendetur,
   In hoc modo! *

If any one takes this book by stealth,
He shall hang by the neck--Thus!

A *Mendoza keepsake, in this version the reputed work of*
Christopher Morley.

Chris was a constant visitor in the store, of course, and this brought him the friendship and interest of the family, but he was most popular and widely read as a journalist, playwright, and essayist, and his works soon became collectible to a wide audience. Dave's brother Aaron especially became addicted to the Morley brand of writing, and he was an early and dedicated collector of Morleiana. The rarest of Chris's books is certainly *The Eighth Sin*, which had been published by Blackwell's in 250 copies in 1912, while the author was a Rhodes Scholar. Chris was somewhat embarrassed in later years by these youthful poems—his first book—and he was not unduly sorry that so few copies were known. But there must have been a secret horde, since no fewer than two copies were in the office safe, and Aaron had an author's presentation copy in his library. Aaron's Morley collection in general was outstanding of its kind. It included all the published material, proofs of various works, letters, correspondence, and manuscripts, and all the publications were inscribed. (One is, of course, constrained to mention that old canard to the effect that the only really rare Morley item—like those of A. Edward Newton—is one *not* autographed by the author, who was a compulsive writer, especially in copies of his own books. As the years pass, however, I find that this chestnut comes from Chris's circle of friends and acquaintances. Their copies surely were inscribed; but as they drop from the ranks and their books go into institutions, the autographed copies have become suddenly fewer.) As happens in families, harmony was not always present throughout the Mendoza clan, and this became strikingly apparent with the fate of the Morley collection on Aaron's death in January 1960. His widow rapidly disposed of the library at a low price to another dealer, Lew David Feldman (himself since gone), and El Dieff sold it to the University of Texas at Austin, where it is a substantial and important part of the Morley collection at the Humanities Research Center. Morley in his days was the New York man of letters par excellence in the view of the reading public, and he is singularly apt as the literary patron saint of 15 Ann Street.

* * *

BUT enough of this history of empire. My topic is, after all, a book shop and the man who ran it, and I should like to talk about some of the books which he directed into my possession. The first acquisition of which I have a clear memory is typical. I wanted a nice copy of Walton's *Angler* which it would be pleasant to have and which I could afford. It was years before I realized that Dave had come up with a copy of the Bagster first edition of 1808, extra-illustrated by Gosden in his typical fashion, and bound by Riviere. I soon developed a craving for early printed books; the incunabula were long beyond my means, but the sixteenth-century productions of some of the famous printers were not, and the books of the seventeenth century were in those days crowding the shelves of all the antiquarian booksellers in town. Splendid Estiennes came my way, the first Gryphius was a pristine Palladius *De re rustica* lovingly "bound by the Booklover's Shop, Cleveland" (an emporium long gone, I fear) at the turn of this century, and Wing's titles, short or long, were no longer entirely a mystery to me. The only noteworthy gap was the Aldines which have since formed the core of my collection; I never had one of Dave, for some inexplicable reason, but some of the books which he practically gave me have since been exchanged elsewhere for the Aldines. Soon followed the books on books, an insidious addiction for the bibliophile, and the handsome older facsimiles of those books known in the original, it seems, only to the Morgans and the Huntingtons. Then there were the things like the first editions of Washington Irving's *Sketch Book* in the original boards, a copy of Thomas Hughes's *Tom Brown's School Days* presented by the author to George Birkbeck Hill, the Johnson scholar, and Dana's *Two Years Before the Mast* (which I read, in part, on the Staten Island Ferry—the vanished one, which used to cross from Bay Ridge to St. George—

[296]

while I sat out on one of the deck benches, salt air everywhere, and the fog drifting by). My perspectives were being increased, and the shop was a great, eclectic treasure-trove. There were the days when one of those phenomena, the book scouts, came by with something which increased my pulse markedly. Dave dealt with one eye on me, over the scout's shoulder, until the (need one say? modest) price was agreed upon; the scout left, and the book left with me at the same price Dave had paid the scout. Often the treasures piled up faster than I could manage to acquire them, and Dave moved them out of harm's way behind the cellar door and reserved them for me, so that I could diminish the pile at the rate of a book or two a week. Books from Ann Street were my constant companions, and I only hope that they enjoyed me as much as I them. I traveled much in the subway in those days, and the hours and miles vanished without notice of time and noise. The Fridays were undoubtedly the best. During my years at college I would get away from Fordham typically in the early afternoon on Friday, arrive at Dave's door as soon as might be, and stay until the homeward rush had left Fulton Street and environs, and Dave put up the shutters at dinner time. The books I bought were of all kinds, and often not so very rare, but that was and is scarcely to the point. I remember vividly, for example, one bitterly cold Friday evening in early December of a year which ought to have been just gone but is not, when I left with a stout copy of D. B. Wyndham Lewis' mesmerizing biography of François Villon. It was typical of book-making of half a century ago: lavish production, good paper kind to the eye, and a wonderful blind-stamped buckram binding; slip-cased, to boot. The season and weather accorded perfectly with Wyndham Lewis' theme, which he laid out in his opinionated and enthralling prose. It perfectly suited my then romantic nature, gave several directions to my future interests, and its influence has remained with me since; indeed, I am quite certain that I shall never be, or want to be, for that matter, entirely free of its spell.

[297]

An item of Americana brought with it interesting local significance. One of the times when Benedict Arnold proved himself worthy of his country's admiration was during and after the gruelling march which culminated in the Battle of Quebec, and in the battle itself, early in the Revolution. The actual assault soon miscarried, because the man who commanded Arnold, a young Aaron Burr, and all the other Continental Army and militia soldiers, Major General Richard Montgomery, was killed in practically the first moments of the major attack on the city's defenses in a New Year's Eve snowstorm. The whole campaign fell apart almost instantly, despite Arnold's efforts, and many of the Americans had to endure horrendous conditions in captivity. A young lad with the Americans was John Joseph Henry; he survived, eventually to return to his native Pennsylvania, where he died years later as a judge. Late in his life he wrote his reminiscences of the entire campaign, and his daughter saw to their posthumous appearance, in Lancaster, Pennsylvania, in 1812. The book was printed in what can be described charitably as rather primitive fashion, and copies of Judge Henry's *An Accurate and Interesting Account of the Hardships and Sufferings of that Band of Heroes, Who Traversed the Wilderness in the Campaign Against Quebec in 1775* are inevitably very heavily foxed when in original condition. My copy was at Ann Street for a brief time before I acquired it, and I soon learned the appropriateness of the location. Years after the Revolution, the State of New York saw fit to cause the remains of General Montgomery to be disinterred. His bones were brought back to New York, and they have lain at rest since 1818 in a martial tomb sculpted by order of Congress in Paris in 1777 and later built into the east porch of Saint Paul's facing onto Broadway and, at a slight angle, toward Ann Street.

But what is book-collecting without the occasional disappointment, or even mistakes? The other side of the coin shows the books I ought to have bought, but did not. One of them I recall simply as a large quarto of seventeenth-century English vintage, but reputed to be known in only three copies. That I no longer know the title shows that I was tempted merely by acquisitiveness, and it is a good thing that I let it go. I do remember two other books, though. One was a post-incunabulum edition of Cassiodorus, printed in Paris by Jean Petit around 1510. I hemmed and hawed over buying it for the best part of a year, and it was not at all expensive; so I have only myself to blame for the loss. The second was then simply beyond my means. A very fine Bible printed at Basel by Henricpetri in 1482, it was handsome indeed in its beech boards and pigskin. It also had received marbled edges later in its career: an unusual pattern of blues, reputed to be of the oldest type of marbling, and certainly a style otherwise unknown to me.

While I am granting equal time, I ought also to report that Dave had early guided my steps uptown, particularly to the Fourth Avenue dealers—most of them since vanished, too. My sole abiding disappointment there was the two-volume Aldine Homer which never did surface in the back room at (as I think of him, fondly if slightly disrespectfully) Old Man Hershbain's next door to Biblo and Tannen.

Dave was not immune from the collecting bug himself. There were handsome French royal bindings of the seventeenth and eighteenth centuries, which he kept at home, complemented by his very extensive collection of bookplates, some of which have been reproduced in reference works. He also kept an Ireland forgery of Shakespeare for many years, even though mention of it showed up in the occasional newspaper item about the store, and brought in potential buyers.

There came a time when I could manage to add incunabula to my library, and the finest one I have passed through Dave's hands. He called me one January day eight years ago, saying that he had something interesting for me to look at. He was right, of course, and the book changed hands on a freezing Saturday, under the usual informal circumstances, including a simple and hilarious lunch nearby. The book proved to be a very

[299]

large copy of a Eusebius published in Rome in 1476 by Johannes Philippus de Lignamine, the first native Italian printer, and one responsible for the *editiones principes* of Quintilian and Suetonius. Complete with the original blank first leaf and restrainedly gilded and rubricated throughout, it preserves the manuscipt quire signatures intended to guide the first binder, who fortunately did not cut them away. My copy is of the version with the dedication to Guillaume Cardinal d'Estouteville, who was of the same Norman family as the Robert d'Estouteville who had been Provost of Paris during the years when Villon raised hell and the art of poetry in the university quarter (Villon and the Provost were personally acquainted in both areas). As Papal Legate of Nicholas V, the cardinal had presided over the university reform achieved in 1452, when Villon was finishing his arts studies.

* * *

IT was to be only a year from the following Wednesday that Dave and I parted mortal company. The end came swiftly: a heart attack in the early morning, while he and Gil were alone in their apartment far uptown on Broadway, and it was over in a few minutes. The psalmist's threescore years and ten were long behind him. We took our formal farewell on Friday, January 21, 1972, another day of bitter cold. First there was a Masonic service, conducted by members of the lodge to which Dave had belonged for over half a century. Then the rabbi spoke of David Mendoza the man, of his family and friends, and of his devotion to all the people who passed through the door at 15 Ann Street. But he prayed, in Hebrew, for the soul of David ben Isaac, thereby closing significantly the circle of the years that midday.

I would not end on this note, however, since doing so would leave important things unmentioned, and I would close on anything but a sad note: that is not the way anyone remembers Dave. For one thing, I have said next to nothing of Gil (the *g* is soft), who was the most important element of Dave's life during his last quarter-century. She was a widow with grown sons and he a seemingly convinced bachelor already in his fifties when they married, but they were more like a pair of teenagers than old married folks: in other words, that rare commodity, a happy marriage. ("When I asked her to marry me," said Dave, "I told her that I had half-a-million books as assets. How was I to know that she thought I said 'bucks'?") Gil's background was Italian, and her father had been an artist. She brought warmth in sufficient abundance into their lives to leave a good bit to spare, and their friends benefited from the overflow. A memorable cook and gracious hostess, she presided over their huge, airy, old-fashioned apartment at the corner of Broadway and 106th with a style which complemented nicely the sunlight which brightened the place during the day. She also shared much of each day at the shop, from the early '60s, and upon Dave's death 15 Ann fell to her lot; she then saw to its future, in a way which I shall mention in a moment. Gil shared a rather dramatic moment with Dave one day a couple of years before his death. A nearby restaurant, which ran through at an angle from Ann Street to Park Row, blew up and burned spectacularly when an employee ignited a gas line which had been tampered with. Some pedestrians fell victim to flying glass, and the book store took on the appearance of a field dressing-station as Gil and Dave helped the injured, and saved at least one person from bleeding to death.

Another matter which should be mentioned is the milieu of the shop. Always crowded in, it became more so with the years. I can easily remember when the new Western Electric building went up across Ann Street in 1961, because it blocked out the sunlight forever. Indeed, Dave and I were standing outside in the resultant shade one summer's afternoon when he looked over to the latest racket to the west and said, "George, what are they doing to my little old New York?" What "they" were doing was putting up the banal World Trade Center, in an area which used to contain a welter of small buildings with old restaurants, army surplus stores, and all the electronics outlets which earned the place the nickname of Radio Row. They went, but then so did everything beneath them, and that meant the prime subterranean archaeological heritage of New York City. What was

[301]

not dug up and dumped in the Jersey meadows was entombed—forever, as far as that goes—in the huge concrete "bathtub" which had to be constructed to keep the water away from the enormous foundations of the twin towers. Eventually, business fell off in the entire financial district, and it has never recovered properly. One neighborhood victim was Whyte's Restaurant. Typical of the older restaurants which used to populate the Wall Street–City Hall area, it was built of real wood grown honestly dark with age, smoke, and use. It closed under unhappy personal circumstances which do not warrant repeating here, but it repaid whatever not inconsiderable debt it had owed the folks at 15 Ann Street. For years, the captain there had maintained as a side interest a mail-order book business, specializing in modern literature, which he operated out of a loft on Chambers Street. Walter Caron—for such is his name—was in daily attendance in Mendoza's for longer than I can recall, and the most steadfast of friends. When Dave died, he helped Gil with the funeral, and she reciprocated by asking him to come in with her to keep the shop alive. He has for half-a-dozen years been the owner (Gil having sold out to him and then retired to the country) of what continues to be called The Mendoza Book Company, and he has done handsomely by the old place. To his great credit, he has refurbished rather than altered. The changes are obvious only to the initiated: paint, mostly, but one can now browse comfortably in more distant reaches of the shop. I well remember returning from the second floor gloom and dust one sunny day with what I thought was just an indifferent copy of Horace which I nonetheless wanted. Both Dave and I were surprised to see in the ground-floor light that I had found Nathaniel Bowditch's copy, which the American navigator had autographed and annotated when he purchased it on December 5, 1793. The only darkness remaining on that floor now is the subject of the books arranged there: mystery and suspense. Walter's real care for the place is not apparent to anyone, since it consists in the complete renewal of the electrical wiring and the plumbing, and a new roof to keep out the weather. It is gladdening to know that the place is in such good hands.

* * *

THE old Ann Street book shop is not the same place for me now, but that is mostly because I am no longer the enthusiastic young fellow who used to spend so much time there. I would not trade that past for worlds, of course; it helped to frame my interests along lines which provide a constant source of enjoyment. I have been schooled in a number of institutions here and in Europe, but I have been educated a bit, as well. A measurable part of that education can be traced directly to a musty old book store and a generous, kind-hearted man who included me among his concerns. Thanks, Dave.